Redecentralisation

Ruth Wandhöfer · Hazem Danny Nakib

Redecentralisation

Building the Digital Financial Ecosystem

palgrave
macmillan

Ruth Wandhöfer
Industry Expert
Sevenoaks, UK

Hazem Danny Nakib
Industry Expert
London, UK

ISBN 978-3-031-21590-2 ISBN 978-3-031-21591-9 (eBook)
https://doi.org/10.1007/978-3-031-21591-9

This Palgrave Macmillan imprint is published by the registered company Springer Nature Switzerland AG
The registered company address is: Gewerbestrasse 11, 6330 Cham, Switzerland

You take the blue pill, the story ends, you wake up in your bed and believe whatever you want to believe. You take the red pill, you stay in wonderland, and I show you how deep the rabbit hole goes.

(The Matrix, 1999)

To Ruth's children Leni and Maxi and her family.
To Hazem's family.

Acknowledgements

We would like to express our deepest gratitude to all those who have helped us bounce ideas around, comment on drafting and provide their insights on this journey, but also for discussions and inspiration which led to this book. In particular, we are very grateful to Vivienne Artz, Prof. Ron J. Berndsen, Prof. Rick Chandler, Andrew Churchill, Prof. Jon Crowcroft, Dr. Geoffrey Goodell, Dann Toliver, Martin Walker, and many other great supporters whose many conversations and contributions have been, directly or indirectly, invaluable.

Introduction

The world is becoming hyper-centralised. More and more is controlled by fewer and fewer to the detriment of the many. We see increased centralisation whether we look at the economy, technology or society—from large tech companies and financial institutions that have become more akin to territory-less, virtually augmented states, to central banks that have been left to reign free only to get to a point where their bag of monetary policy tricks is empty, leaving behind a market without guidance and without confidence. When we look at the digital financial ecosystem, which is the focus of our book, the banks, payment service providers, value networks and supporting technologies continue to centralise further, whilst simultaneously the workforce which these systems serve splinters into a micro and gig economy. On top of this, the path towards Web3 and the Metaverse has begun to develop and once again it looks like it is created and controlled by the few on behalf of the many, the start of the real-world Matrix!

What has become apparent in the last decade is that consensus is increasingly difficult to reach on established models like capitalism, communitarianism, democracy and nationalism—all being jumbled up with trade-offs and balancing acts as our local and global communities become so much more interconnected. It is difficult to understand what is what, as boundaries blur between these different models, and indeed between how we view our own selves as we interact under different personae across the digital and physical worlds. Perhaps, there is no better alternative and we ought to accept the least worst option of the status quo, or perhaps, we can do slightly better.

We also observe the acceleration of a growing divide between rich and poor and the privatisation of profits in the face of the socialisation of risks and harms. This state of affairs is creating deep-rooted discontent in many quarters, which has the potential to easily spill over into further division and strife, making this a crucial matter for public policy, national security, human rights as well as an economic and technological challenge.

It is therefore no surprise that people feel left behind and lose faith in each other, in governments and in large companies, whether these are financial institutions or tech companies. The COVID-19 crisis has been a sharp reminder of, on the one hand, 'everyone for themselves' and the erosion of trust in centralised institutions, and on the other, a great success in combating a virus through collaboration of the public and private sector in the pursuit of getting through it together. That is right, we did this together!

It is this state of affairs that has been fuelling a most interesting new trend, the trend of redecentralisation. This trend started in the financial sector, one of the ripest sectors for digitisation and the application of technology. At this point in our lives, we are stuck between Scylla and Charybdis: on the one hand, the emerging world of cryptocurrencies and Decentralised Finance (or DeFi), based on decentralised autonomous organisations (DAOs) that are (or appear to be) resistant to regulation and control and on the other hand totally centralised systems that are able to operate decisively and rapidly, but not necessarily for the benefit of humanity or mother earth. New forms of governance, ways of making collective decisions, through but also outside of financial institutions and governments are beginning to emerge. Tensions, conflict, challenges but also opportunities are becoming clearer in a new and more integrated digital financial ecosystem with areas such as Open Banking venturing into broader Open Finance and Smart Data where a whole new data ecosystem is becoming a possiblity.

For us the big question is this: "Is there a new way in which humankind can truly live in a democratic and inclusive way, and could financial services, supported by technology, be a model for this to the benefit of society as a whole?"

This is where redecentralisation comes in. Increasing the application of decentralisation as a concept, vision, premise and underlying operating model and ultimate ideal will have the potential to provide more efficient coordination in the financial sector, greater privacy protection and fairer interactions between three spheres: the public sector, private sector and people sphere and help us put the people sphere back in the centre of decision making and priorities.

Through globalisation and greater access to technologies, more and more interactions between the public sector, the private sector and people have become digitised. There is now a digital fabric that connects people, businesses and states, whether enabling access to public goods, one's digital identity, financial affairs, ecommerce or social media—everything connects people everywhere. However, this has also brought about additional control, manipulation, coercion, risks and costs. As we as individuals interact with each other and other entities in an ever-growing number of personae wearing different hats, this complexity is set to snowball, as we shall see, into a mass trust crisis.

Amidst all the great developments in technologies, there is a deep erosion of trust going on today, where people everywhere are questioning the state, corporations, firms, the news and one another, whether as a result of the Global Financial Crisis of 2008–2009, the disastrous handling of the COVID-19 crisis in some places and for certain decisions from 2020 onwards, the rise of populism around the world, the hacks into technology firms and data breaches, the mismanagement of our personal data and information (regularly!), or the feeling of divisiveness and voicelessness that seems to seep into the digital echo chambers that we all appear to inhabit more and more frequently. We are living in the midst of a trust crisis,[1] apparently stuck in this rabbit hole of deepening mistrust on all fronts, which threatens the fragility of many of our existing and longstanding social institutions. Some may need to transform, others will need discarding, and some may be kept with slight changes.

Our journey in this book will begin with an explanation of what we mean by redecentralisation and provide a qualitative framework for how redecentralisation or decentralisation can be best thought through to equip us all as the system designers, creators and builders that we are, with a new tool. Once this is in place we will look specifically at the areas of technology, money and payments as well as identity and data to see where on the spectrum of redecentralisation we find ourselves and what is really happening right now in those areas. We will assess steps, if any, that could be taken to create and be part of better systems in a digital world. Finally, we will draw this all together to ascertain whether the financial ecosystem is an appropriate model for broader societal reform.

This will naturally lead us into a discussion of future scenarios, accompanied by recommendations for the public sector, private sector and people—our three spheres that comprise nearly every system, whether legal, technical, societal or political. We will highlight what steps could and should be taken in order to rebalance the management of our collective affairs.

Concluding our journey, we will be going into some deeper philosophical thinking (call it sociotechnical futurism!) and ponder what would and could happen if we continue on the trajectory that humankind has been pursuing thus far. In doing so, we will propose a vision, or rather a meta-vision, for a new digital social contract that we feel is needed for the digital world that we live in today in order to support our collective future.

Let the journey begin!

Note

1. Edelmann Trust Barometer 2021, https://www.edelman.com/trust/2021-trust-barometer (last accessed 22/10/2022).

Contents

About the Authors

Ruth Wandhöfer operates at the nexus of finance, technology and regulation and is passionate about creating the digital financial ecosystem of the future. An expert in the field of banking, technology and regulation she is a public speaker and provides training and coaching for the finance industry as well as the Fintech community. Following her banking career at Citi, Ruth is now an independent Non-Executive Director on the boards of a bank, an exchange and two technology firms, a Partner at Gauss Ventures and Chair of the UK Payment Systems Regulator Panel. She is also an advisor of the City of London Corporation, the British Standards Institution and the European Third Party Provider Association (ETPPA). She is a Visiting Professor at Bayes (formerly CASS) Business School City University London where she gained her PhD as well as at the London Institute of Banking and Finance and occasional lecturer at Queen Mary London School of Law. She published two books: *EU Payments Integration* (2010) and *Transaction Banking and the Impact of Regulatory Change* (2014), both Palgrave Macmillan.

Hazem Danny Nakib is a financial and digital technology expert, having worked in different roles at the Royal Bank of Canada and in secondment at the Boston Consulting Group. He is an honorary researcher at the University College London, Fellow of the Royal Society of Arts, Associate at the London School of Economics Systemic Risk Centre, and Visiting Researcher at the University of Cambridge and sits on the Digital Strategic Advisory Board of the British Standards Institution. He holds a B.B.A. Management Specialist from the University of Toronto, B.A. in law from the University of Cambridge and BCL from the University of Oxford, as well as an M.A. (ad eundem) from the University of Oxford.

List of Figures

List of Tables

Chapter 1
Three Definitions

We are starting our journey with something that sounds quite tedious and boring: 'definitions'. But don't be alarmed. Definitions are essential to set the scene and to put everyone reading this on the same page—literally (as my children would say!). It turns out that all good things, as usual, are three and so we will walk through these three key definitions, which will provide us with the red thread that runs through this book.

Much has been written about the concept of 'decentralisation'. The term originates predominantly in political theory. In the days of empires long past when these expanded by seizing more and more land, they needed to consider the management of what they owned, their property, land and estates in order to stay in control. Decentralisation became a topic within such nation states in terms of governance. It had to be determined how and where decisions would be made and what types of decisions would be devolved and passed down to more localised and subordinate entities to manage affairs. The monarch wasn't keen to be concerned with the plights of certain folks in a village somewhere in his kingdom. That same village likely had a vassal that was empowered to collect tax and inflict punishment, for example in case of poor crop yields.

Similar principles apply today to decisions relating to tax or health care where some should be or are taken at a more local level, for example whether at the federal, state, provincial, municipal, council or household level. All of this speaks to the organisation of society, of affairs and of our relationships with one another.

To cut a long story short, the question is that of power structures in any given system. Where does the power reside?

Now, this was the typical question of decentralisation. Though, as should already be apparent, it had to do with two things. On the one hand, finding the right model to govern efficiently, so that decisions were actually made in a timely way, as well as effectively, ensuring that action was taken after decisions were made. On the other hand, it had to do with how involved everyday people are in decision-making and their ability to actually get things done.

R. Wandhöfer and H. D. Nakib, *Redecentralisation*,
https://doi.org/10.1007/978-3-031-21591-9_1

As the world becomes more global and more connected, hyperconnected even, and as people in a small village become part of a nation state, trading bloc and the like, they are less able to get things done well without reliance on others, on a centralised Tower of Babel monolith that reigns supreme … or so we might think. And as the individual in the first village interacts seamlessly with another individual in (or believed to be in!) another jurisdiction, how do the technological and legislative interpretations practically manifest themselves?

To what extend should power to get things done, be centralised versus spread out more to the people allowing them to directly manage their affairs and have greater choice and optionality without reliance on a central authority that can force or prevent them from doing something? And how do these balances change on a global level where conflicting philosophical models online clash up against actual conflict between geographical enforcements?

One easy-to-use heuristic is asking yourself 'do I need someone's permission to do what I am about to do?' or 'can someone stop me from doing what I am about to do?'.

In our increasingly digital world, it should come as no surprise that the concept of redecentralisation is more and more relevant in the field of technology. The ability to digitally communicate and share information facilitated by the inception of the Internet and the Web is becoming an extension of oneself—or indeed 'one selves' as we explore later when we delve into our increasing multiple personae. The Internet became centralised in many ways across its different layers, and the Web, which was intended to be decentralised soon also became centralised according to one of its pioneers, Tim Berners-Lee. Search engine monopolies and governments' ability to restrict what we can access and use based on where we are in the world in order to fit their policy requirements are all demonstrations of centralisation at play.[1]

Following the centralisation of the Internet came the push towards digitising and redecentralising the exchange of value, and value itself in its most obvious form, money. This was clearest with the arrival of Bitcoin, and the more recent emergence of what is called 'decentralised finance' or DeFi, which tries to push for people, anytime and anywhere being able to exchange value without the risk of needing to face up to a single intermediary that is empowered with unlimited censorship and surveillance. This is extending further and much more deeply into the fabric of society complemented by trends such as data sharing and digital identity.

The surge in interest and hype around redecentralisation and the whole Web3 narrative of a decentralised Internet of value has also raised fundamental questions about a much more age-old set of debates around decentralisation within organisations, political governance and civil society. For us, this is at the core of our message in this book! How can technology, as a tool, deliver a better state of affairs between the three spheres that make up our system: the public sector, the private sector and people, so that we can find the right balance between centralisation and decentralisation for a new and fairer digital economic fabric that connects us all.

The world is changing, and it is changing fast through technological innovation. Lots of centralisation was needed, and yet, some of it no longer is and we are caught up in a race between the opposing forces that push for decentralising everything against further centralising everything. We need to go back to basics and ask ourselves, as technological change provides the tools to reorganise society, what might we want society to look like? And ultimately: how do we re-democratise society or finally introduce democracy for those who have yet to attain it within their nations?

1.1 Centralisation Versus Decentralisation and Everything In-Between

Every single day we all interact with a number of systems, the economic system, political system and financial system, for example. This can, at times, be misleading though because it assumes, in some way, that these systems operate in a vacuum, which, we can very confidently say, is not the case.

When our two miscellaneous adventurers, Leni and Maxi, go about their daily affairs, they might use cash, which is one system, and they certainly could not buy any illegal substances without getting into trouble, which is where the legal system comes in, and when they use their email to schedule a meeting, they use the Internet, a technological messaging system. These systems are interconnected, and they press against each other in a number of ways. Leni and Maxi are the connective fabric that get these different systems to press against one another and interconnect through their actions as they go about their day.

Now, each of these systems, as we shall see, has a number of different dimensions, involving a number of stakeholders: the public sector, private sector and people. Systems, of all shapes and kinds, are pervasive, even ubiquitous across our lives, and many technical systems have social dimensions, whilst social systems in turn also have technical dimensions. Putting these terms together, we get concepts such as techno-political, techno-economical and techno-legal.

Technology trends cut across most systems in today's world, and most systems have to do with people, relationships and decisions and so what we are talking about in the twenty-first century are all techno-social systems in nature.

Why do we say this you might ask? Well, it's because decentralisation is not just about technology, or society or politics, it's all interconnected, just like our lives are. We can try to isolate and just look at this one ant hill, or locust swarm and speak about decentralisation. But today, we are a techno-social system, social in essence and technological in action.

Now let's get on to definitions. There are really three that are most important to our story: centralisation, distribution and decentralisation. Each of these three is usually used to represent network topologies, that is, the shape, size and connectedness of the nodes and interconnections that determine the characteristics and properties of a network's architecture. The most familiar depiction of this was put together by Baran in 1964 in connection with communication networks.[2]

Understanding Centralisation

To begin our story, we need to take a closer look at centralisation before we can get to redecentralisation. According to the Cambridge English Dictionary, centralisation means:

> the act or process of centralizing a system, company, country.

The origin of centralisation when we take the dimension of a country, has everything to do with the principle of sovereignty. Sovereignty was coined as a result of the peace Treaties of Westphalia, concluded in 1649 after 30 years of civil war in Europe between the Protestants and Catholics and which today underwrites the entire international order. Apart, of course, I hear you cry, for those of us living and operating internationally under Common Law. Primacy of Parliament over Crown had been established in the English Civil War, a decade before Westphalia. And what of Magna Carta, and the limitations on the absolute power of the Crown over four centuries earlier? These are indeed interesting dimensions, and the differences between Common and Civic Code legal views are intriguing ones as we look to the global techno-economic interpretations of disputes, and feed into the philosophical mindset behind a majority of the major international technology and financial services players. But for this book we will focus on a continental legal frame of mind and rather explore the Common Law dimensions at another point in the near future.

Sovereignty has been the key driver for centralisation when we think about the arrival of today's iteration of nation states as centrally controlling the affairs in their jurisdiction within their map-drawn borders. They have centralised a number of things—first and foremost, the use of military force. Though the Treaties of Westphalia do not mention anything about the principle of sovereignty per se, they are seen historically as representing the beginning of today's order of equal and independent states. At an international level, it is a decentralised system, whereas at a domestic level of any nation state it is centralised within its borders.

This shift to national sovereigns is only the historic tip of the iceberg though. Traversing through history from ancient philosophers like Plato to Hobbes, the central authority has always been one thing or another. Typically, a monarch or a sovereign, a central figure whose word was law. And at the basic level, if we pick up Hobbes, the perception of individuals—importantly to note here that this perception was born out of 'fear'—was that delegating their power to a central ruler would reward them with protection by the ruler. Now, we all know that anything done in response to fear is likely to be fraught, though as Machiavelli puts it in 'The Prince' 'It is better to be feared than be loved, if one cannot be both'. Whilst we look to a potential future that is more democratised by technology, it remains to be seen whether both can be attained globally or perhaps even reverse a somewhat medieval mindset!

Today, things are a little more complex. Our day-to-day activities, from communication to trade, social media and more, are borderless in many ways. The companies and businesses we interact with are not totally linked to just one place, but instead, are more and more similar to territory-less and borderless states that we need to go through to message, sell, buy and interact with others. This is the new layer that cuts across the centralisation of the nation state.

Moving into finance, one of the clearest depictions of centralisation, and one of our playgrounds in this book, is money. Money, of the fiat kind, like bank notes and coins, is issued by the central bank of a country in a centralised way and backed by and supported by that central bank and its centralised government. In reality though, 90% of money in circulation is created by the private sector, via, you guessed it, banks, and that money is called commercial bank money. We might think, woah, so money is not that centralised when it comes to its creation? Not so. Commercial banks rely on a central bank allowing them to create commercial money—and that at a multiplier, which is called fractional reserve banking. A central bank in turn requires commercial banks to hold part of their monies as reserves at the central bank in central bank money (which is a direct liability of the central bank).

But something else has emerged over the last years, something of a rather less centralised type of money—and it is still arguable whether it can be labelled as money at all. You know what we're talking about here, cryptocurrencies like Bitcoin of course. As we shall see later on, this comparison is more complex when we unpack what exactly decentralisation is. To plant a seed early on, maybe it's all centralisation, just of different forms and kinds.

Centralisation in its essence, when we look at the world of economics, has always been seen as a way to create efficiencies. For example, a centralised process of production is more likely to enable scale and thus reduce cost of production overall. Simply put, if everything is either in one place or at least governed by one rule and way of doing business, then it is more likely to achieve a practical outcome and success for any given system and its users.

The first thing to clarify if we talk about a system is its governance, i.e. 'who is in charge?' 'How are changes made to the rules?' 'Who or what can allow or prevent a particular activity from taking place?'.

In a centralised system, we encounter a single decision-maker or central authority or small group of them. Naturally, this makes decision-making and reaching consensus rather easy and thus fast and cheap when compared to decentralised systems—effective and efficient. Apart from that though, are there other drivers for centralisation? The key one to point out here is the network effect. The more participants that join, the more positive the utility and value of the network. The Internet itself is a case in point here, as are payment systems.

Centralisation was the best answer we could fathom to the question of globalisation and hyperconnectivity. When you have a lot of people in different places you wanted to connect, it wasn't effective for them to physically interact, communicate, buy, sell and exchange things. Instead, we needed centralisation combined with digital connectivity to allow for the kind of scale that was required to accommodate this changing social fabric.

Centralised systems in computing terms are those where we have one central server and one or more nodes—a device or connection in the network that transmits information—which are directly connected to this server through a communication link like WiFi, cable and the like. In this system, a node can send a request to the server and will receive a response—a system with one master. At the end of the day, there is a central point of failure regardless of how many connected nodes there are in the network. So, if the central server (which is a node) gets disconnected or crashes, then none of the nodes can connect to each other, and they cannot communicate.

Such a system is thought to be easy to physically secure because we 'know' the location of the central server and the client nodes. Nodes can easily hook up or disconnect, and updates only need to be applied to one entity, the central server. These systems are easy and efficient to set up, and data analysis can be applied quite straightforwardly as all data is stored in one place. Everything in a centralised system operates on the basis of one global clock, which is dictated by the central server node.

On the flipside, if the central server is down, everything goes down and this can be a real challenge for back-ups, i.e. in case the central server node has failed to back up and is down, the client nodes lose all their data. As the server has to be running non-stop, any software or hardware updates and upgrades will need to be done on the fly, which can also cause issues.

Importantly, another drawback is the fact that these systems are difficult to scale beyond a certain point and can suffer from bottlenecks at high peak activity. The limit to scale is a key problem in a world where the amount of data continues to grow exponentially as does the need for computing power necessary to store and analyse it.

A system that is not set up to cope with increasing amounts of data in terms of storage, maintenance and analytics will likely become obsolete over time, whilst on the edges, where small amounts of localised data are being captured, such as through sensors, it may still continue to be relevant. Such systems are also increasingly vulnerable to attacks. Instead of having to fight street by street, attacks only need to bring down one house, through so-called Denial-of-Service Attacks (DDoS). In other words, the attack surface is large and attack vectors are many. A useful analogy for protecting such systems is fire safety in buildings—we are all used to basic fire safety features like fire doors, smoke detectors and the like to protect property, but there is always the risk of arson from a thankfully very limited number of local individuals of such a persuasion. With hyperconnectivity, the world's arsonist community is not only chatting amongst themselves and urging each other on, but they've all just moved in next door.

Now, a personal computer is a great example of a centralised system in operation, and there are large known organisations that operate such centralised computing systems. It is also interesting to note that cloud computing is another example of a centralised system. It leverages distribution—by spreading the operation of the system out geographically—but it is still one organisation and one decision-making process. Everyone thought cloud computing was the best thing since sliced bread, but what we have found is that servers can be incredibly centralised and unsecure (and give rise to a number of legal issues around data storage). As a consequence, some businesses are beginning to make a move back to on-premise data centres, aided by the development of better chips and computing capacity, more compact facilities, and responding to regulatory issues around data storage. More on cloud computing that later on.

Running any kind of computer network, whether it is strictly speaking a distributed system, or not, requires some degree of organisational centralisation. An example of this is the Internet Engineering Task Force. This Task Force creates and coordinates changes to technical standards of the Internet. Historically, nobody ignored this or its predecessor bodies because if you attempted to ignore these standard changes you would lose the ability to communicate with other users on the Internet when it came to transmitting little packets of data. That is, there would not be interoperability and the Internet, which is comprised of many different networks, would no longer be as efficiently connected.

The Bitcoin blockchain, which utilises a public blockchain architecture, where no one is officially in charge of standards and there is (generally) no dependency on any one central system, still needs users to conform to standards, as otherwise people would not be able to communicate with each other. What this means in practice is that when a group of people—in this instance developers—decide that they are not okay with one system, they create another system, a new public blockchain network. This is referred to as a fork in the blockchain. In essence, you have a deep sense of coordination that serves a centralised function.

We observe, as will become clear in later chapters, that the Internet has a much higher degree of centralisation at the commercial and organisational level. Certain platforms have become near monopolies in their given area of functionality and there has been a higher concentration of ownership in the facilitators of connectivity rather than providers of specific functionality, i.e. the Internet Service Providers (ISPs).

Now, the arrival of 'cloud' technology creates another dimension of centralisation versus decentralisation. At the logical level, the Internet is still a distributed system because different parties control their own systems including the code, which runs on them. However, we now see centralisation of hardware ownership and management by cloud providers. There is also a centralisation (in some ways) of the utility software like operating systems and databases.

In business terms, centralisation can be encountered in two ways. The first is merely the central bureaucratic decision-making that most businesses undertake—the bigger the business the longer anything takes, something we've experienced all too well. The second is in the form of a centralised or general ledger, which records all data, information and transactions such as a company's assets, liabilities, costs and revenue. This is nothing but an accounting system and the underlying means of running this system has evolved from manual to computer driven. Of course, this also includes central databases like a Microsoft Excel spreadsheet or Hyperion database recording anything really, like customer information, or the UK's initial Track and Trace Application that was using Microsoft Excel to capture COVID-19 cases and their proximity to others, alerting users of quarantine requirements.[3]

From an organisational perspective, centralisation is at the heart of government structures such as a country's army or a central bank—reflected even in the name! It is also found at the core of corporations. The fact that the user has no control over the single decision-maker that runs the system and the resulting possibility of censorship can become a real issue. Or from a military perspective, the degree of Command and Control dictates the operation of the overall system, leading to the modern-day principles of C4ISTAR, augmenting traditional C2 with Computers, Communications, Intelligence Surveillance, Target Acquisition and Reconnaissance! But even in modern warfare, there are still cultural differences in approach and adoption, though it is perhaps ironic when we look at these cultural approaches on the battlefield that it is the often more flexible 'Anglo-Saxon' cultures that historically adopted a precise centralised control of 'Befehlstaktik' as opposed to the other Germanic Bundeswehr creation of the more localised results-based '**Auftragstaktik**'.

As computers and other systems are at the core of our digital world, de facto extensions of ourselves, this has far reaching societal implications—just recall the fact that a very known social media platform can cancel user accounts at their leisure, as done with former US President Trump's account whilst he was still acting President! With a centralised system and a centralised authority, that authority can arbitrarily block, say, IP addresses, people it doesn't like, change the rules whenever it wants to, modify the records of information, use that information for one thing or another, prevent individuals from accessing payment systems, and with the onset of the Internet of Things (IoT) from turning on the lights. And the list goes on...

This Other Thing: Distributed Systems

Decentralisation is often confused with distribution. Whereas governance and decision-making are key dimensions to assess as to whether a system is centralised or decentralised, the distributed nature of a system is quite different and chiefly determined by elements such as the location of participants and or data. A system may be distributed and centralised or distributed and decentralised.

Therefore, we will, for example, need to ask: 'Are all actors (or nodes in computer system terms) in the same geographical location?' A system with geographically dispersed nodes is a distributed system, where distribution refers to the geographic location of the 'nodes' and the storage of the recorded data, as well as the location of the requisite computational power being utilised. Control by one or more entities has no bearing on whether a system is distributed. Unlike in a decentralised system, as we shall see, distributed systems operate on the basis that every node is in communication with every other node such that they all behave as a single unit. This is the point of common purpose. At the same time, they may be entirely centralised.

Imagine if you have a distributed system that controls a production line. There may be one central system that controls whether the line keeps moving but multiple sensors (each controlled by a different computer system) monitor different parts of the production line. A sensor system may detect that something is going wrong with a particular machine and send a message to the central system telling it to stop the line. Many distributed systems may consist of some elements that are largely independent from one another (the censors) but have elements that are highly centralised (the system that switches the line on or off). The designers of distributed systems do not generally care about how centralised or decentralised something is. They just try to define the most efficient and resilient system relative to the objectives and goals of that particular system, which, if being created by a central authority or system, will nonetheless be centralised.

The key feature of distributed systems (which have been around for many decades) is that the multiple different systems, which are typically loosely connected (generally communicating via asynchronous messaging), perform some combined purpose, but different individual computing systems, within the overall distributed system, perform different tasks. Here are some definitions:

> *A system in which hardware or software components locatedat networked computers communicate and coordinate theiractions only by message passing.*[4] [Coulouris et al.]

> *A distributed system is a collection of independent computersthat appear to the users of the system as a single computer.*[5] [Tanenbaum & Van Steen]

> *A distributed system is a system that prevents you from doing any work when a computer you have never heard about, fails.*[6] [Lamport]

> *A distributed system is a collection of autonomous computerslinked by a network with software designed to produce anintegrated computing facility.*[7] [Baran]

Now, the Internet is a classic (but huge) distributed system. Many systems interconnect with each other to provide a wide variety of functionality. During the history of the Internet (going back to its original ancestor—Arpanet), there have been various elements of centralised functionality to keep the whole thing going.[8] Whilst the original Arpanet was designed to link together four computers with each operating independently to keep communication going, as more computers were added, the degree of centralisation increased over time.

With the Internet, we have to distinguish between all those decentralised computers that offer various types of functionality (where these do not impact the overall operation of the Internet) from the systems that keep the Internet itself going. For example, one of the main technologies that underwrites the Internet, the Border Gateway Protocol (BGP, more on that below), is in fact more centralised than is often conceived, though the Internet taken as a whole is distributed because what keeps the system running is geographically spread out.

By being distributed, a network or system is less reliant on any given node. Of course, the nodes remain connected to one another, but the problem of having one central node is solved in the sense that there can be several failures in the network, but some nodes can still communicate with one another. By being distributed, ultimately centralised organisations and networks have sought to reap some of the decentralisation benefits of network architecture whilst remaining centralised overall.

And Then: What is Decentralisation?

So far, we've been talking about what decentralisation is not, i.e. centralisation and distribution. And most probably, that is the best way to think about decentralisation.

We know it when we see it and can compare systems intuitively with a few helpful heuristics for the end user.

Let's start way back when, with us, human beings. Would we be considered decentralised? Well we have a brain and if that brain is turned off, we likely would not be a 'being' anymore. So, it's probable that we are centralised, unlike a sea star that does not have a central nervous system (like us) or a jellyfish that has a nervous system spread throughout their body. But if we turned everything else in our body off and kept the brain on, we might still 'be' but maybe not in the fullest sense. Perhaps we have a handful of loci, each one being necessary, a bit of a hybrid, where nothing works without the other. We need the heart, the brain and other organs to really 'be' and have these central loci. We may thus neither be totally centralised nor totally decentralised. This is a difficult question but precisely the kind that decentralisation touches upon.

Turning to the evolution of modern humankind for inspiration, let us briefly reference the Harvard University biological anthropologist, Richard Wrangham, who has spent his life studying violence in the evolution of mankind.[9] Wrangham hypothesises that around 300,000 years ago, reactive aggression, the type of aggression where one loses their temper, began being suppressed and down-regulated in homo sapiens. Alongside this down regulation of reactive aggression came abandoning the typical constitution of tribes where one alpha male, that had defeated all other males in physical combat, governed total centralisation. Once the alpha male was gotten rid of in favour of less reactive individuals (beta males at the time), early cultures were better able to focus on things other than conflict and could cooperate and support one another in ways that made the group more effective, and becoming slightly more decentralised.

This is also likely one of the reasons for how Sapiens were able to expand at the expense of the Neanderthals because Sapiens were able to cooperate in larger groups in the hundreds, whereas Neanderthal tribes were only made up of 15–20 individuals. Thus, Neanderthals were less formidable against the Sapiens. The power of human tribalism is the evolution of cooperation coupled with the reduction in aggression.

At some point after that, perhaps greater decentralisation into disparate nomadic groups and tribes came to a turning point where it was thought that the only way to settle down and for civilisations like Sumeria, Egypt, Greece and Rome to emerge, would be through centralisation. National Geographic pinpoints six key characteristics for a civilisation as we know them today and include large population centres, architecture and art, shared communication methods, ways of administering territory, some division of labour, and social as well as economic classes.[10] Egypt, for example, had the Pharaohs at the top, followed by priests and somewhere at the bottom had the unskilled workers.

Everyone's favourite philosophers and political theorists, Hobbes and Locke would likely attest to the need for centralisation to really kick off civilisations. For Hobbes, nature was a horrid state of meanness, cruelty and violence, and for Locke, the state of nature was not so bad but the cooperation through a centralised political estate was better. Of course, the state of nature for our budding philosophers was not a real thing or place, but a helpful device to rationalise centralised institutions and rightly so!

But then came the demand for democracy. Some kind of set-up of society where everyone's voice was heard and where the many did not out-rule the few and the few did not govern the many. Actually, the very principles of a pure democracy are that decision-making power is passed to citizenry. The way this is done is through the decentralisation of governance itself, where participation in civil society is open, accessible and inclusive, irrespective of different values, thoughts, creeds, colours or circumstances.[11]

Moving to technology and in order to place decentralisation into context, we need to also look to the inception of different Internet-related infrastructures on the one hand, and society on the other. This provides the first lens through which we can look at decentralisation today.

Internet-related infrastructures began as a distributed and predominantly decentralised architectural exercise but inevitably became more centralised due to various pressures, whether commercial, security related, economic or technical. It turned out that it was technology that did not enable the scale that was necessary and it emerged that certain actors wanted to have authority over the system to monetise it, which meant that decentralisation's time was counted.

The Internet Protocol (IP) is an exceptionally relevant place to start, and it is one whose inception is fiercely debated. The Internet consists of a series of tubes that carry packets of data and information connecting a number of different networks. Originally, this was the main innovation, a way in which computers were able to communicate with each other. Paul Baran's RAND paper[12] on distributed networks highlighted that each computer that forms part of a network should not share the same fate and should be separated from other computers, so that each one could survive some attack, destruction, failure or malfunction. This led to the architectural design principles of stateless routers, connecting connectionless protocols known as, what we called out above, the Border Gateway Protocol (BGP) for the purposes of the following uncoupled tasks: end-to-end communication over the network, hop-by-hop forwarding by routers based on a distributed periodic computation of routes over which to forward data between end systems.

None of the aforementioned tasks were designed to have a central authority.[13] Where the network is decentralised, the nodes represent a kind of swarm. So, where a few nodes go down, it is not the end of the world because many of the nodes remain fully connected and can still communicate by sending information to each other.

With any kind of system, we need to first of all ask: 'Are there several decision makers, which ensure that no single individual or entity is in control?' If the answer is 'yes', we are likely dealing with a decentralised system where there is no central authority that acts like a monolith for decision-making in that system. There might instead be several decision-makers, and the more that there are, the more spread-out decision-making is, the more decentralised that system might be.

In a decentralised system of the technological kind, we have a network of computers that make up the system. Within it, we encounter a plethora of authoritative nodes (connection points) that power and keep the system running, i.e. where each node makes its own decisions and the result for the system is represented by the aggregate of these decisions. A system with fully decentralised decision-making would be attributed across all participants and therefore imply the absence of any form of influence, power or control over developers or contributors. Everyone participating in the system is participating in the governance of the system (if they want to) and there are minimal, if any, barriers to doing that, whether technological, social, political, legal or otherwise. Based on the aforementioned list, we shouldn't ever think of decentralisation in a vacuum.

We can imagine a global network where instead of servers and data centres storing our information, we would have devices in our homes, or just our mobile devices where we contributed computational power to prop up a system or network which we use for messaging, sending money, communicating and all the rest. The difference between this and what we have today is that each and every one of us would be contributing to keeping the system up and running. And similarly, we could all participate in its governance, in the rule-making of that global network. We would have a globally connected digital trust layer. That would be pretty cool, and more on this later.

Contrasting the previous examples, decentralisation operates on and within a spectrum. Whilst a particular system can be denoted as 'decentralised' because there is no central decision-maker or authority, one decentralised system may be more or less 'decentralised' than another system. This is critical as different variables and parameters arise internally and externally within and around a system, especially as it interacts with any other system, cutting across the social, political, technological and legal.

Let's consider a simple example, the influence of a particular individual over all the developers that are contributing to the code of a decentralised system, or all nodes being operated by one particular corporate entity or individual. Quite akin to how there might be one hundred water wells in our city open to all, but secretly controlled by five different fractions of thugs that collectively decide how and when the water wells are used. Sure, that's more decentralised than one royal emperor controlling all 30 of the wells, but it is still quite centralised.

Similarly, if Barack Obama, the former President of the US, Celine Dion, the famous performer, and Vitalik Buterin, one of the founders of the Ethereum blockchain each amassed large communities of developers as followers that did their bidding or were devoted to their social and political policies. If you had some system that may be technologically decentralised, or have the capacity to be decentralised, it would be wrong of us to characterise it as decentralised when these three developer groups play paramount roles in the up-keep of that system. This would be because at any given time the available developers would be listening to each of those three people for guidance on what to develop and how. Any changes to the code to, say, make an upgrade or modification would be influenced directly or indirectly by Barack Obama, Celine Dion or Vitalik Buterin. Therefore, the system would be centralised amongst those three developer communities.

Now that we have a broad perspective on centralisation, distribution and decentralisation, let's see how we can create a framework that allows us to measure these three different variables in our day-to-day lives.

Notes

1. Clarke, K., "Tim Berners-Lee is on a Mission to Decentralize the Web", Tech Crunch, 9. October 2018, https://techcrunch.com/2018/10/09/tim-berners-lee-is-on-a-mission-to-decentralize-the-web/ (last accessed 22/10/2022).
2. Baran, P., "On Distributed Communications: I. Introduction to Distributed Communications Networks", Santa Monica, CA: RAND Corporation, 1964, https://www.rand.org/content/dam/rand/pubs/research_memoranda/2006/RM3420.pdf (last accessed 22/10/2022).
3. Kelion, L., "Excel: Why Using Microsoft's Tool Caused Covid-19 Results to Be Lost", BBC news online, 5 October 2022, https://www.bbc.co.uk/news/technology-54423988 (last accessed 22/10/2022).
4. Coulouris, G., Dollimore, J., Kindberg, T., Blair, G., "Distributed Systems", Pearson Education, 2013.
5. Tanenbaum, A. S., Van Steen, M., "Distributed Systems", 3rd Edition, Distributed Systems Net, 2017, https://www.distributed-systems.net/index.php/books/ds3/ (last accessed 22/10/2022).
6. Lamport, L., Famous Quotes on A.M. Turing Awards, https://amturing.acm.org/award_winners/lamport_1205376.cfm (last accessed 22/10/2022).
7. University of Edinburgh, School of Informatics, Lecture Notes, http://www.inf.ed.ac.uk/teaching/courses/ds/handouts/part1.pdf (last accessed 22/10/2022).
8. Mathew, A. J., "The Myth of the Decentralised Internet", *Internet Policy Review, Journal on Internet Regulation*, 5(3), 30 September 2016, https://policyreview.info/articles/analysis/myth-decentralised-internet (last accessed 22/10/2022).
9. Wrangham, R., "The Goodness Paradox: The Strange Relationship Between Virtue and Violence in Human Evolution", Pantheon, 2019; and Wrangham, R., Peterson, D., "Demonic Males: Apes and the Origins of Human Violence", Houghton Mifflin Harcourt, 1996.
10. National Geographic Resource Library, "Key Components of Civilization", https://www.nationalgeographic.org/article/key-components-civilization/ (last accessed 22/10/2022).
11. Manor, J., "The Political Economy of Democratic Decentralization", The World Bank Group, 1999, https://doi.org/10.1596/0-8213-4470-6 (last accessed 22/10/2022).
12. Baran, P., "On Distributed Communications: I. Introduction to Distributed Communications Networks", Santa Monica, CA: RAND Corporation, 1964, https://www.rand.org/content/dam/rand/pubs/research_memoranda/2006/RM3420.pdf (last accessed 22/10/2022).
13. Ibid.

Chapter 2
Redecentralisation

One of the features of the twenty-first century is a new race between centralisation and decentralisation. On the one hand, we see the world centralising further, even recentralising through monolith type structures with states and companies using new sophisticated technological tools. On the other hand, with equally sophisticated technological tools, we note an increasing ambition of some parts of society and business to decentralise, notably in the world of finance and identity.

Whilst early centralisation has been conceived as a solution to being able to solve for difficult coordination problems, decentralisation has continued to come in to lessen the constricted nature that centralisation can have. At the same time, centralisation and decentralisation do not operate in a vacuum, and each may have benefits to any given system and its objectives. And yet, the concepts of centralisation and decentralisation remain opaque at best. This chapter looks to provide just a little bit more clarity to understand them.

2.1 From a Decentralised Past to a Centralised Present

Now, it is worthwhile digressing slightly here and reminding ourselves that decentralisation has been the primary form of organisation in the past. What do we mean by that? Well, before we had the creation of nation states, borders and central authority and decision-making, we lived in a world of small groups solving their own problems themselves with minimal reliance on others, the so-called hunter-gatherers. Things were more if not fully decentralised and decision-making was localised. This translated into the way of living, like local sustainability when it comes to food and water, different localised ways of managing agriculture, cattle and commerce. Whether it was growing ones own crops, bartering with one another to exchange and trade things of value, or even communicating a message by speaking directly or handing over a handwritten note. Many things happened between one person and another, directly,

R. Wandhöfer and H. D. Nakib, *Redecentralisation*,
https://doi.org/10.1007/978-3-031-21591-9_2

with limited reliance on a third party or intermediary, without help, and without institutional structures that could say 'yay' or 'nay', that could forbid or censor. There was minimal reliance on others that could force you out of a system. People just did it, rightly or wrongly.

The same applies to money. Before governments began to issue centralised tender as fiat money, money was a decentralised affair. Starting with shells that were used as a method of exchange in order to reduce the complexity, cost and friction of barter. When shells made way for silver and gold coins, as any numismatist will tell you, a plethora of tribal kings minted coins in their own image, but the underlying value was based upon the amount and purity of the metal. As nation states coalesced and the gold standard gave way to fiat currencies, it is interesting to pause and to reflect as to what extent these fiat currencies are merely 'locally centralised' or whether currency markets, where they are permitted to operate freely, provide a decentralised model, albeit one intrinsically intertwined, be it to the US dollar, or the value of dollar-based assets such as oil—or indeed to the price of gold! A parallel example would be the time before print and digital communication was invented—a time when information was flowing through stories, face to face encounters or by writing down on papyrus, cotton, or rock and handing it from person to person, sometimes trekking months if not years through the desert, across oceans, and around mountains to pass it on, with each and every person adding their own contributions to that story. Perhaps, that is the epitome of decentralisation.

Some thinkers such as Thomas Hobbes, the infamous political theorist, defined that period (whilst imaginary in their writing) as a horrible and brutal state of affairs, the so-called state of nature before modern states, whereas the equally infamous John Locke disagreed and instead thought that actually it was filled with mutual collaboration. At the same time, both of these political philosophers saw the immense value in the coming together to form centralised institutions.

At some point, we went from decentralisation in all these different activities to centralisation. Why is that? Originally, decentralisation came with a variety of quite extreme shortcomings. Most obviously, the decentralisation of yesteryear was difficult to coordinate and inefficient to scale. In order for large numbers of activities, exchanges or transactions to take place, some central authority, entity or group of organisations needed to manage those activities, to be the go-between so to speak, or at least that is what we have thought to be the case until now. For example, we wanted to be able to send money or messages across every ocean, sea, mountain and desert. We wanted to be able to settle disputes easily and efficiently. We wanted to live our lives with ease, and let someone else worry about the tough stuff, the difficult questions about the organisation of society.

The real objective of the inception of centralisation therefore has been to manage things and solve the problem of coordination when it comes to large numbers of people, groups and societies working together. How is it that we could get a lot of people in our modern metropolitan cities to do the same things you might ask? Well, a central arbiter as judge and jury certainly makes it easier to do so by setting the rules, deeming what is and is not right, and setting standards that solve coordination problems across a given community or society.

Take the example of the 250 Volt AC Europlug that is used across many different countries in Europe. It is certainly better than everyone using an entirely different adapter and brings conformity, consistency and coordination. We also cannot think of any reason for why everyone should use entirely different adapters. As far as we know, it also does not come with that many costs. Now, our answer might be different if we needed to register every device or appliance we used a Europlug for, that would be odd and rather inefficient.

The issues with decentralisation are exacerbated by two main things. Firstly, in order to scale beyond the local, the face to face, the direct, let's say in small communities, intermediaries are needed to help do just that. For example, the banking system was created precisely to solve this challenge; a series of pitstops spread out across Europe where people's written promises to pay could be redeemed for what was owed anywhere along a trade route. Solving this problem is answering the question: 'How can we be larger and faster when we are no longer just local?' That is the exact history of the shift of money from token money like beads, pearls and coins to paper promises and later bank accounts tied to identity that use messaging to verify the identity of the parties involved (today we call that the SWIFT messaging system). So far, the current centralised set-up has been thought to be the only or the best way to coordinate large-scale coordination problems.

The second issue is the fact that people and organisations can be quite untrustworthy, which necessitates some kind of intermediation to verify that what is going to be done is actually done, to enforce it if it is not done and to prove that what is claimed to have happened has in fact actually happened. This is why we talk about trusted third parties. A central trusted authority and intermediary that is able to stand up and say 'Yes! This is what happened, I can enable it to happen, stop it, or permit it. I certify, verify and authenticate'. That central party can do all those things so that no one else needs to, people get peace of mind, at least as long as they trust that third party! An example of such a trusted third party would be judges and courts applying the 'Common Law', originally derived in England to provide a common approach across the King's courts. Common Law is used for international arbitration as the English courts are the global trusted third party, long before we entered into the technology context of cryptography and technological governance.

Until now, decentralisation has been difficult, clunky and did not make much practical sense. With developments in technology, decentralisation can become more of a reality in many areas where this can deliver real benefits.

Having said that, a word of caution. We must not be taken hostage by great sounding terms and bland platitudes. As with everything, some things are better left centralised, and others decentralised. In some instances, there is a balancing act and finding the third way of decentralising certain bits (pun intended) whilst centralising others. In fact, any given system may be best centralised in certain aspects and decentralised in others in order to optimise the interests and goals of the parties or stakeholders at hand, of the system itself and its purpose. It will come down to what one is trying to achieve, and what the values at stake are, for example: 'What is best for users, consumers, and everyday people?' and still aligning interests across the public sector, private sector and people. Technology can help with this alignment.

Quite clearly, we all come from a shared history of decentralisation that morphed into increasing centralisation where today we find ourselves with a lot more centralisation across economic, political and social relations around us. Technology is an enabler and enhancer of centralisation, just as it may be with decentralisation. Whether it is where our money is, how our identity is managed, or how supply chains are set up. At the same time, things have become more complex, and technology has developed more rapidly than ever before. In fact, technology is now getting to a stage where you can do all the things you want to do, in a way that is more decentralised than having one central intermediary that needs to be wholeheartedly depended upon, and that is why we talk about redecentralisation! Technology allows for a previous state of affairs that was enjoyed in the real world to be reflected into the digital one.

Of course, this picture we are painting is not static. It is not as though there was just one thing that happened that centralised everything, or one thing that could decentralise everything. History reflects an ebb and flow between centralisation and decentralisation along different dimensions touching on different systems at different points in time and in different ways. A frequent recentralisation and redecentralisation over and over ad infinitum. Though, knowing us humans, we happen to fluctuate towards extremes at either end. Sometimes, the ambition for decentralisation can lead to a despot-type figure chanting the hymn of decentralisation that makes them the central focal point of an entirely centralised system, something we have seen repeatedly in the more recent cryptocurrency and blockchain space but also in politics.

Today, many societies, in general, are quite decentralised. We can all, generally speaking, decide and have the ability to make choices about what we want to do, to decide for ourselves what is right and what is wrong and then act on it. We have the autonomy and agency to be able to do so. In fact, this is one of the most important aspects of our civil society, personal autonomy that is especially fragile. We have the ability to choose what to do and what to think and when. To us, this is really the heart of decentralisation.

As we know, there are laws, regulation, standards and controls. And yet, we have the ability to decide at any given point, more or less for ourselves, what it is we believe to be the right course of action and act upon it. We may be held to account or be liable if we do something that conflicts with laws, rules and social norms, yet we can still do so. In this way, many systems in our society are decentralised from that standpoint. At the same time, this is not as true in the digital realm. There is a deep disconnect between how our lives are lived in the physical world versus the digital world. In the physical, we find a mix of centralisation and decentralisation, whilst in the digital, it may have begun with decentralised ambitions through the Internet and the early World Wide Web, but nobody would today consider either to be decentralised, at least when it comes down to the way everyday people interact with it.

As the digital fabric of technologies continues to interconnect the three spheres of the public sector, the private sector and people in different systems, that agency, autonomy and independence are at risk of being slowly chipped away. Sooner or later—and for the cynics—already today, we will or are no longer able to choose for ourselves and solve our own problems as we deem fit. We can no longer choose.

This provides us with a little bit of a dilemma. We spoke earlier about the move from decentralisation to centralisation at a meta-societal level by looking at the move from a state of nature of the pre-state and hunter-gatherer kind to a more centralised state-oriented way of managing our affairs. Of course, there has been an ebb and flow between centralisation and decentralisation in the meantime, all within this meta-period of centralisation. That early shift from decentralisation to centralisation, as argued by the likes of Hobbes, Locke and in particular the French political theorist, Rousseau was based on a social contract, a kind of hidden agreement between people and the state where people gave up their ability to use violence and would welcome being governed, and an authority would reign supreme and protect them, settling their disputes and protecting their rights as and between one another with a monopoly on the use of force. The rapid hyperconnectivity of everyone, everywhere, at all times through technology has changed this dynamic and put pressure on this, perhaps underlying, social construct that underpins our current social reality. The digital world has its own rules, and new actors, organisations, businesses and people (even digital nomads) that span different countries, spaces and roles. The traditional social contract between the private sector, public sector and people is under pressure to accommodate a new digital world that has not found its footing; beginning itself decentralised, it transformed into heavy centralisation, and now is moving towards redecentralisation.

2.2 Demystifying Decentralisation

Without naming names, we'll use our experiences interacting with various peoples to bucket what they are often focused on when it comes to decentralisation. Most people, whether academics, politicians, economists, regulators, executives, technologists, futurists or finance professionals are usually using the word decentralisation very differently from one another. In fact, it covers a slew of different things to different people at different times. Most commonly, it is a vacuous term thrown around to bring people together either to work on something, or to work against something.

To start off with, many conflate decentralisation with distribution which we covered in Chapter 1. Namely that decentralisation has to do with data being stored in many places instead of only one place. That is not decentralisation, though it may certainly come hand-in-hand with it and comprise a part of it. It is perfectly possible to have distributed and centralised models combined together.

Some people, in particular from the financial services industry, take decentralisation to refer to a wide variety of services being provided to some group or market segment instead of only one service being capable of being offered to them.

Regulators on the other hand take decentralisation to refer mostly to individuals having some kind of control, including indirect control over things like bank account access by being able to use different technologies to ensure they can access it without being prevented from doing so by a central authority. This is certainly a part of decentralisation, but not the entire picture.

Some others treat decentralisation to be about how things of value, like money, data and all the rest are spread out amongst users and locations instead of in the collection or the hands of the few. This might be a small part of decentralisation, but in reality, how spread out or concentrated value is has also to do with other things in a system that contribute to equality or inequality—the level of decentralisation of a system being one such factor and an important one at that.

We have also seen a number of stakeholders refer specifically to technologies as being decentralised, e.g. blockchain (which however is not always decentralised). This too misses the point. The design of a system may take decentralisation into account as a design property, and yet, when the system is actually in use and is live, clear points of centralisation may appear.

One thing that we have found is that the majority of those discussing decentralisation see it as a switch. Something, usually referring to network topology, that either is or is not decentralised. This too misses the point that the majority of systems fall somewhere on a spectrum between centralisation and decentralisation.

There are also lots of instances where systems are considered decentralised, that are not. This might be because decentralisation has become the latest fad, again, or because it is thought to generate greater usership, or of course, it may just be a mistake in the use of the term. We will see that it is important to look at a system from several different angles when considering its degree of decentralisation. For example, it would be difficult to say that some technical system is decentralised where it relies on the use of something of value, like a coin or token, when all those coins or tokens are owned by one person. In this case, the system itself may be decentralised, but the fact that such a centralisation exists in ownership of the main unit of value in that system is a point against how the system can actually be used in practice, i.e. be decentralised. This is made worse where those tokens come with certain rights to participate, let's say, in governance. Even though the system allows for decentralisation, sure, the reality is that it is quite centralised because that is just the reality of what happened for the system to get off the ground. We look to the reality of the matter, the possibilities and the potential.

One needs to step back and make sure we are asking the right question. Here, it is not whether we should have more or less centralisation, or how we can bring about total redecentralisation. Instead, it is that the race between centralisation and decentralisation is raising the question of how society should be best organised with new technologies. And in our more specific case, how the financial system should be best reorganised.

An obvious place to start would be to measure the level of decentralisation of any given system. As decentralisation considers the location of power, there are a range of metrics that could be used to consider it, which would require settling on how to quantify power and then looking at the system, like a political system—e.g. the Canadian political system—or a technological system, e.g. the Bitcoin blockchain, and assessing the distribution of power within it.

John Leslie King, a professor for management of information at the University of Michigan, when considering computing systems, put forward three dimensions along which power relations should be considered to measure decentralisation.[1] The first is whether decision-making is centralised by way of being concentrated in one single individual or entity, a group, or if it is much more spread out at all levels of decision-making. The second is whether the facilities that are being used, such as data centres and others are spread out or not. The third is whether there is a locus—a centralisation—of operation. Rightly, King posited that every system has to find its optimal solution by mixing and matching across these three dimensions.

When it comes to the Bitcoin blockchain—one of the systems that we will be discussing in more detail in this book—the authors Srinivasan and Lee looked to quantify whether Bitcoin is a decentralised system or not.[2] They consider clients, miners, exchanges, nodes, accounts and developers. If any one of them is overly centralised, then the aggregate degree of decentralisation would be lower. They refer to this as a system's Nakamoto coefficient to pay homage to Satoshi Nakamoto, the person(s), if at all, responsible for authoring the Bitcoin whitepaper in 2008. What the Nakamoto coefficient supposedly tells us is that the higher it is, the more difficult it is to compromise the system because the more hostile parties and factors are required to be able to compromise it. There is actually a website that does something quite similar and considers a number of different blockchains and measures the number of different client codebases, which account for the vast majority of nodes, the groups that control the majority of mining power that keeps the system afloat, the number of public nodes and the distribution of money or value within that system that is held by the top one hundred accounts.[3] According to them, 19% of all Bitcoin sits within one hundred wallets. We do not know if the same person owns all these wallets. It also points out that only four mining pools control over fifty per cent of Bitcoins mining power, making the operation of this system rather centralised. An interesting revelation given that it is widely thought, and consensus appears to be, that the Bitcoin blockchain is an example of 'decentralisation'.

Though we could go down the route of taking a more quantitative approach, it does not really capture the essence of what we are looking for. Decentralisation has an important qualitative function that is part and parcel of the organisation of our society. In many ways, it is an ambition, an ideal, and a goal.

One of the founders of Ethereum, the second most popular blockchain protocol, Vitalik Buterin proposed a different way of thinking about decentralisation. In Buterin's view, not too far apart from Professor King, there are three dimensions: architectural, political and logical.[4] The architectural has to do with the number of actual computers that a system is made up of. The political considers the number of individuals that are in control of those same computers, whereas the logical dimension looks at the data structures involved and whether, if you cut the system in half, each half of the system, covering users and providers could continue to function independently from the other.

Whilst helpful, these views only begin to scratch the surface of the systems we face every day. To get to a better way of looking at it, we need a few more tools to frame our thinking when zooming in on systems in all sectors, including the financial.

2.3 The Three Spheres

Systems do not operate in isolation, they tend to be connected. We can even go so far as to say they are interconnected, by and through each of us, our actions and day-to-day lives. This is amplified through the connective fabric of technology that pulses through our interactions. At the same time, any given system is comprised of different parts. From that standpoint, we find it necessary for working through larger problems to be equipped with a heuristic that we call the three spheres. Any given system, or multiplicity of systems with their connective technological fabric, cuts across the three spheres.

These three main spheres are: (i) the public sector and government; (ii) the private sector and industry; and (iii) the people and community. These are our three Ps. Each sphere has sub-spheres and components of their own. As an example, the sphere of people and community has micro-spheres within it at the individual, household and village or town level that may cut across different jurisdictions and be either local or global. Similarly, the public sector and government sphere has an internal dimension domestically and an external dimension internationally.

This interconnection and intermingling of systems is actually how most people go about their daily lives with overlap across systems, whether the financial system, social systems, legal systems and so on and so forth.

When thinking of decentralisation then, we need to be able to account for this systems-rubbing-against-each-other and the role of technology within them. This is particularly true the larger each of these systems becomes because they will inevitably affect each other just like law, technology, finance, politics and the Internet do. Similarly, the more valuable any system becomes the more value is created and extracted within the system such as Big Tech companies and Internet Service Providers (ISPs) with the Internet or cryptocurrency exchanges and wallet providers with Bitcoin.

By taking this framework approach to systems, we can examine where and how the three spheres interact and when they are in line or out of sync. Fundamentally, different things matter to each of the three spheres as they engage in and through any given system. Technology can influence and modify the relationships between them, leading to either greater alignment or misalignment.

A driver for the public sector may be re-election in modern democracies, driving economic growth and maintaining control over its territory to ensure monetary, financial and military sovereignty. For the private sector, profits and year on year growth to satisfy shareholders are often key objectives, whereas people themselves demand to be treated fairly and ensure that their needs are satisfied to a certain degree, to have the choice of doing things privately, to be respected and not have their agency encumbered, and to have a multiplicity of options available to them in the market so that they can do things efficiently at limited cost.

We can say that each sphere values different things, notwithstanding that there may well be overlap across some of their interests and preferences. As these three spheres

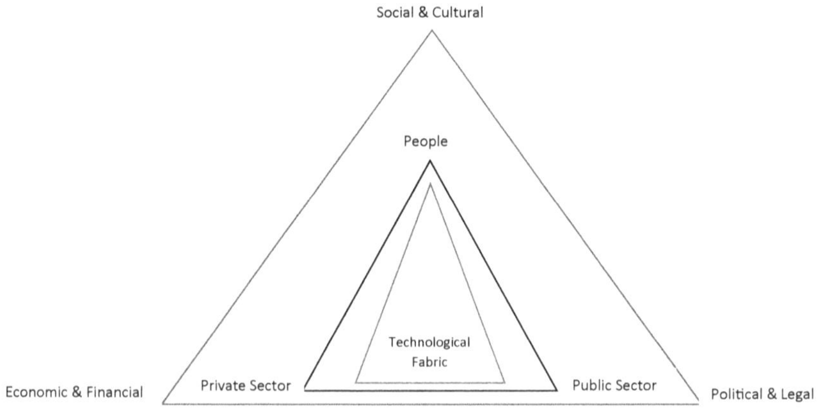

Fig. 2.1 Our system with an underlying connected technological fabric

interact, whether in cooperative, anxious or hostile ways, those interactions have social, economic and political implications. This total picture gives us our Fig. 2.1 as a starting point for examining, in our case, select areas of financial services like money, payments, and identity.

The ultimate aim should be alignment across each of the spheres in order to enable resiliency and sustainability across our systems and our society. This is the ideal, complete value alignment. What is usually the case is more of a turbulent friction that shifts and turns ever so often.

However, we would argue that we instead tend to experience misalignment between the three spheres and that at an accelerating pace. Just as though the tectonic plates beneath the surface of the Earth can lead to a tsunami, the same is true of value misalignment across the three spheres with drastic economic, political and social implications. These are typically the result of underlying and long-standing misalignment.

One obvious example is the 2008–2009 Global Financial Crisis where creative financial instruments were the result of profit seeking by the private sector sphere. The other interests at play at the time included the relaxed approach taken by governments around the world to foster innovation, as well as the interests of the people sphere for buying homes they could not afford. It may be thought that there was value alignment when it came to profiteering, though it was of the wrong kind. The 2008–2009 Global Financial Crisis shows us that there was short-term value alignment of certain interests at the expense of long-term value alignment across the three spheres. At the heart of it was also a question of trust. The private sector was trusted with lax regulation not to be too creative, and people relied on the private sector not to give them loans that would be impossible to ever be repaid. No one would have bought into the scheme knowing the outcome, and what mattered to the three spheres was overlooked, with the people sphere suffering most.

2.4 A Framework for Redecentralisation

Until now, there has been little thought given to creating a clearer way for understanding decentralisation and for applying it to any system, whether social, political or technological. Rather, decentralisation has become a catch-all term, sometimes referring to there being no one central authority or point of failure, or there being no or minimal gate-keeping for the ability to transact and access some system, or still further, that there is little to no intermediation. The more astute observers have taken decentralisation to operate along a spectrum. And although decentralisation has been seen by proponents as good, and by the centralisation proponents as bad, they are both wrong.

Decentralisation, both as an idea, and as an ideal toward a way of organising our affairs, our society and the relationship between different stakeholders, can be realised because of technology. It can sometimes allow things to become better. But what exactly do we mean when we say 'better' or 'good'? This is an interesting question that takes us on a detour into the concept of values to inform us on how we think about what this transformation *should* look like. Without spending too much time there, it returns us to the question of what matters to each of the three spheres, and how and why certain things matter more than others based on some conception of what is good and what is bad in building the resilience, not only of the people, private sector and public sector spheres but the resilience in their alignment.

The concept of decentralisation has two main aspects:

First, decentralisation is a spectral concept. That means it operates along a spectrum where the far end is dominated by centralisation and the near end represents full decentralisation. Second, decentralisation as a concept is relational, meaning that it has to do with the relationship between one or more people and some system, whether political, social, economic or technical. It is also a concept that is best understood when looking at actually doing something. For example, asking if any given system is centralised or decentralised can be more clearly defined where something needs to get done, like making rules, transferring money, voting, managing one's information and so on. The level of decentralisation in one system is also most easily considered by comparing it to another which may be more or less decentralised, whether a real one, or a potential future system.

In the previous section, we highlighted what many people presume or are thinking about (without telling us!) when referring to the concept of decentralisation. Instead of arguing about these different points of view, we are looking to characterise decentralisation's different dimensions, which can help to develop better tools and debates that we can think through when considering questions about reorganising society and building the digital financial ecosystem. In some places, centralisation might be helpful for speed or efficiency, but the trade-off might be consumer and user privacy in relation to their personally identifiable information. We might also perceive a trade-off between efficiency and privacy or security when there in fact is no trade off but it is a mere ruse and all we have is a situation of intermediaries trying to defend data access and use.

Note again that the ideal measure for a given dimension in a given system depends heavily on the system: its goals, its participants, its internal structures and the external environment it finds itself operating in. So, when we look at cash, bank deposits, the Internet, Bitcoin or civil society, the general framework is, at a meta level, more or less the same, and the specific dimensions of the concept can be quite similar and will only change across each of them because sometimes certain things just aren't relevant. For example, why would we be thinking about who can stop you from transferring something of value to me when we are looking at voting rights (though caveat many of the ballot box issues).

The question that has been agitating many people in recent times, in particular as technology innovations such as blockchain and the social phenomenon of Bitcoin appeared to suggest that things could be done differently, has been: 'why do two people looking to exchange value, information or just to communicate with each other have to go through a bank or some other intermediary?' The inception of the Internet also comes to mind that looked to answer: 'how can computers communicate with each other, anywhere at any time whenever people want them to?' It is at its heart about not having to be forced to trust someone else because, generally speaking, you cannot trust what you cannot verify!

Our story then is really a question of power dynamics and power relations that give rise to important economic, political and social questions. It is about considering spreading out power to best enable people to manage their affairs in a more connected environment and build resilience against external environmental and human-made shocks. This ultimately has the potential to rewrite the rules and the organisation of business and society, and for readers to be able to find what is best left centralised and what should ideally be decentralised in building the digital financial ecosystem.

Decentralisation's Seven Dimensions

Now let's jump into the core of the decentralisation framework that we are putting forward here by discussing some of the important dimensions that need to be considered by any system.

These dimensions act like heuristics to help us short circuit the process of understanding where a system lies before considering whether that is a good thing or not and the fact of the matter as to whether a system should be more or less decentralised overall or rather in one particular dimension. The dimensions are our mental shortcuts. In itself, this framework, made up of different dimensions, is entirely neutral. It does not posit a right or wrong view and so strips out some of the baggage we see when these words are thrown around.

The dimensions are in themselves objective. This is helpful because it means that they don't presuppose any answer for what is best, and they are descriptive to understand the state of a system, whether centralised in certain ways and decentralised in others. Equipped with this framework, we hope that system designers, those contributing to technical, social, cultural, legal, regulatory and government systems, can have a better idea of what they want to achieve and why. We are all system shapers in different ways.

The underlying question of decentralisation is really this: 'How reliant or dependent is a particular participant on any other party to successfully do something, that they have decided they would like to do?' In many ways, this is how far someone is forced to trust another party by the design of a system to be able to get something done. The more decentralised, the less reliant on a particular individual, entity or group and the more open to a plurality of diverse participants a system is likely to be. At the same time, a system with decentralised aims or design may lead to centralised outcomes where that plurality is non-diverse. Further still, a system may look decentralised and not be, or it may be decentralised but incredibly cumbersome that it is ineffective in doing what its creators and its users expect from it, making it decentralised but wildly inefficient.

We are interested in the reality of decentralisation and centralisation. A system may begin decentralised in its design from a system architecture standpoint, but end up centralised once people use, interact and engage with it. Our focus is to consider the case of real systems we can see, which will inform us in how systems change, how to change systems and in creating new ones.

When it comes to our framework of dimensions, we have the following seven decentralisation dimensions:

1. *Governance/Rule-making*

This is one of the most important dimensions to look at. It has also become one of the main dimensions that is used when thinking of decentralisation. Which parties in the system make decisions in that system, enforce the rules of that system and sometimes create those rules? Part of this is looking at how governance or consensus is reached across all decision-makers. Consensus refers to the way in which decision-makers involved, that have been granted power for whatever reason, actually come to a decision.

There might be one specific decision-maker over things that happen in the system. For example, when it comes to payments, the payment service provider is the ultimate entity that decides whether a transaction is valid or not. However, there might be a much larger number of participants involved in making that type of decision. If there are, then there is less reliance on any single one of them, making it more decentralised. Where a distributed ledger is used to validate a transaction through some consensus process, the operators of the system that determine the validity of a transaction might include many different system operators that come to a consensus through a particular process. This applies equally to the creation of rules in the system that one or more parties are empowered by the creation of the system to promulgate. Just like your bank can set terms and conditions on you, or a social media platform can decide on a policy with which to suspend accounts, which would all be very centralised. However, other systems, like the English language have a much more fluid and dynamic rule-making process, for example when it comes to the rules of grammar that are not set by any one given party but change over time. It is also possible for a group of people to come together and begin using a new word, that could catch on and become widespread, making it more decentralised.

In some ways, the remaining dimensions, though standalone dimensions in their own right, fit into how decisions are being made in the system and the concentration of authority and power.

2. *Action/Process*

Although connected to the dimension of *Governance/Rule Making,* this is really where we zoom into what can be done with the system. It has to do with the day-to-day operational control within a system. Every system has an action-related or operational purpose that went into why it was created in the first place. We are not asking the esoteric 'why?' it was made, but what was it made to allow users, customers, consumers, or people to do. By looking at it that way, we come to some interesting insights. If we take somewhat democratic political systems, we cannot overlook that one of its purposes is to enable all people to be able to contribute to electoral processes through civic participation by voting for someone somewhere and in some way.

Similarly, the banking system should be serving the purpose of a safe place to put money, to take out loans, to make transfers and payments, to get guarantees and all the rest. The Bitcoin blockchain has to do with making transfers of value in the form of Bitcoin, unencumbered by a central intermediary. At the same time, it is encumbered because, whilst decentralised in design, the reality is that around four mining pools—effectively groups of miners that keep the system running by solving mathematical problems—maintain over fifty per cent of the mining power and voting of the Bitcoin blockchain.

On the basis of this, this dimension is considering, whatever purpose of the system is, being delivered operationally on a day-to-day basis. When we identify that, we are looking at whether dependencies exist to be able to execute and do that thing, like sending a message, transferring some Bitcoin, placing a vote, or executing a bank transfer, and then the concentration of those dependencies (if any).

3. *Structure/Design*

This dimension is an added heuristic that asks us to take a step back and look at the shape of the system. It is not dissimilar to Vitalik Buterin's logical dimension we discussed earlier. It focuses on looking at the system in question schematically. When we consider the make-up and set-up of the system, its design and structure, does it look like a monolith, like a tower of Babylon type structure? Is it more spread out, or does it have a swarm like shape with little to no hierarchical structures? One easy way to think about it is if you broke it up into many different pieces horizontally, vertically and diagonally across all the different stakeholders and participants involved, could the system survive? If it could, we are likely looking at something that is more decentralised because there is an element of self-sufficiency in and of itself with minimal reliance and dependencies within the system. However, if it would shut down and be rendered totally useless, then we know it's definitely a more centralised design that we have in front of us. Banknotes and coins are a great example. Whilst using banknotes and coins is quite decentralised because all you need to do is hand them to someone else, thus the *Action/Process* dimension is extremely decentralised, they still rely on a central bank to be issued and a government to say that they represent something. By slicing and dicing the system, it would not be able to sustain itself because, although we could still hand notes and coins to one another, they would be the equivalent of any other piece of paper or metal.

4. *Access/Entry*

If we think about access and entry in our daily lives, an example that comes to mind is considering a shop that we frequent down the street. Most stores nowadays have a security guard of some kind, or at least a CCTV camera. Subject of course to whatever policies that store may have, the managers of the store could prevent us from entering and instead keep us away from participating in the system of, say, grocery shopping, maybe because of how we are dressed, because we had not been negatively tested during the COVID-19 pandemic, not being vaccinated, or for many other reasons. The ability to access or enter is limited. This is pretty important because the ability to interact with a system unincumbered and take part in the operations of a system is a part of the decentralisation exploration. If you wanted to use the banking system, entry and access to that system to, for example, make a wire transfer is limited and restricted to only a subset of people, namely those that hold an account with a particular financial institution. From the standpoint of the unbanked or underbanked, or other more excluded individuals and communities, and even those that do not wish to have an account with a financial institution linking their identity to their transactions, for any reason, it may be quite difficult, if not impossible to access such a system, making it extremely centralised.

This dimension considers the degree of dependence and the concentration of that dependence to access and enter a system. In our technological world, there is a growing list of difficult-to-use-systems, some of which can only be used with a particular bandwidth, Internet connectivity or technical proficiency. Regardless of this possibility, which could and should be solved in some way with better education and technology access, some systems go further, making it exceedingly difficult to use or enter, to the extent that users are sometimes discriminated against or outright excluded. When we take a look at banks, you have to meet a variety of criteria in order to become a customer. You have to meet different Know Your Customer (KYC) and Anti Money Laundering (AML) requirements which, whilst important to undertake certain actions such as making a payment, may not be required for all operations provided for by a bank. On the other hand, with cash, there is an extremely accessible system with low entry barriers since anybody can hold it, use it and exchange it.

The same is true with our more online social lives. Consider email, file sharing or social media. In the social media context, there are only a few corporations. Each of them could prevent you from using their services if they wanted to, and they have high entry requirements for access, such as sharing all your data and information and its ownership with them and removing you from that ecosystem if you behave in a particular way. The more relaxed a system is about who can use it to do whatever the purpose of that system is or what it was made for, the more decentralised it will be along this dimension.

5. *Change/Lifeline*

Systems are prone to change. Sometimes they do so overnight, for example when a technological system is upgraded. Equally, a political system can effectively change or end within a very short period of time, for example as a consequence of a coup d'état. Other times it takes much longer for a system to disintegrate and self-implode on its own or to evolve into a completely different system, and even split into another system. Clearly, in order for a system to meet new challenges, opportunities and demands, it will need to change, often iteratively over time. This dimension comes in two parts. First, it looks at who can make such a change, and second, for those changes to become fully adopted into the system, who and how changes to the system that effect the lifeline of the system are allowed to be made. It gets into the critical nature of a system to find out who can modify it, change it and upgrade it at its deepest, most essential level.

If we take Meta—aka Facebook (we will be using these terms interchangeably)—for example, to be able to modify the Facebook Messenger app on your Android smartphone or iPhone, we are quite certain that you will need to be a Facebook employee for starters. You would probably have been vetted and have restrictive access to make specific modifications that are reviewed by different teams before being pushed out into the app. Of course, it would naturally be a collaborative process internally. At the same time, no one external to Facebook could ever dream of modifying the application. The same is true for other well known applications like Alphabet's Google search. When we take a look at the Bitcoin blockchain, there is a pre-existing process called the Bitcoin Improvement Proposal whereby any developer can access and modify the open-source code of the Bitcoin blockchain, which is freely available and accessible online to propose a change or upgrade to the underlying code, as is often the case with open source projects. From that standpoint, it is remarkably decentralised on the first part of this dimension. When we move to the second about actually pushing out the upgrade, it is not. This is because it requires immense support across the network of miners and node operators to get any given change through the hoops of the Bitcoin Improvement Proposal and ultimately adopt it as the new version across the system.

6. *Problem-solving*

This dimension is about disputes. Problems arise, they inevitably do, and typically we need to go to an intermediary, a someone, somewhere to settle that dispute for us and decide who is right and who is wrong. Whether the village chief, tribal leader, judge at the local courthouse, arbitrator or mediator. If a problem arises, then what? Who do we trust to settle it for us? We might trust a centralised legal system, or a distributed form of dispute resolution that is spread out globally, such as normally occurs under Common Law. We might instead trust in technology, in trusted computing that can provide us the answer or help us avoid a dispute in the first place. Whichever way we cut it, the more concentrated the dispute resolution mechanism on which we must rely on to be made whole, seek redress or vengeance, the less decentralised a system is because when things go wrong, as they inevitably do, we turn to the judge to rule on who is right (and even that is centralised, i.e. one judge).

7. *Knowledge*

Part and parcel of decentralisation is the notion of diversity. An aspect of diversity is that there are different forms and kinds of knowledge within a system. Knowledge may manifest in different ways. It might be the knowledge of a client that's being used in a technological system, or an ideology or methodology within a political or scientific system. The more diverse the knowledge base of a system is, the more decentralised it effectively is.

Take the system of the English language. Although there are bodies that have become widely accepted as the determiners of what is and what is not an English word—we call them dictionaries, with the Oxford and Cambridge English Dictionaries being the more well-known—culture plays a tremendous role. As if to prove this point, one should note that Oxford and Cambridge are both English dictionaries, if you will, whereas on a global basis many other English speakers, indeed probably most, might defer to an American English dictionary, such as Collins or Merriam-Webster. One need only to use TikTok to see how culture and generational change modifies the English language on its own and how widespread it can be. This reflects the diverse knowledge base that can participate in the direction of the system, in this case language. The more differing knowledge bases are represented, each of them with a clear enough voice to express their frustration and enthusiasm and participate effectively without being entirely subdued or rendered voiceless, the more decentralised a system will be. For example, the Bitcoin blockchain and many other blockchains have one single agreed upon state of the entire system, or one body of knowledge, and that is what helps it act like just one computer as opposed to many different ones, making it extremely centralised along this dimension.[5] Returning to our spoken language reference of English as the global lingua franca, ironically itself a non-English term, and turning to the financial lingua franca of the dollar, it is primarily the US dollar to which we assume we refer, and the degree of trust in 'the dollar' certainly precludes reference to say the Zimbabwean equivalent!

2.5 Why Redecentralisation?

When we ask ourselves, whether as policymakers, regulators, industry practitioners and executives and each and every one of us: 'Why should we care about redecentralisation?'.[6]

Well, redecentralisation could be a way to:

- Increase the bargaining power of users.
- Enhance economic efficiencies by eliminating rent seeking or value extraction.

- Reduce vulnerabilities to security threats and build resilience.
- Make a system faster, quicker and less beholden to bureaucracy.
- Make a system more responsive to users.
- Make a system more transparent, achieving better information symmetry.
- Reduce the concentration and misuse of power unilaterally.
- Give people the ability to contribute to the systems they participate in.

In our view, across many of the benefits of decentralisation, there are (at least) six fundamental categories of reasons for why decentralisation is an important consideration that is valuable for the reorganisation of the financial system and a new digital financial ecosystem.

1. *Diversity*

The more centralised a system, the less we will hear of differing viewpoints. The more decentralised, the more diverse the viewpoints will become because more people or groups are empowered to voice themselves and contribute to the system. This inevitably results in more diverse schools of thought, bodies of knowledge, participants and rationales leading to increasingly complex systems that progress and innovate. The more centralised, the less differing viewpoints there will be and the more prone a system is to becoming static, uncreative, monopolistic and uncooperative, uncompetitive as well as corrupt and oppressive.

2. *Privacy*

It is no accident that when Tim Berners-Lee, one of the pioneers of the World Wide Web, along with several of his co-authors, was proposing the best strategy (according to them) for online social networking in 2009, that they together chose increased decentralisation as the best route forward.[7] Their view advocated for decentralised outcomes in a social networking system whereby it should allow users to maintain privacy of their own personal data, control over how it is owned and used, spread and accessed, and that people should have total ownership and control over all of their data, much like your own property in the real world, whether your slippers, your hat, or the dollar bill in your pocket.

In general terms, decentralisation can help alleviate if not avoid circumstances where an individual can be censored, surveilled, discriminated against and their personal data and information, which in today's world is really an extension of everyone's person, misused or sold (or both!) without their knowledge and complete consent. The benefit of decentralisation is that it has the potential to offset the possible risks and costs associated with threats to privacy.

This is, of course, not a guarantee, though as centralisation increases across each of the dimensions, the likelihood of threats to privacy materialising significantly by a unilateral actor that may have all to gain by engaging in initially innocent behaviour that may turn sour when unfettered. This is because intermediaries are more prevalent, a simple sum of operational risk and a pinch of potential nefarious tendencies will always give you a level of baseline threat that is ever present.

This is particularly clear where requirements are imposed by those intermediaries for some kind of safekeeping or handholding, whether making our use of their services dependent on opening an account and therefore having to provide personal information, which means our activity can be monitored, our data analysed, and our personal and non-personal information used to feed us, for example, advertisements, or being sold on to other parties to do the same.

In today's world, a small number of companies process most information, communication and transaction flows between people, both domestically and internationally. The channels through which that information flows are concentrated amongst an equally small group of organisations that store, track, analyse and use that information with limited restrictions. Indeed, the very and continued existence of some of these organisations in fact relies on the ability to effectively collect, process, store and use the data and information of their users and sell it as data brokers to third parties.

That is not to say that companies that track and use data for advertising do not provide any value at all. Any time we use any third-party service provider or interact with an intermediary, it is usually for peace of mind, great user experience, and because it is so well integrated with a whole range of other services we also use. It makes our lives easier (or at least appears to do so until things go wrong). There is a lot of value there but at the same time it comes at a cost that is beginning to matter more to people.

Take cash, for example. One of the beautiful properties that is increasingly valuable of having the choice of using cash is that we can go about our affairs without being mandated to open up an account in order to have access to the economy and have everything we do with it tracked, a choice that has long existed (and as we have mentioned, when it comes to the operational use of cash of handing it to one another, it is extremely decentralised). The more decentralised a system is, the more opportunity there is for privacy to be preserved. Where the network is uber-centralised—meaning all information and data need to go through a central node such as a central server—that node or server can monitor, prevent access, change, impose rules on, censor or surveil and discriminate against those trying to use the system.

3. *Disintermediation*

In addition to risks to privacy, the very concentration of intermediary services amongst a small number of organisations and entities is another key risk. It means that any one of our banks, platforms, custodians, Internet Service Providers or utility providers can take unilateral action on their own behalf or on behalf of a group. That action may well be entirely arbitrary. Decentralisation can prevent this type of unilateral action or unilateralism because you could solve your own problems without having to rely on others.

This unilateralism can take any number of forms, whether directly or indirectly charging a new toll or fee for anyone using a service or making a change to the historical record about something that had happened like your bank changing a past transaction you made, or having you conform with certain new, seemingly arbitrary policies and requirements. The intermediary can change the rules at any time, and if it is not entirely benevolent, it can arbitrarily treat you however it likes.

We've each received different notifications either in our mobile applications or via email from different service providers changing their terms and conditions. One of them even increased the fee by one hundred per cent. Another requested additional personal information to maintain an account with them. And another still was asking a lot of questions about our use of their platform for no good reason (well definitely good reasons for them!).

Consider the example of being able to go to the local well to get some water, and let's say that works just fine. It's a bit of a pain, but as a community we work together to have a schedule and built the needed infrastructure to get water to our homes. It's not the best of high end well, but it works okay. Outside of the possibility that a local gang of thugs comes around and blocks use of that well, no one really is going to stop us using it, whereas our utility provider, the only one in town, can stop our water at any time (they even once threatened to do so).

What decentralisation also brings is making it that much harder for the members of a system to collude together and act in a way that is exclusively in their self-interest and contrary to the interests of others. This should bring out alarm bells since at any point in time, people, companies and politicians have the potential to act in ways that can turn out to be pretty bad for everyone. If it were more difficult to do so, things would be quite different. That is really the inception of having checks and balances. There may still be overreach but it is limited and there must be accountability. At the same time, perhaps there are some powers that no one entity or person should be ordained with.

Another way to see it is through the emergence of Internet of Things or IoT. There is a lot of excitement around it and for good reason. However, one of the risks is that the providers are going to be heavily centralised. Imagine forgetting to make a payment for your car and suddenly your car stops working (for old school fans this is what happened to taxi driver turned hero Corbyn Dallas in the 5th Element!) and so does a variety of other things until you make your payment, even when the mistake is in the system, a glitch, a unilateral nefarious show of force to show you who is boss, or with an intermediary provider making an error and you had actually made the payment!

4. *Security and Resilience*

The more centralised a system is, the easier it is for cyberattacks to successfully cripple the existing system, particularly in cases where robust cybersecurity measures to limit there being a single point of failure are absent. It is easier to take down one system that is centralised with a strong attack to take down the entire castle, than it is to have to take down hundreds of thousands of walls, towns and villages where the surface of attack is significantly more flattened and spread out.

Of course, this has actually been one of the main focuses of the aim of distributed computing, discussed briefly earlier. At the same time, we note though that the central authority remains the same, as without it there is no system continuity.

Looking at it from the standpoint of a database or ledger, if the database is centrally managed, a centralised ledger would necessarily rely upon some central authority that would have an operational role in transactions or in maintaining the shared historical record of all things that have happened. This role would mean that the central authority operating the system would hold administrative responsibility for system reliability and resolution of disputes. The central authority would also, because it is the central authority operating the system, be in the perfect position to influence how transactions are carried out and recorded. The central authority would therefore expend significant costs in trying to make sure that transactions, whatever they are of, whether payment transfers, voting, or any operation, action, or activity that is being recorded, are done as expected. It would also incur the risks of being accused of acting arbitrarily, negligently or with vengeful intent, whether or not transactions take place and are recorded as expected. The central authority is also the grand decider and can determine, on its own, what is allowed and what is not, what is correct and incorrect within the system and could be accused of not following the rules in the system. Each of these responsibilities demonstrates the responsibility a central authority has, and where they are subdued, the responsibilities it holds for operating the system are left vacant. Thus, external environmental or human-made shocks can totally disrupt a more centralised system than a more decentralised one, if only because of the less resilient they are to shocks to disrupt it.

Quite simply, a system that is more decentralised is more difficult and more expensive to attack, modify, coerce or change because it does not really have a central point or authority that can be taken down. That makes the network much more resilient because there is no dependency on one single node or one single entity or thing. Authority as well as information is shared, which means that a system can live longer than it otherwise would. What we mean by this is that some nodes might be down, offline or cut off from the rest of the network, or even large parts totally damaged, and yet, because the information has been replicated across many nodes, it remains available and functioning.

5. *Value Creation*

Every given activity, action or set of connected systems that is looking to solve some problem or make it possible to do something by way of exchanging information, communication or exchange something is engaging in some activity or operation that has something of value at its heart. That value is part of a value chain. If our two adventurers Leni and Maxi want to exchange a dollar, every step of the way can leak value, have it extracted or have it protected, stored or distributed, based on the costs, risks and benefits involved as well as the dependencies, number of steps and types of stakeholders along the value chain.

The more intermediaries there are, whether data brokers, search platforms, financial brokers and the like, the more value is leaking out of the system that Leni and Maxi are paying for because it is being extracted, often not in return for commensurate value. On the other hand, we cannot simply dispel intermediation outright as a bad thing. Those intermediaries provide people with jobs, they may protect and preserve value that would otherwise be at risk of being entirely lost, stolen or corrupted and charge a fee, just like having an armoured truck transfer your gold bullion instead of carrying it around with you in duffle bags. That being said, intuitively, it seems difficult to deny that there is a lot of leakage that does not seem entirely fair across the board. And then there is the illusion of 'free of charge', where many companies allow users to use their platform for free, a great deal, right? Well, that depends. It depends on the importance of all the data that is given in exchange for using their services.

It may seem unfair, though a pretty large fraction of the global population is perfectly okay with it, right? That could be right, but it is equally right that the value of, for example, all our data is priceless on its own, or priceless when not used, or priceless in the really expensive sense to each and every person as their property and part of their identity that businesses are owning more and more of. At the end of the day, in the digital world, more is becoming of value and more matters. Decentralisation offers the possibility to turn things on their head and make the people sphere the central component, the important thing in the middle that can decide what it wants to do with what it considers valuable. Equally, it means that there are less people in the middle providing services which are not needed in return for some fee along the way of your being able to do something like buy a product or service digitally, send a message, submit a form and so on.

6. *Trust*

One of the major trends that the blockchain and Web3 wave has mustered is that, instead of trusting some central intermediary, trust is instead placed in code, that will (or should) inevitably protect one's interests. This is a slight fallacy. It is not code that is being trusted in. Alternatively, there has been the parallel wave claiming that blockchain is trustless, meaning that trust is not required or it is somehow automatic. Instead, it's all about the underlying consensus or decision-making process that spreads it out of a central monolith structure into a less concentrated form of decision-making where no one party can supposedly unilaterally decide what the correct version of the truth is, where this truth becomes the shared history of transactions of Bitcoin in the case of the Bitcoin blockchain. But as mentioned before, in this particular instance, we really need to trust four mining pools that are responsible for over fifty per cent of the votes (however, most of us are unaware of that state of affairs) in the Bitcoin blockchain. Nevertheless, the underlying principle is increasingly helpful in spreading out instead of concentrating the decision making process in a system.

Decentralisation can increase trust, and trust is the focal point of a functioning system, any functioning system; remember our Fig. 2.1. It requires a small emblem at the centre that represents trust. All systems strike a fragile balance between people, the public and private sectors. Whilst centralisation may come with benefits such as speed (sometimes), or scale, decentralisation can help in avoiding the ailments of centralisation that lead to mistrust such as lack of transparency and accountability, but also increased collusion, corruption and more because unilateral action is more likely and more possible.

It is safe to say that we are living in an era of mistrust, a trust crisis. Indeed, the Edelman Trust Institute thinktank, which publishes an annual report called the

Edelman Trust Barometer found that in 2022 there was a collapse of trust in democracies as well as companies.[8] Whilst the report did not make a connection between centralisation and the decline of trust, it is the current decision making that is problematic, and that is stemming from more and more centralised institutions, which are capable of operating unilaterally. It is fundamental to the future of the cohabitation of our three spheres that solutions to trust arise, and perhaps, further centralisation is not the best solution. Trust in institutions continues to decline as we centralise further. Decentralisation can complement a concerted effort to rebuilding trust across the social, political and economic system and realign the people, private sector and public sector by ensuring that no one party or group in one sphere can deeply infringe on the interests or rights of the other spheres.

2.6 Nuovo Era: A Perspective on Technology and Finance

It is fascinating to trace the evolution of centralisation and decentralisation when looking at technology and finance in particular. The first half of the twentieth century is really a story of centralisation. In the field of finance and government, we see large bureaucracies building up with a lot of physical and manual processes, whether these are card files, machines or paper invoices. Bureaucracy allowed for better centralised organisation to maintain order—just like it did in earlier civilisations such as ancient Egypt where what were called priests were at a higher social hierarchical level than the workers. Societies experienced massive progress through the centralisation of technology and government.

In the 1950s, we see an even bigger boost to centralisation with the arrival of the first computer. Using computers enables better organisational control. This was also the origin of the information society.

But then a new wave of decentralisation begins to make an appearance on the technological side. This was triggered by the arrival of the Internet, the origins of which and the reason for it being decentralised were of course the threat of atomic war. The US Department of Defence in collaboration with several universities created the Internet as a decentralised and distributed network in order to ensure that it could be resilient enough to withstand a nuclear attack. This was really the start of the new era or Nuovo Era of decentralisation in modern times with technology in the digital world, as opposed to the more ancient forms of decentralisation. This new way of working was driven by and through technology, with less and less of a hierarchical view of the world. Instead, the world was beginning to divide into little pockets of information all around where people look for ways of managing their affairs without reliance or dependence on others, where the trust they had to place in parties they do not know and cannot influence is minimised.

From the first computer towards personal computers (PCs) becoming mainstream, allowing the world to get more and more connected, we are moving away from the centralised management of affairs. Now, everyone can connect with everyone via computers and smart phones and this is how the technology wave of decentralisation really begun. Yet, the underlying Internet, and certainly the Web has, over time become centralised when it comes to how everyday people interact with it. Decentralised ambitions can still lead to centralised political, social, technological and economic outcomes. The hyperconnectivity of everyone, everywhere, requires new and better solutions that are faster and easier to use, but also accessible in a non-discriminatory way.

What we see at the same time in the field of finance is that centralisation is further gaining ground. From the 1960s onwards, the financial industry is still working its way out of paper-based systems and towards the adoption of computerisation. These are the days when centralised utilities such as national payment systems, clearing and settlement systems and other financial market infrastructures were built. But as PCs are making their way into finance, we see the arrival of new financial products including more Over-The-Counter (OTC) and derivatives trading, all facilitated by PCs. This is when the decentralisation wave begins to hit finance with new financial products being offered to more people.

After that, we enter the Dotcom era of the 1990s. The arrival of e-commerce and social media are great examples of the network effect at play. Everyone wants a platform; in other words, everyone wants to be a monopoly and so we are back into the centralisation of the Web, that is, control of everyone's access to information, commerce and value.

Even technology converges more on centralisation as we observe the arrival of cloud technology from 2006 onwards (though the concept already existed in the very early days of computing when we look at the time share phenomenon).

Before as well as after the Global Financial Crisis of 2008/2009, finance further succumbs to centralisation as banks get bigger and regulators seek more and more centralised control following the clear let down by the private sector.

The concoction of technology, finance, financial crisis and regulatory responses moves us deeper into centralised control akin to those last seen in the late nineteenth century in the US with monopolies like Robert Baron but this time across the private sector and public sector sphere.

The development of cryptocurrencies and the current evolution of Decentralised Finance or DeFi and drive of Web3 are reactions to this centralisation. However, as they stand today, they are not viable models for the future on their own, sometimes filled with risks and shady characters. Evading AML checks is diametrically opposed to the demand of visibility by regulators, whilst at the same time risking fraud and negative implications for the broader public—neither viable nor sustainable. But, new technologies can find a bridge to balance the interests of all spheres to provide regulatory supervision and, for example, privacy (like zero knowledge proofs).

Every once-in-a-while though, something happens that has the potential to rewrite the rules of society. That 'something' that is of interest here is an innovative idea. For any innovative idea to have teeth, it needs to come along at the right time with the right tools; only then is it true innovation. That 'something' in and of itself can rewrite the rules of society for better or for worse. Take double-entry book-keeping developed in the fifteenth century by Luca Pacioli for example. This allowed the

Medici family to efficiently scale their business endeavours in a way that had not yet been done before, thereby enabling the Medici family to fuel and underwrite the Renaissance because of their love for promoting culture and funding artists across what became their conglomerate. The idea behind double-entry book-keeping was efficiency and reach, which enabled other transformational projects in art and culture.

The surge in the technological and cultural blockchain wave and the cryptocurrency community has led to the creation of widespread networks that are often open source and lend themselves to or provide for the ability to modify, replicate, and grow. Many of them may not be all that decentralised across all our dimensions, but it cannot be denied that they have transformed a lot of the understanding of how digital systems function. They have revamped methods of authentication that are more seamless and automated than those of central governmental authorities, big banks, giant payment service providers or social media companies. In fact access to some of these networks requires no enrolment at all. The databases that they employ also do not sit on that company's servers or the company that has been outsourced to or with the cloud provider.

Today, we live in an ever-changing fast paced and technologically driven world. In many ways, everything is becoming digital, and everything is becoming smart through the use of data, or so we think. There are more and more digital representations of things, like land titles, currency, commodities and contracts that are recorded, exchanged and stored digitally. We live in a Digital Economy, but the people sphere has not been at the centre of building the digital financial ecosystem.

The main message is that redecentralisation can rewrite the rules of society by alleviating frictions between three spheres: the public sector, the private sector and people, so that we can achieve an alignment of their interests in the digital world that we live in today. The only way this can have a lasting impact is by being able to identify 'what matters', that is, what is most important to the public sector, the private sector and people spheres, and to work towards alignment across all of them by using technology and keeping the people sphere at the heart of a new digital social contract, where 'what matters?' is built into all systems.

Notes

1. King, J. L., "Centralized versus Decentralized Computing: Organizational Considerations and Management Options", *ACM Computing Surveys*, 15, 319–349, 1983.
2. Srinivasan, B., Lee, L., Quantifying Decentralization, Medium, 2017.
3. Are We Decentralized Yet? Available at: https://bitcoinera.app/arewedecentralizedyet/.
4. Buterin, V., The Meaning of Decentralization. Medium, 2017.
5. Buterin, V., 2017, The Meaning of Decentralization. Medium.
6. Hoffman, M. R., Ibáñez, L.-D., Simperl, E., "Toward a Formal Scholarly Understanding of Blockchain-Mediated Decentralization: A Systematic Review and a Framework", *Frontiers in Blockchain*, 3, 35, 2020. https://doi.org/10.3389/fbloc.2020.00035.
7. Yeung, C.-M. A., Liccardi, I., Lu, K., Seneviratne, O., & Berners-Lee, T., "Decentralization: The Future of Online Social Networking", In W3C Workshop on the Future of Social Networking. Barcelona: World Wide Web Consortium, 2009.
8. Edelman Trust Barometer, "The Trust 10", Edelman, 2022. Available at: https://www.edelman.com/sites/g/files/aatuss191/files/2022-01/Trust%2022_Top10.pdf (last accessed 07/11/2022).

Chapter 3
The Universe of Technology

Technology is a central pillar of this book because we got to a point where technology is permeating our everyday lives, our work and our social experiences.

When we start from the core of our thinking with the spectrum ranging from centralisation to decentralisation, technology is a very interesting example of change that effects social and commercial discussions around the governance and decision-making of more efficient social institutions.

We have already shed some light on the evolution of technology ranging from concepts of centralisation, distribution and decentralisation across the previous two chapters. In this chapter, we will provide a more detailed account of the technology evolution of our more recent past, picking out distinct technology areas that are on the one hand essential pillars of our evolving digital economy and life and on the other great test cases to understand their degrees of decentralisation and examine whether a change of direction on the spectrum could support a more balanced and positive impact.

A particular focus will be placed on the Internet—as our digital highway—cloud technology, DLT or blockchain and AI. We see these broad technology pillars as the basis of our evolving digital world.

Let us begin with some historical context setting to frame technology innovation.

3.1 Waves of Technology Innovation

Many different economists, sociologists and innovation experts have attempted to understand the sweeping trends over the last several centuries as these relate to the connection between economics and technological innovation. The idea, broadly speaking, is to be able to identify, based on a variety of factors, how markets, products and players are driven through technological revolution, which disrupts the status quo and leads to advances in the form of long-term waves. The criticism of this type of thinking or analysis is that it is often difficult to support with the appropriate data

R. Wandhöfer and H. D. Nakib, *Redecentralisation*,
https://doi.org/10.1007/978-3-031-21591-9_3

and consists of a variety of short-term factors that influence them. Nonetheless, one of the most notable pioneers of this thinking is economist Nikolai Kondratiev who posited that ultimately there are long waves, known as cycles that were driven by technology and innovation. These cycles are composed of three phases: expansion, stagnation and recession, which have all been confirmed through spectral analysis by the work of Kondratiev and Tsirel[1].

The economist Joseph Schumpeter, for example, argued that these long waves were indeed caused by innovation, which contributed significantly to both economic growth and cyclical instability, where innovation was the most fundamental aspect of economic change. Schumpeter viewed certain time periods to result in the aggregation of technological innovations, which he referred to as 'neighbourhoods of equilibrium'. Such periods were at equilibrium when innovators, creators and entrepreneurial thinkers viewed the risk/return inflection point to be aligned to generate the greatest levels of commitment towards innovation. Schumpeter's theory of 'creative destruction' was aimed at evidencing the onset of a new wave whereby the old assumptions are destroyed to make way for new ones. Table 3.1 identifies Schumpeter's waves of innovation, as put forward by Moody and Nogrady.[2] Each of the waves ended in some form of crisis, for example, the Napoleonic Wars at the end of the first, the Great Depression at the end of the second wave, and the Oil Crisis at the end of the fourth. Each of these waves resulted in the influx and growth of new industries and businesses, and the disappearance of older ones. The change from one wave to the next, while due to technology innovation, it is the driver of innovation as a result of changing market configurations and changing needs of consumers, technology and society, and the only way those needs are satisfied is through new market and technological configurations. An example is the technology of the "smartphone" and more specifically the consumer need of the "selfie". The same is true of communication and instant messaging, voice and video conferencing, and now Zooming. This simple facility transformed personal data communication globally and enforced the upgrades to the underlying network infrastructure well beyond any original plans. We should be asking, what will be the next selfie?

More recently, Šmihula identified six of these long waves that he believed were caused by technological revolution.[3] Šmihula argues that each wave would necessarily be shorter than its predecessor due to the accelerated rate of innovation. For Šmihula the major contributor to any long-term economic development was technological innovation and each of his waves comprised a technological revolution

Table 3.1 Schumpeter waves of innovation (according to Moody and Nogrady)

	Wave	Period
1	Industrial revolution	1771–1829
2	Steam and railways	1829–1875
3	Steel and heavy engineering	1875–1908
4	Oil, electricity, the automobile and mass production	1908–1971
5	Information and telecommunications	1971–?

Table 3.2 Waves of innovation based on D. Šmihula

	Wave	Period
1	Financial-agricultural revolution	1600–1780
2	Industrial revolution	1780–1880
3	Technical revolution	1880–1940
4	Scientific-technical revolution	1940–1985
5	Information and telecommunications revolution	1985–2000–01/2008–09/2020
6	Possible wave of informational technological revolution (decentralisation, resource efficiency and clean technology)	2000–01/2008–09/2020–?

and an application phase. The application phase is related to circumstances where the number of new innovations decreases and the ability to apply those innovations increases. The application phase results in greater investment into that particular technology and the phase itself is identified through the area in which the greatest technological revolution occurred. Naturally, this would also relate to where the greatest application phase has occurred. The end of a phase typically results in economic stagnation. For example, the 2008–2009 Global Financial Crisis could be seen as the end of the fifth wave identified below by Šmihula in Table 3.2, although that is unclear. It could easily also be 2000–2001 dot com bubble and burst, or more recently the 2020 and even 2022 downturns during and following the Covid-19 pandemic, given the economic downturns, or possibly a combination that results in a wave that is still ongoing. Moreover, Nogrady and Moody suggest, for example, that the sixth wave will be focused on general resource efficiency and on clean technology.

And as an important side note, we now live in a world of smartphones, where Moore's law enables these phones to process ever more data. As a consequence, the transmission spectrum is moving to higher frequencies, which do not transmit easily over extended distances. This is a potential barrier to 6G growth, but it is being addressed by the development of new materials.

There are applications of both optical and radio-frequency (RF) metamaterials, which enable opportunities in reconfigurable intelligent surfaces (RIS) in telecommunications, meta-lenses for smartphones and automotive radar beamforming. Reconfigurable intelligent surfaces (RIS) based on metamaterials offer a unique solution, promising wide area coverage at low energy consumption. RIS reflect and potentially even direct signals directly to end users, increasing signal range and strength.

These will deliver the next frontier—6G! We should now be asking ourselves where we stand in the grander scheme of these waves, where are we now? Anyone could argue, based on different supportive data that it is now the onset of clean technology, semiconductors, the metaverse, augmented reality, quantum computing or some combination of them. Perhaps it is new RIS technologies that were just mentioned. Who knows really. Maybe it is not something that can be predicted and only known retrospectively. In light of this, it appears to me, at least intuitively that the current wave, or phase, or cycle, is deeply intertwined with trust and so far as we do not know for definite, we are best off treating the current or next wave of technological innovation to be one of technology redefining relationships toward rebuilding trust.

Digitisation Versus Digitalisation

Digitisation technologies convert traditional forms of information like photos, documents and others into computer code, ultimately ones and zeros. But digitalisation is so much broader than that.

It also involves the transformation of social, economic and political interactions. Over the years, digitisation, data and computers seem to have become more of a utility with the majority of services now being offered digitally, businesses spending significant amounts per year on digitising their workflows, and a surge in online marketplaces, social media, and digitally native content across every sector.

What humans as a species have been naturally adept at identifying is certainly how a particular technology could disrupt a particular industry or how such technology may be used, but the creativity of the human species ends with the mode with which this is done. A mode relates to the medium of delivery of value. For example, the shift from physical to digital was rarely if ever identified until it had become much more widespread. By being able to understand the historic trends categorically, we will also be in a better position to understand the modes with which disruptive innovation occurs and their possible mediums.

As with all things, technology trends and changes of modality do not exist in a vacuum, they tend to have a large and long history and provide us with an understanding of where such trends may lead us. Yet, this too may be difficult to consume, and perhaps too simplistic, as it may lend itself to theories such as embedding a microchip, connected to a host's neurological pathways, having the new mode being digital and brought closer to consumers, with computational power, data and information, similar to moving from a paperback to a tablet. However, and although this is important, it remains simplistic and largely suffers from what we term 'leap orientation', that is, the ability for people to think in leaps and bounds without applying their creative faculties to implementable and practical modal changes of innovation.

Standards bodies are already defining international standards for brain-computer interfaces. Contact lenses, which can present augmented video to the wearer are in the final stages of development and the "Hyperconnected human" is already becoming the subject matter of industry conferences (curiously alongside longevity!). We then have smart cities developing in parallel where cities are totally interconnected, available in the physical worlds and virtual worlds where everything can be done digitally. And then there is the metaverse boom for totally immersive virtual experiences where more and more people will spend more and more time that will feel more and more real (but isn't!).

To help us make sense of all of this, there is a methodology, which we have termed 'modal architecture', a simple and effective tool, which looks like this:

- *Mode*: Physical, Digital, Biological, Other
- *Operative Mode*: Human, Technological
- *User mode*: Human, Technological

At the time of the printing press, the designer and creator would be an individual human, the physical technology would come in the form of printing, and the receiver would also be an individual human. Regarding photographs online, with the first photograph uploaded to the Web by Tim Berners-Lee (which depicted the pop group *Les Horribles Cernettes*—four of his colleagues), the mode was digital, the operative mode was human but could today be technological (an Artificial Intelligence or AI model) and the user mode also had a human receiver but today this could be technological (an AI model).

The Internet in combination with developments in computing, provided a transformational way, first for digitising information, data, books, and documents, and second, for the transfer of information, data and the like. However, what modern-day computing in combination with the Internet has failed to do effectively is to provide an efficient way for the digitisation and transfer of value in all of its forms. In fact, digitisation is a process of making the inefficient marginally and incrementally more efficient. Nothing more. After decades of this, and specifically when looking at the financial industry, the outcome is a Frankensteinian nightmare of legacy systems, middleware, a multiplicity of data silos and convoluted processes that net or batch transactions to circumvent failures of digitisation, requiring intermediary layers and outdated processes to operate, where no one who helped create these systems is still around. The overhead of legacy was for decades ignored by banks and FIs. As businesses moved from mainframes with terminals to networked PC's and then to Wi-Fi connected laptops they left their mainframes in their basements and did not invest or innovate. Only now when smartphones with strong identification and authentication technology are in the hands of large numbers of their customers (individuals and businesses) are they forced to invest and build. Digital financial alternatives with cryptocurrencies are seen by some as alternatives to over-restrictive and slower banks that are keeping up with, not only digital, but digitalisation.

What is needed instead is actually digitalisation, the thing that replaces inefficient processes with efficient fully automated and fully integrated digital ones. Yes we first need digitisation, turning information into digital format. But then the real story begins: changing business models, creating new business models altogether based on the use of technology, which allows for new forms of value generation!

3.2 This Thing Called Internet

Computing and the Internet form the backbone of the digital revolution that we find ourselves in. Computers allow individuals or groups of humans to be able to interact with digital processes. They provide the connection between the physical and the digital to be conducted in a way that is conducive to people generally, as opposed to those with specific expertise alone. The digital access is no longer local but rather global in nature, opening up the world of information and knowledge as much as misinformation and fake news.

In this section, we will explore a brief history and description of what the Internet is and how it has reshaped our commercial as well as personal interactions over the last decades. And yes, we will take a view on the question of whether it is centralised or decentralised, or whether parts of it are or aren't in order to assess if things should change for the better.

A Few Words on the Internet

The Internet has its origins in the 1960s when the US State Department of Defence created the basis for time-sharing of computers (in those days computers were few and very expensive, so you had to book your usage time, a bit like a laundrette machine). The predecessor of the Internet, the so-called ARPANET, emerged in the 1970s as a network connecting military and academic computers, primarily for the purpose of research. It was a bomb-proof, self-repairing network, allowing the exchange of information through trusted private networks. Secure international public networks such as X400 were developed through global collaboration between telecommunication operators and governments. They were resilient and secure for business users but not adopted for open access by everyone. Once the US government stopped funding, in the 1980s, the behemoth of US technology power jumped on a commercial Internet and X400 dies. Usage rules were initially respected in what was termed "netiquette", but these rules disappeared once commercialisation took over and particularly when advertising started to pay all the bills.

And before we delve into more detail, here a quick clarification of the difference between Internet and World Wide Web (WWW) (something we know is often mixed up by people). The Internet is the infrastructure and the WWW is the way in which users communicate—information interface on the Internet.

The core Internet fundamentally provides what are called "packet services", a means to break up data transmissions between individual computers and/or networks into small packets of data, specifying the format of those messages through IP, the Internet Protocol, and how those packets should be transmitted and/or re-transmitted using the Transmission Control Protocol (TCP).

The decisions about the design of the relevant protocols and changes to them are still agreed these days by the IETF global committees representing multiple parties democratically, so you could argue that the standards element of governance is more centralised.

The management of the network is hierarchical. There is no central party controlling the operation of the transmission of data but some Internet Service Providers (ISPs) are more important than others and they form into a hierarchy. The highest tiers were traditionally national operators in their role as ISPs. It is the national domain registrars that set the hierarchy. They control the Domain Naming Service

(DNS) which maps every IP address to a URL name. For example, in the UK the internationally agreed name was .GB. This is now owned by the UK government as under international pressure the registrar issued the .UK and a whole lot of subdomains .co.uk .biz.uk, etc. In recent years, these subdomains have become crowded so new domains have been opened such as .space, .sport. If one wanted to use a domain name in another country, e.g. .com from a UK business, the UK registrar would agree with the American registrar who controls the .com domain. The business name, which fronts the URL, is bought from the network of international registrars and for international businesses has to be negotiated for each country, e.g. Sainsburys.uk, Sainsburys.cn, Sainsburys.de.

Publishing the DNS Map, which links every Internet name with an IP address, can be done in real time by top level tier one ISP's and the new names trickle down to lower subdomains in due course. Errors in this name to IP address mapping have occurred and when they do happen, they can sometimes take large parts of the Internet down.

Understanding that the Internet manages the transmission of data is the first step to understanding that really what most people regard as the Internet really isn't, notably services provided such as search engines, social media and shopping sites.

Instead computers or networks of computers provide these services. The Internet is the fundamental mechanism by which you communicate with these computer-based services but each is essentially run by a company, a person or some other form of organisation. No central body determines what can or can't be provided as a service that communicates with the rest of the world via the Internet, though local authorities or ISPs can try to block them.

Rather than trying to govern the Internet globally, the UN instigated the Internet Governance Forum (IGF) as a quasi-regulatory organisation. Governments send representatives to annual IGF conferences where governance issues are discussed and although consensus can sometimes be reached, no mandatory actions are forthcoming.

Technical standards, protocols, etc. have always been the prerogative of the Internet Engineering Task Force (IETF). This was the initial body, which designed and delivered the Internet. Its democratic procedures rely on the submission, discussion and finally agreement of Request For Comments (RFCs). These are proposed, numbered, debated and finally agreed democratically amongst the members. Meetings are generally quarterly but a considerable amount of discussion is now carried out remotely. The stakeholders in IETF used to be from academia and the military but now include many large companies with vested interests.

Policy and regulatory issues are ordered by the Internet Society based in Geneva.

The Intricacies of the Internet

The Internet is often thought to be the prime example of decentralisation, namely the most democratic form of organisation, allowing people to interact and communicate digitally. Typically, when this statement is being made, the underlying assumption is quite simple, that the Internet cannot be controlled by any one central authority. So much has been written about the Internet as being decentralised and it is true that the Internet is not a centralised global institution per se. In fact, the success of the Internet is precisely due to the fact that it is not institutional or entirely centralised.

Before the commercialisation and opening up of the Internet, most computers were connected by proprietary communications links and networks (such as token ring for IBM). The growth of TCP/IP-based Internet services was met initially by these proprietary networks developing gateways to the TCP/IP network. This allowed Internet services to be routed to these proprietary machines. In this way, businesses and even government departments became able to share data between previously unconnected devices and built services we now take for granted, like the e-mail! This growth of the pre-web Internet did not restrict small companies or even individuals from taking. It was the web browser that enabled even the smallest companies to showcase their business and of course web-based advertising that paid for it. This is what started the "dot Com" boom (which became a bubble and ultimately bust!)!

So, when it comes to the Internet, what exactly is it that we want the Internet to do? Simply put, we of course want to get information to some place automatically, that is, without needing to give anyone direct instructions about how exactly to do that and where to go.

Interestingly, the Internet does not need any kind of agreement or consensus to function or for people to use it. All that is needed is agreement on the underlying protocol that is used, and that is exactly what the Internet Protocol (or IP) represents (a set of agreed upon rules for routing information from one place to another). There also is no central organisation or authority within the Internet that can unilaterally force one rule set upon its users.

The Internet also doesn't really have a way to ensure that the information sent from point A reaches the destination point Z from an assurance standpoint. There is no guarantee. Individual Internet service providers (ISPs) do compete on the basis of the performance and reliability of their service but they are not mandated to do so.

Perhaps this is the reason why the Internet's success has come quite as a surprise. Now, when a device is connected to the Internet, it uses its IP address (that is why we always talk of IP addresses). The Internet is further divided into autonomous systems (AS), which is, for all extents and purposes, the denomination used to ascertain large collections of devices or networks that use one particular routing policy.

In terms of our investigative question, Geoffrey Goodell does an excellent job at highlighting three areas that represent aspects of centralisation in the Internet.[4]

The first has to do with the allocation of IP addresses. So, how are IP addresses and AS numbers generated? There are actually five regional Internet registries that assign them (AFRINIC, LACNIC, RIPE NCC, ARIN, and APNIC). Whilst there is no real or material difference to the allocation of those IP addresses and AS numbers, there can be when it comes to carriers doing the allocation and managing the delivery of information based on IP addresses. What this means is that anyone using the Internet has to be comfortable with that centralised set of entities that allocate the IP addresses and AS numbers (which is how devices and collections of devices are identified and consequently, information being routed to them). Now in practice, carriers can actually further allocate IP addresses to those devices that are part of its network and thereby route data and information between those devices that are connected to its network and those that are not, however, it would like. As Goodell highlights, this creates a disparity in the types of users of the Internet.[5]

Let's move to another innovation: routing. This is where the Border Gateway Protocol (BGP) comes in, which is what AS's use to pass on information about how they can be reached.[6]

The early Internet was much simpler and consequently much smaller than it is now and simple routing was possible. As the Internet grew BGP became a necessity. It was first described in 1989 in RFC number 1105 and has been in use on the Internet since 1994.

There are many ways of getting from any AS to another. But any of these routes need to actually be found. When a route is selected after being advertised, packets of data can then move from point A to Z.

Things can, of course, go wrong. For example, where the messaging application WhatsApp was advertising some routes but there was a network in Switzerland named Safe Host that advertised those routes to everyone, thinking it was a good network to route to WhatsApp, which was then picked up by China Telecom which then passed them to Cogent, who thought the best route to WhatsApp was to go through China Telecom, and was then blocked.[7]

The second area has to do with naming. When it comes to naming (the actual domain names of websites), it is the primary responsibility of the Domain Name System (DNS) to assign different domain names, who further rely on a number of organisations like the Internet Corporation for Assigned Names and Numbers (ICANN), a non-profit organisation, as well as others. The registrars register domain names, and there are usual third party providers that we use to go about registering them to get the name we want. Hence the .com boom. So, who determines if someone gets a particular name or not? We rely on each of these registrars doing the right thing, including keeping a record and adhering to certain policies.[8]

The third area highlighted by Goodell has to do with verification. Since Internet routing is fundamentally decentralised, how can one be sure that the other party to a conversation, as identified by its IP address or domain name, is authentic? This is a question of security, and we know that we can use cryptography not only to protect our conversations from eavesdropping but also to verify the authenticity of a conversation endpoint using digital certificates (such as SSL).[9] Certificate Authorities come in here as trusted third parties (there are six main certificate issuers). These Certificate Authorities sign certificates so that they are accessible and reachable when using different operating systems and web browsers (and often come preconfigured with them).

These act as trust anchors by providing security and authenticity. At the same time, these trusted third parties can also fail even though we refer to them as Certificate Authorities, meaning that they are in principle trusted by default. One prominent example of where things have gone wrong is the example of the Stuxnet worm, which was apparently developed by government bodies in 2010 and had been used to infiltrate and compromise an Iranian nuclear facility but then took on a life of its own. As it spread across the wider Internet, it infected DigiNotar, a Certificate Authority.[10] This ultimately led to the interception of some Internet services provided by Google.[11]

Centralisation does by definition pose risks, which are acutely obvious when we consider the cyber space. This is where the argument for redecentralisation becomes stronger and stronger as cyber security challenges are increasing exponentially on the path of digitisation. Recent improvements in the security of edge devices like biometric authentication of users to their phones through fingerprint, face recognition and other forms are to some extent rebuilding trust. AI and DLT are building on this with predictive analytics and value exchange services.

The Three Waves of the Internet

Having established some of the background, we also need to understand that the Internet has been changing its nature since inception, and that in waves. The first wave of the www was what we call Web 1.0, which began roughly in 1991 and ended around 2004. The Internet before and including Web 1.0 was made up of static websites, and primarily text-based data sets, enabling users to only view and thus consume digital content. This was followed in 2004 by Web 2.0, coinciding with the arrival of Facebook, which enabled interoperability of platforms and allowed users to consume, create, upload and engage with content. It remains the Internet we still use today. It is still funded by advertising but this advertising is guided by AI-based predictive analytics these days. Our online activities are watched (whatever our privacy settings) and targeted advertising, based on a prediction of our needs, is delivered.

With the arrival of blockchain and DLT, and other technology systems creating networks, Web3 is in the making. All circles are around blockchain, cryptocurrencies, DAOs, NFTs and the Metaverse. This changes how we connect with each other, as it permits peer-to-peer connections, rather than forcing users to pass through intermediaries. Distribution of data across all network nodes—once fully in place—will make it harder to hack. Also, the tech stack transition to DLT will move more and more transactions on-chain, thus putting in place transparency, which will hopefully make fraudulent behaviour, amongst many other mischiefs, much more difficult (with off-chain capabilities for ease and efficiency). For example, we have decentralised applications or dApps. dApps also have native tokens associated to them and users are enabled to vote with these, a new method of user engagement.

Web3 also offers the opportunity to improve efficiency. Today users either have to pay for services or, if services are seemingly free, they actually pay with their data, which is harvested by various data brokers. Web3 promises to provide more freedom, decentralisation and privacy. However, global viewpoints on privacy differ widely. The National Security Agency (NSA) in the US assumes a right to the personal information of all citizens globally. This is challenged by other countries and regions, e.g. Max Schrems has successfully done it from an EU viewpoint twice and is about to do it again. This could hail the arrival of decentralisation to the benefit of all but the proof will be in the pudding. We are still early in this journey. The metaverse, whilst immersive, is only at the start of its ability to be as realistic as possible. So too, is a new, fully integrated network across many technologies, and everything we do day-to-day, from playing games, communicating and messaging, purchasing, selling and all the rest, where these elements are brought together in a way that is at your doorstep and under your control doing to all value what the Internet did to information.

3.3 The Advent of the Cloud

Because of the increasing ubiquity of 'the Cloud', or so is our impression of the current state of technology in the industry, we felt that it would merit a separate section in order to demystify this concept, unless you are of course very familiar with it.

With the increasing dependence of many companies on global Internet coverage and the expense of providing that as an internal service, businesses started "outsourcing" some of their services to third party providers (usually their ISP). Eventually for economic and security related reasons large data centres were built. These sit on massive fibre networks and maintain the highest levels of security. Various data services, which businesses might need, can be housed in one datacentre as services (e.g. banks, Microsoft, Salesforce, Government, Logistics, Marketing). By making a local connection to one of these data centres, a business can economically access a diverse set of "services" according to its needs. These services are now known as "Cloud Services" and are provided by specialist cloud providers.

Cloud has become a sort of sales and marketing buzzword in the industry with the suggested implication that using the Cloud is inherently better than not using it. When you try to dig deeper, confusion often starts to erupt. Core business critical services can be kept within the company network for security and resilience reasons but most of the other computer services are usually cheaper in the Cloud.

Talking to technologists the Cloud is seen as an exciting opportunity, in particular because it is not only about on demand computing power, but the many tools and services offered by Cloud providers, such as Amazon, Google and Microsoft. A term used for the all-in is to go 'Cloud Native', where the whole gambit of Cloud is being deployed, including serverless computing, containerised web applications and security solutions. The Cloud is a clever thing, leveraging the subscription model to create an on-demand culture of computing. It is big revenue for a handful of players, the top three being Amazon, Microsoft, Google, followed by more narrow propositions by Alibaba, IBM and Oracle. Cloud computing, however, is from its beginning until to date a rather centralised phenomenon. And as you may already guess at this point, decentralisation is likely to feature in what we consider to be a better way forward for both industry and individual users.

How Clouds Have Formed

Over the last decades, computers and software became cheaper and cheaper, leading to mass adoption in the financial industry. In the first phase, the focus was on mainframes and internal time-sharing, but over time every employee was able to have their own computer, further decentralising computer usage during the 1980s and 1990s. With more breadth of new products and solutions appearing, including in the trading space, in turn more demand for PCs and workstations became the response. Along the way data became more and more fragmented up until the millennium as different data would sit across many different workstations and PCs without any connection between it and no data normalisation and standardisation efforts that could be applied in order to make sense of it at an organisational level. Of course, protecting data from theft also became a real issue as those were the days where PC security wasn't taken too seriously—cybercrime and risk training really only came into the daily lives of organisations a good 15 years later. The plethora of systems and hardware also increased costs, all of which pushed towards the central server model and increased limitations and controls for PC users. These servers are expensive and with the amount of data exponentially increasing, more and more servers would become necessary, increasing demand and challenging supply. Also, next to the hardware, software configuration was not an easy task. This is when the business model of outsourcing these servers would become a more pressing need for the industry and Amazon Web Services (AWS) having moved on from the initial concept of turning the bookstore online began to offer virtual server access, based on an underlying shared pool of servers in 2004. This was the same basic economic concept as Time Sharing, which emerged in the 1970s and enabled many computers to share the same resource at the same time facilitated by multi-programming and multi-tasking. Single computers tend to use small but very variable quantities of computer resources, i.e. storage, memory and processing power. Tapping into a big network of servers by many computers can significantly increase utilisation and thus reduce cost.

In terms of basic vocabulary, there are two terms that are key to the Cloud. First, we have the Private Cloud, which means a Cloud computing environment dedicated to a single customer. Many organisations still prefer this concept as it combines many of the benefits of Cloud computing with the security and control of on-premise IT infrastructure. Secondly, we have the term Public Cloud, a Cloud shared between many customers.

The financial crisis of 2008/2009 made the appeal of cost reduction through outsourcing to become a business priority. As long as something was 'non-differentiating' to other competitors, outsourcing would almost become the norm. It started with computing power via the Cloud but today we commonly see various permutations of services—more on that below. Suffice to say that we are witnessing an ever-increasing list of outsourcing options, which are all supported by the Cloud.

Ingredients to Running IT

Businesses that run applications, let's say a bank, need of course computer hardware and software. In a simplified view, software can come in form of an operating system, a database management system and web servers, where the latter might run on specific software depending on the nature of the business (e.g. in investment banking you would have trading applications).

To run the hardware, software and necessary human resources, various options and combinations are possible.

Business systems can be written by bank IT staff and managed internally. But over the last two decades, we have seen that IT systems in banks and other financial services providers are not specialised enough for the demands and opportunities that new technologies and new forms of coding and data science enable. Therefore, buying business software from third party vendors has become more common. This can be either installed and managed internally or completely outsourced to the vendor and run on their infrastructure, and it can be a bespoke solution or one that is shared also with other customers. Utility software itself can either be managed by a vendor or in-house, but is almost never written by a firm's IT team.

When it comes to hardware and here we speak about servers, they can either be allocated to specific applications or used as a pool to support many software services, the latter being the Cloud we are talking about. Management of course can be outsourced or insourced.

Looking one further layer down, server centres, these can equally be owned and managed in-house or outsourced to a third party. Increasingly, third parties may also outsource these to another third party—layering of outsourcing!—such as AWS.

Depending on what is outsourced and insourced, this may also lead to more flexibility with regard to human resources, where increasingly we see less fixed staff in some areas of IT as a consequence.

There are many types of concepts that can be delivered as outsourced solutions. One that we hear about very often is Software as a Service (SaaS). So, what is behind that? SaaS is when software is provided by a third party and also runs on that third party's hardware. The hardware could be the third party's own server, an internal network of servers—i.e. a private Cloud—or provided by a public Cloud provider such as AWS or Google or Microsoft Azure.

Then we have Infrastructure as a Service (IaaS) where a third party provides the hardware, managed inside its own service centres. There is also Platform as a Service (PaaS). In this model, core utility software, such as operating systems, web servers, databases and even versions of blockchain technology, is provided in addition to hardware. Typically, today this is done on a Cloud of servers. By now we even have Exchange as a Service (EaaS), where technology is provided as underlying infrastructure for new forms of exchanges, such as digital exchanges.

These examples already show us that the popular labelling—for example of SaaS solutions as Cloud solutions—is incorrect and confusing.

Economics of the Cloud

Now the good thing about the Cloud is that it can truly bring efficiencies and economies of scale. Where dealing with all the server buying, set up and maintenance is a protracted, painful and expensive exercise, tapping into the Cloud—on demand—feels a bit like magic. The more users there are in a Cloud, the more varied user profiles there will be in the mix, which means that overall a smaller amount of resources would be used more intensively. And the fact that more resources can be added quickly, e.g. memory, Central Processing Units (CPUs), etc., also means that the Cloud model is elastic.

Now we have already seen that Cloud services are really a commodity set of products. All the things that institutions do not consider as their 'secret sauce' in this area are increasingly outsourced to the Cloud. We also know that a market of commoditised products or services would be competitive if customers can move easily between different suppliers. Now is this then the case for Cloud services?

Well, and here is the thing. It's not that easy and certainly not that cheap. Because today Cloud providers charge money (not always cheap) if you want to transfer your data to another Cloud provider. But that's not the biggest issue. In fact, the clever part of the un-competitiveness of providers in this market is due to the practice of the so-called Cloud Nativc functionality. Whilst many developers rave about these as they make their life easier and surely create many other benefits, the fact is that most types of the Cloud native functionalities are inextricably linked to a specific Cloud provider. In practice this means that if software is specifically written in order to benefit from tools for let's say Google Cloud, then if you want to move to another Cloud provider that is cheaper, in addition to paying a fee for the move, you could end up having to re-write your software as well! A bit of a hidden problem if you don't read your contract, product descriptions and other relevant documents in detail.

Many companies also moved to Cloud providers in addition to their normal ISP in order not only to access SaaS economically but to give them a backup connection. A recent development to help with this has been the emergence of overlay providers that allow you to connect to multiple Clouds. But whether this will also permit the use of all Cloud provider-specific functionalities is not so clear.

The Cloud is a great example of centralisation in action. Injecting redecentralisation by leveraging blockchain could potentially be a way to rebalance this space in favour of users. And indeed, more recently, we have started to see the attempt to provide decentralised Cloud services. This is something that we will be elaborating further on in our final chapter, when we look into the future. A space to watch.

3.4 Making Sense of Blockchain and Distributed Ledger Technologies

In the early days of computing (1960s), the world was centralised with mainframe computers. It took a good 20 years through local area networking (LAN) and client server stages for distribution to become more prevalent with the broader adoption of stand-alone personal computers. The next step was to connect the Internet to these personal computers, which then became smaller and smaller over time until we saw the smartphone, a tiny supercomputer, in our pockets. Since Bitcoin appeared on the scene in 2009 the terminology of decentralised and distributed systems has increasingly made inroads into our mainstream vocabulary, notwithstanding their long history in academia, political theory, economics, and the origins of the Internet. The underlying DLT, however, is not so new, and goes back to the 1970s with the Merkle Tree as explained in Table 3.3 below. As we will see in this section, there are various technological building blocks of DLT, which date back in some instances as far as the 1970s. With regard to our spectrum, one could argue that the first comprehensive DLT application with Bitcoin was not only focused on the aspect of distribution but chiefly aimed to decentralise the system against the backdrop of a perceived mistrust in intermediaries within the financial system, inspired by the shortcomings exposed during the 2008 financial crisis. Since then, however, we see that elements of centralisation are increasingly creeping in. In particular as the regulated financial industry is looking to leverage DLT, decentralisation of decision-making and operating is not centre of mind. Bitcoin and its version of DLT—the Bitcoin blockchain—did manage to unleash a new era of technology, where almost any sector in the economy has become to be questioned in terms of the need for intermediaries, threatening to potentially take them out. It brought forth a shift in thinking, an idea, enabled by technology, for other architectures, technologies, and processes that may have nothing to do with blockchain, that can do the same to other sectors and other industries. However, the forces are clawing back and we observe in many areas the phenomenon of re-centralisation, rather than redecentralisation.

Let us briefly examine blockchain and the example of Bitcoin that will illustrate what we mean by that.

An Excursion into Blockchain

DLT is just a new kind of database where any given update to said database is made as an entry to the end of the database. In regular databases, you can change the database at any time by modifying an existing entry and saving it. Now, when it comes to corporate and government databases, there are of course very strict rules around who can do what. Nothing is generally deleted; the previous versions of the database can be seen in history tables and there are logs of specific actions and who took them. You can set up a database in a sloppy way that does none of that but it actually requires a bit of effort to be that sloppy. Still, the fact that someone could technically go back and change anything is a risk. And if you are in an environment where there are no rules and controls, you need to ensure that no one can arbitrarily change the shared history of records. This is what the Bitcoin blockchain as a type of DLT was able to do.

There are three main things that blockchain can deliver in a novel and interesting way. A record, a timestamp of that record and the proof that the record is authentic. The way this works is by adding data in a new block to the end of the database or chain of blocks, stamping it with a proof that identifies its unique order so we know its chronology, which is the timestamp, and then 'hashing' it together to demonstrate that the block should be added to the chain of blocks. Every new block—updates to the database regarding some record—can be identified and is validated by its 'hash', which was created from data that includes the block before it. By doing this over and over, you have a connected chain from the very first block, referred to as the Genesis Block to the block that's just been created, recording the most recent transaction. Of course, those records could be records of everything and anything.

By thinking about it this way, blockchain is really a pretty cool way of time-stamping something so that you can prove when something happened and prove that it has not been mucked around with and also affixing a digital signature to something. In essence it is really just a new kind of accounting that can be verified: in other words: 'verifiable accounting!'

The idea then is to combine data, which could be anything like records of transactions, healthcare records, social media records, news records, historical records and pictures which are then stamped in a block in the blockchain, much like having these records notarised. Only those records or 'transactions' that are validated by the network are added to the record history, which is the 'chain' in 'blockchains'. In that way DLT really replaces centralised decision-makers/notaries with communal decentralised notaries, and the data record on the chain is meant to reflect the trusted data outcome of this process. Once these records are validated—stamped so to say, like a notary—they are distributed to all the members in the network that then verify them and update their own version of the database providing an updated version of the history of records. This means that one person or a small group of people cannot arbitrarily make a change because all members of the network have copies of the original. Instead of one company like your local bank, or a tech company or a government being the final arbiter and instead of this record residing in one place only, it is now in many places with many people. Creating a new record that is updated in the

Table 3.3 The Merkle tree

Patented by Ralph Merkle in 1979, the Merkle tree, otherwise known as a hash tree, serves as a tool to securely verify the contents of large data structures. Every node, also called 'leaf' of a Merkle tree, represents the cryptographic hash of a data block, whereas every node that is not a leaf, but rather a branch or inner node, is a cryptographic hash of the labels of its child nodes. Such a hash tree enables efficient and secure verification of contents of large structures of data. In very simple terms, a Merkle tree is what we call a 'cryptographic commitment scheme' where the tree root is considered a commitment and the leaf nodes can be proven to be part of this original commitment. Merkle used the Merkle tree to provide digital signatures … more than 40 years ago!

network requires the majority of members of the network to accept it, typically 51% of the network. To make a change that previously was recorded and verified would require convincing a lot of people in the network to agree to your version of history instead of the history recorded and publicly made available to everyone else on the network.

An important feature of the blockchain is the use of the Merkel Tree (see Table 3.3 above) as this can show evidence of tampering. But in addition, specific forms of consensus such as Proof of Work are required to make the blockchain 'tamper resistant' (Fig. 3.1).

Other ingredients, such as the invention of public-key cryptography by Diffie and Hellmann in 1976, used to provide security to plain text and clipboard attacks, as well as timestamping of digital documents in 1991 by Stuart Haber and W. Scott Stornetta, which prevented the ability of users to backdate or forward date those documents, were also essential for the blockchain to appear.

So was David Chaum's vault system for trusting computer systems of 1982, which already included many building blocks of the blockchain, even though that ultimately came along in 2008 when Nakamoto presented the architecture for the Bitcoin blockchain in which he introduced the concept of a 'chain of blocks', enabling new blocks to be added without the need for these to be signed by a trusted third party (thus removing elements of centralisation!). The Byzantine General's Problem by Lamport and Shostack[12] is another key challenge that modern DLT has begun to solve (more on that in a later chapter). By combining these key inventions, Nakamoto also created the concept of a 'chain of digital signatures', which enabled owners of coins to transfer these directly to the next owner via the process of digitally signing a hash of the previous transaction and combining this with the public key of the next coin owner in line and adding this information to the end of the coin that is being transferred.

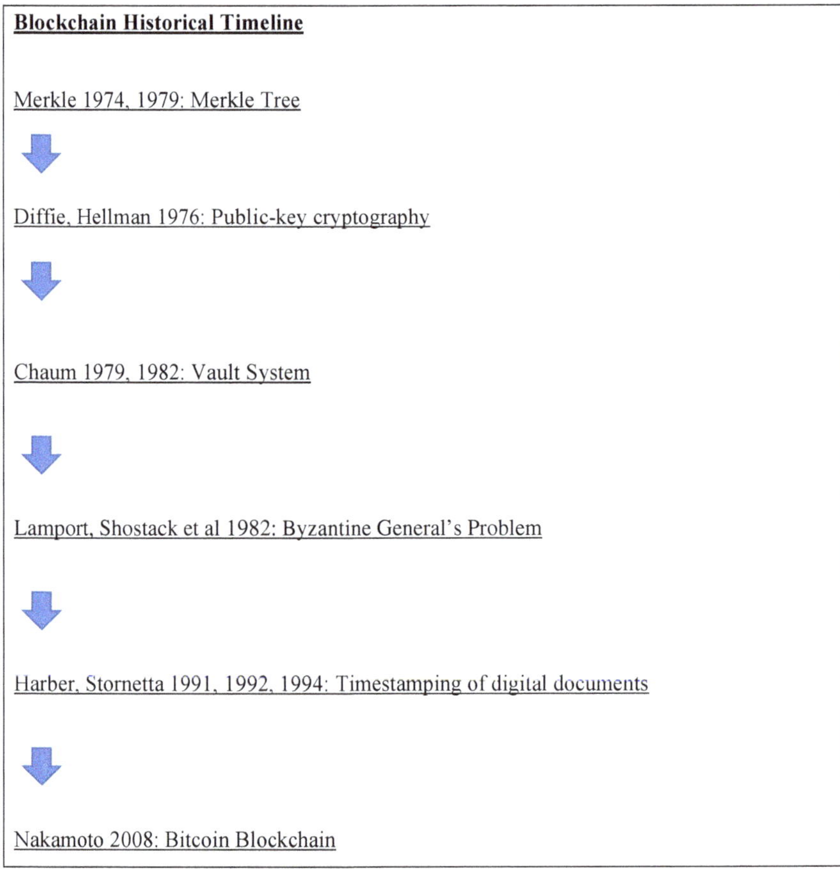

Fig. 3.1 Blockchain historical timeline

For a historical timeline of blockchain, see Figure 3.1 above. To complement the above overview, it is useful to provide a snapshot of how a distributed ledger is structured.

In a nutshell, we have four key elements as follows:

Protocol Layer. The set of rules that define the system and its architecture as a whole including: (1) system code; (2) architecture; (3) how changes are made to the system code; and (4) modifications and developments to alter the system architecture.

Network Layer. The operational use of and implementation of the set of rules to; (1) use data; (2) store data; and (3) join, leave, or participate in the system's network.

Consensus Layer. The implementation and decision-making that is the result of the set of rules and used by the network in implementing that set of rules. The consensus layer also consists of part of the technology governance framework, occurring on-chain.

Data layer. The categorisation, use, storage and meaning of the data that is being collected.

Application layer. The applications that all participants use in order to participate in the network.

DLT and Decentralisation

To be able to create fully decentralised systems, the only overarching architecture or type of governance that would allow for it in the space of DLT is through public/permissionless ledgers. A public blockchain also typically aims to provide anonymity or pseudonymity, the governance structure is cooperative, and the network aims to be democratically controlled based on the consensus mechanism employed. Truth be told, the reality has shown that this aim has thus far largely failed. Those with the most hash power also happen to have more real power in practice. This is the case in Proof of Work (PoW) blockchains. Similarly, in a Proof of Stake (PoS) blockchain, a voting group that construes a supermajority can control the governance. Essentially, such governance structures can be viewed as cartels or oligarchies within the network that prevent true decentralisation.

In practice, however, it is not simply permissioned or permissionless as there also exist various hybrid versions that may be both public and permissioned and are not fully decentralised because of the gatekeeper functions that still exist, thus limiting participation in the decision-making system. Examples of these types of hybrid architectures are Hedera Hashgraph and Ripple, Hyperledger and Besu.

In terms of permissioned blockchains, there are also state-run distributed ledgers that are used and operated by governments for the purpose of different services or functions. It is interesting here to call out Estonia's digital identity management, which has been labelled as a blockchain system more for marketing purposes than anything else, but under the hood is essentially centralised, despite using a Merkel Tree structure. Other DLT use cases cover land registries, court records and healthcare records in order to provide ease of use, access and reduce the centralisation risk inherent in having one database that stores all data, but also to better enable data transfer, exchange and access across multiple parties. These types of state-operated permissioned DLTs typically have stakeholders elect different board members, and where a broad set of stakeholders is allowed to view but not edit (read and not write) the ledger, whereas only a few entities can validate and process transactions. Private blockchains are actually pretty pointless because you have thrown away the decentralised consensus mechanism. Basically, you just have the 'tamper evident' feature of Merkel trees, but things are not 'tamper proof'. However, you can also argue that private blockchains can be useful for specific use cases. Whilst the highest form of transparency is public facing, private blockchains do provide a facility for extending trusted data across a value chain.

There are also private blockchains whose purpose is typically linked to driving efficiencies and improvement of process management. This involves creating applications for the business itself where the management board of the organisation or the committee established across multiple organisations are the main stakeholders, operators, and owners that govern the direction of the system. We have, of course, seen the milieu of different consortium blockchains that are private and permissioned such as R3s Corda, as well as many others that have a predetermined process for electing and selecting members to be part of the system that operate nodes to validate transactions.

It is important to note that the type of system, whether permissioned, permissionless or hybrid in combination with the consensus/governance model employed is directly correlated to the degree of decentralisation of the particular system. The consensus model governs the process by which transactions, and therefore activities are allowed, the rules to which any actions on the system need to adhere to in order to be taken. (De)centralisation is by no means a binary concept, but as previously mentioned consists of two linguistic steps. Firstly, whether centralised or not as determined by having a central authority or not, and secondly in comparison with one another against two main parameters, namely whether permissioned or permissionless, and the type of consensus/governance model. The major consensus mechanisms, which we want to mention here as a manifestation of governance, are Proof of Work and Proof of Stake.

Proof of Work is commonly seen as the first type of consensus mechanism that was used in a public blockchain, specifically the Bitcoin blockchain.[13] Proof of Work uses a process of mining where the nodes which keep the network operational solve complex mathematical problems through the use of computing power. The more computational power is used, the faster the asymmetric mathematical problems that need to be solved in order to calculate the hash of a new block.[14] For solving these problems, miners are rewarded with coins in return. This is the protocol used in the Bitcoin blockchain. In order for the miners to make a successful attempt at identifying the winning block, they need to solve for what is termed the nonce—"number only used once".[15] Node operators are incentivised in the proof of work model by being provided with rewards of transaction fees and block rewards if and only if the block they have identified is included in the chain.[16] Due to this architecture, it is often assumed that it is difficult for any one party or entity to control the majority of total computational power and thus prevent a Sybil attack from occurring.[17]

Proof-of-Stake, in most implementations today, utilises a randomised process to identify who or what will determine the consecutive block. In order to be considered by the process, a certain number of tokens must be staked/locked up for a particular duration. Once this is done, the entity will become a validator on the network whereby it is able to discover new blocks of data and receive a reward if it is included in the chain. This is the Protocol that is used in Ethereum which has undergone a shift from the PoW mechanism to a PoS one in 2022. PoS is considered to be more energy efficient than PoW.[18] The central tenet to the various PoS mechanisms is that the node, which is allowed to propose a consecutive block is determined by the proportion of a particular digital asset being staked. This assumes that the more an entity, individual, or group stakes the less likely they will attempt to sabotage the decision-making process because they have 'skin in the game'.[19] And also, part of staking is that if you try to cheat the system, you will pay a penalty of some or all of your stake. This is a disincentive against bad behaviour. PoS basically rewards you by paying out tokens as a function of your stake size (like an interest payment) for good behaviour.

A more recent consensus mechanism is the *Convergent Proof of Stake* algorithm, which creates a conflict-free replicated data type that provably converges to a stable ordering of transactions, effectively solving the double-spent problem in a very fast and Byzantine fault-tolerant way. This decentralised consensus mechanism may well be the foundation for a future decentralised ecosystem of digital assets of any kind. There is a provider that operates this consensus algorithm on the basis of lattice technology, which can replace blockchain as the underlying substrate for decentralised payment systems, particularly in the retail context with up to 30,000 transactions per second. Something to watch more closely!

And then we have the famous 'forks'.

Soft-forks are software updates for the blockchain or DL being used and are often implemented in order to refine governance rules or fix bugs in the system's underlying code software. Soft-forks, unlike hard-forks, are compatible with the previous blockchain. Soft-forks are also completely optional for the users of the system and participants in the network. Thus a soft-fork does not result in the creation of a new cryptocurrency or asset. However, soft-forks are examples where people like miners can exert enormous power. If the miners don't take the updated software, the soft-fork will fail and even turn into a hard-fork.

Hard-forks result in the splitting up of the blockchain system into two parallel networks which results in two unique crypto-assets on each system. Typically, the underlying code of the system is replicated with the same transaction history but all future transactions are distinct and run on a new software code with a new digital asset that is not fungible with the old one. In practice, hard-forks occur when there are competing developer groups that are unable to reach agreement or where system critical issues require fixing. Hard-forks also often lead to impacts on the use and pricing of the crypto-asset. These forks are of particular relevance for both digital only stores of value as well as security tokens and stablecoins (more on these later). When these are traded on secondary markets and a hard-fork occurs, the system becomes less conducive or secure, and therefore, the preference is to remain on the previous system, where the other loses its developer, miner and user support. This can pose significant security, and operational usability risks for the platform but also create technical risks, which digital custody providers need to be aware of and accommodate.

There are also a variety of hybrid solutions that have emerged or are beginning to emerge, including private databases on public blockchains, or off-chain storage units with a public blockchain, alternatively open consensus but permissioned governance (e.g. Hedera Hashgraph with their 39 multinational corporates serving as their Global Governing Council and their main node operators) but also Ripple. Although these hybrid models do not allow any individual or entity to participate, they are partially permissioned environments. Due to this there have been implementations of Proof of Authority where the consensus itself is determined by selecting or randomly selecting an authority and it is assumed that these authorities are trustworthy to determine the most recent version of the database (Angelis et al., 2018). There are many other consensus mechanisms that exist and that are being researched, tried, and tested including proof-of-existence, proof-of-burn, proof-of-elapsed time and many more.

Decentralised Autonomous Organisation

A DAO refers to a decentralised autonomous organisation, one of the first of which aimed to enable the creation of a user-controlled venture capital fund (this was also called the DAO), and which suffered a significant hack, where an error in the underlying code resulted in funds being stolen. In summary, first, tokens were sold. Those tokens were accompanied by voting rights in relation to proposals the fund would invest in. Second, after this took place and was created, and due to an error in the underlying code, $60 million worth of ether were stolen.[20] The DAO was entirely governed by code and smart contracts. Once this hack took place, a hard-fork occurred in order to essentially erase the occurrence of the hack. This was supported by the majority of Ethereum miners at the time, but it also resulted in a new coin and in the transactions being completely modified. Since then, the idea of a DAO has become a label for a fully autonomous entity run on a variety of smart contracts and code that is borderless and controlled by its stakeholders. Another early example of a DAO is Dash which is a blockchain that aims to provide additional encryption and anonymity around transactions in their native digital assets, primarily for payment purposes.

Public blockchain systems are not really distributed systems in the conventional (i.e. real) sense of the word, in spite of the use of the term 'Distributed Ledger'. They are really massively duplicated centralised systems because instead of each full node performing a different task, all full nodes attempt to perform the same task, i.e. processing transactions, and creating blocks.

When it comes to the question of decentralisation, public blockchains are the only ones that can display features of decentralisation, subject to the specific consensus model deployed and its effectiveness. But as soon as we see deployment of private blockchains and DLT structures we are by definition looking at a centralised structure. As the regulated financial industry as well as other sectors and government are beginning to deploy DLT, centralisation is going to be the prevalent trend for these applications. In parallel, the building of an alternative financial ecosystem with Defi, or decentralised finance, promises more decentralisation. Still we are at an early stage with this and entering as well as exiting Defi structures does require the deployment of centralised procedures, controls and regulations, such as KYC, AML, identification of users etc. We shall examine later on in the book where this path is likely to lead us, but for now we have to soberly note that the redecentralisation trend was limited to the early days of Bitcoin.

3.5 Demystifying AI

Artificial Intelligence—in short AI—has become quite a hype word over the last few years. From the day-to-day convenience of AI in your mobile phone to the fear of being taken over by machines (as predicted in the film 'the Matrix'), AI is often invoked in many different guises and contexts without necessarily being clear as to what AI is or does and what it could evolve into. This is why in the following section we want to shed light on the mysterium that is AI and we hope that reading it will be far less of a challenge than it was to write it!

The history of AI has not been very long, but certainly very exciting, in particular since the 1990s. Following Alan Turing's famous Turing Test for the evaluation of intelligence in 1950,[21] the term 'Artificial Intelligence' was defined by John McCarthy, who became the Father of Artificial Intelligence, at the 1955 Dartmouth workshop as *"The science and engineering of making intelligent machines, especially intelligent computer programs. Every aspect of learning or any other feature of intelligence can in principle be so precisely described that a machine can be made to simulate it. An attempt will be made to find how to make machines use language, form abstractions and concepts, solve kinds of problems now reserved for humans, and improve themselves".*
One year later McCarthy demonstrated the first-ever running AI programme at Carnegie Mellon University.

In those days, to be more precise, seven areas of AI were defined, describing how AI machines can do what a human can do.

1. Simulating higher functions of the brain.
2. Programming a computer to use general language.
3. Arranging hypothetical neurons in a manner so that they can form concepts.
4. A way to determine and measure problem complexity.
5. Self-improvement.
6. Abstraction: Defined as the quality of dealing with ideas rather than events.
7. Randomness and creativity.

After more than 60 years of progress on numbers 2, 4 and 5 to some degree, 7 is just starting to be explored.

Since those days many advances have been made in AI, ranging from language recognition and programming to vision, drawing and combined abilities to problem solving. Advances have also been delivered in the microprocessors and computing power that provides for the ability to use AI models meaningfully to process large amounts of structured and unstructured data. It is interesting to note here that the first computer-controlled autonomous vehicle was already built in 1973!

AI needs to be differentiated from "Machine Learning" with which it is often confused (see later information). ML programmes for personal computers exist since the 1980s such as Borland's Prolog. These have the ability to basically "learn" from various inputs such as question responses or sensor input and deduce an intelligent response in the same way that a human might. ML programmes do not generally have the power to look forward or predict outcomes.

During the 1990s AI moves into innovation acceleration, further fuelled by the arrival of the Internet, e.g. web crawling. In 1997 the Deep Blue Chess Program beats world chess champion Garry Kasparov. The world wakes up to AI! And even more prudently, digitisation of interactions, exchange, media and more as enabled by the Internet provides fertile ground for AI through new customer facing business models and the extent of the type and amount of data available.

At the end of the day, AI is all about the ability of a machine to (almost) imitate a human being and do something better, in a way that is somewhat similar to a human being. And it is this ability to mimic human beings that is the reason AI is getting so much attention with its possibility for replacing human jobs, turning humans into cyborgs, or the creation of some super intelligence that feeds off of everyone's data through the Internet. But today, and for the foreseeable future, AI is ultimately a model for complex probabilistic decision-making that optimises processes or predicts behaviour of some kind.

Navigating the AI Landscape

Since the 1950s AI has evolved, which means that we now look at these seven elements in a more nuanced way. Today we find three broad categories of AI amongst experts:

1. Weak or Narrow AI: 'Artificial Narrow Intelligence' (ANI)
2. Strong or General AI: 'Artificial General Intelligence' (AGI)
3. Artificial Super Intelligence (ASI)

As you can imagine ANI is the type of AI that we encounter nearly every day. Technologies that are restricted to their scope of application and frankly do their job increasingly well. Narrow or Weak AI-based systems can behave like a human, but it is not clear how this is coming about; for example, we do not understand how the Deep Blue Chess programme managed to beat Kasparov. It is kind of a 'Black Box' where a model is created by which to process data. The data is provided to that model as input and the output is some decision. Yet it is unclear specifically what the decision-making process has been. And this is part of the reason why AI models are not yet used in socially sensitive areas, such as criminal sentencing, the allocation of government resources and the like.

AGI is the aspiration to achieve AI that is able to simulate a human brain itself, so to do things outside a human-defined scope and expected outcome.

ASI today falls in the realm of fiction and so we only hypothesise as to what the future could hold. The likes of Stephen Hawking and Elon Musk have already expressed their concerns over what could happen if we create super intelligence that becomes infinitely smarter than humans and might even choose to eliminate humankind as a social step. The film fantasy world is unfortunately no longer just that and awareness and action, before it is 'too late' will need to be required by all of us.

In the below you will see a list of AI type technologies included with their own definitions:

- A basic form of ANI is what we call Robotic Process Automation (RPA), which is based on rules and actions obtained through observation. Taken to the next level we have Intelligent Process Automation, or IPA.
- Expert Systems are based on rule code that aims to copy humans in their decision-making. A subcategory of this is fuzzy systems which apply fuzzy logic, as a form of reasoning that resembles human reasoning. Expert Systems employ human knowledge in a computer to solve problems that ordinarily require human expertise.
- Focusing on specific senses another form of ANI is computer vision, where computers can understand, interpret and comprehend visual inputs; this is, for example, used in clinical diagnostics for patients or by the police in terms of recognising the faces of criminals. Another example in this field is handwriting recognition software that recognises the shapes of the letters and convert them into editable text.
- An ANI that is in frequent use in terms of commercial solutions we see today (e.g. in financial services) is Natural Language Processing (NPL), which focuses on language understanding, generation and machine translation. NPL algorithms combine a knowledge-based approach, machine learning and probabilistic methods to solve problems in the domain of perception. In such a way, humans can interact with computers that understand their language.
- Algorithms inspired by the neural structure of the brain are so-called neural networks, where performance improves without the need for instruction to do so. Deep Learning and Generative AI are two increasingly important areas of neural networks. In Deep Learning, nodes are acting as artificial neurons connecting information. Generative AI is able to generate new outputs on the basis of data it has been trained on. Generative AI itself has three subcategories: General Adversarial Networks (GANs), AutoRegressive Convolutional Neural Networks (AR-CNN) and Transformer-based models. In the case of GANs, we have networks training each other. More later on Generative AI, which has become a recent buzzwords, a problematic interference in human education and an awfully big risk to personal agency...
- Cutting across robotics and intelligent systems we find Autonomous Systems, which, for example, combine intelligent perception with object manipulation.
- An emerging exiting field of AI, which is in the AGI space, is Distributed Artificial Intelligence (DAI), where problems are distributed to autonomous agents that interact with each other. Agent-Based-Modelling (ABM), Multi-Agent-Systems (MAS) and Swarm Intelligence fall into this category, where the interaction of decentralised independent agents leads to collective behaviours (we will pick this area up in more detail when we discuss DeFi later on).
- Going deeper into human traits, such as emotions, interpretation, recognition and simulation we find Affective Computing.

- Human evolution is also used in the computer science field of evolutionary computation. An AI form here is Evolutionary Algorithms (EA) that mimic biological concepts such as reproduction and mutation to identify optimal solutions. An example of such algorithms would be Genetic Algorithms that search for the 'fittest' solution.
- Decision-making is enhanced with the use of Decision Networks, such as the Bayesian Network, where a group of variables and their probabilistic relationship are mapped out on what we call a 'directed acyclic graph'.
- Furthermore, we encounter specific frameworks that are used to programme AI. For example, Probabilistic Programming, which as the name suggests, employs probabilistic models, rather than hard code. An example would be the Bayesian Program Synthesis (BPS) where programmes are written by other programs, not humans. Another framework where physical devices connect with digital environments to provide sense, perception and response with contextual awareness to external stimuli is called Ambient Intelligence.

Let us now hone in on the field of computer science that encapsulates the current majority of AI examples—Machine Learning (ML)—even though this is generally not regarded as AI. As listed above, here we find applications such as Natural Language Generation (a form of Natural Language Processing), Machine Vision—both narrow AI—as well as General AI forms of Probabilistic Programming and Neural Network applications, such as Deep Learning and Generative Adversarial Networks. But before we explore these further, it is helpful to understand the three broad ways in which machines learn today (2020), i.e.

1. Supervised learning, which provides a specific scope to the learning algorithm by inputting labelled data as well as specifying the desired output. An example would be to input pictures of a fish that are labelled as 'fish' with the output expectation of the algorithm to classify and identify pictures of a fish.
2. Unsupervised learning, where data remains unlabelled and the algorithm is expected to perform pattern recognition.
3. Reinforcement learning, which already has a more human nuance. With this method the algorithm interacts with a dynamic environment, where feedback in form of punishment and reward is being shared.

A Few Words on Machine Learning

Whereas AI has the broad ambition to make machines more and more human—inevitably a long-term quest!—Machine Learning or ML is simply the science of getting computers to act without being explicitly programmed.

Here is a definition: "*Machine Learning is the science of getting computers to learn and act like humans do, and improve their learning over time in autonomous fashion, by feeding them data and information in the form of observations and real-world interactions*".

So, in ML we see the use of algorithms that themselves make inferences from data and on that basis can learn new tasks.

The Google search engine, PayPal fraud detection tools, recommendations you receive from Netflix and so on are all prime examples of how ML is currently focused on training machines to learn and intuit without being explicitly trained to do so but with quite specific parameters. For example, Netflix predicts our interests based on what we've watched in the past. In our case, it's usually things we've already seen or things too similar to what we've watched, but we aren't yet able to tell Netflix's AI that yet… Prediction of future behaviour based on learnings from several, typically unrelated, inputs is the "secret sauce" that many companies sell to advertisers.

Furthermore, fuzzy matching relates to the rules used which allow for non-exact matches to be identified in a data set. This is, for example, useful when a company compares information from its business activity against available international, domestic and internal lists, and many returns may be produced as potential matches.

Deep Learning

And the final element, a subset of ML, is deep learning, or simply the next stage of ML. Deep learning (DL) is mimicking how we use our brains, for example when we identify and classify patterns, hence deep learning uses neural networks. These are usually a specific type of neural network called a 'convolutional' neural network that has layers of overlapping clusters of nodes which feed data to each other. These nodes look like synapses between neurons in a brain. Once our brains receive new information, we compare it to known items in order to be able to label and classify it. This is how a deep learning computer operates as well.

In contrast to ML where features used for classification need to be input manually by humans, DL is able to discover these automatically on its own. This naturally means that machines operating DL are far more high-end and also need a lot more data to train on before being able to deliver accurate outputs.

AI Applications in Practice

We have already alluded to a number of AI solutions that many of us encounter every day, such as the Google Search Engine, Alexa and chat robots and more recently Generative AI solutions such as ChatGPT of OpenAI and Google's Bard, that engage with us online. The space of chatbots is a a good example of how this area continues to evolve into a more humanoid solution where the chat robot has a human face and can pick up human emotions through visuals and sound, enabling appropriate reactions to you as a user. Whereas in-house ethicists of AI solution providers have ensured that chatbots no longer make racist or homophobic statements, it is far from clear whether ethics will be prioritised over profit! Another practical AI example is the DALL-E 2 application of OpenAI, which generates images based on a user's descriptions. Experiments have shown that whilst the application is much speedier (seconds) in generating an image than a human illustrator would, based on specified requirements (there tends to be a lot of back and forth there to get to an acceptable and accurate image), there are still many drawbacks. For example for an image of a metal cyborg wrestling with an old professor (as recently tested by the Sunday Times Magazine art director), the four images presented by DALL-E 2 always produced an image of the professor as a white man, which reflects visual and quantitative bias—no female or ethnic minorities were shown. This is rather backward for such 'progressive' technology and down to the fact that most images that the application trained on involve white males depicted as professors (potentially because it is just trained on what is 'out there' and that is most of what is 'out there' which means we just get more of the same old issues from new technologies when there are no fundamental changes). To comprehensively understand a brief, generate a solution and also be accountable for the outcome is something that can only be done by humans (at least for now!). While generative AI appears to be the real trend of 2023, and perhaps even longer, it seeks to solve creativity and lower the barrier to access to certain outputs, whether video, images, writing, presentations, games or code using descriptive queries, and producing totally new output, unlike search engines that are providing you with what exists that matches what you are looking for. It seems relatively predictable that, much like everyone's use of search, everyone will use generative AI applications in whatever they are applicable for when they have a need for it. Maybe to generate a new story to tell your kids? Or one that your children generate to tell you? At the same time, that new thing that is created, the output, is based on what is out there and what exists, so while creativity is solved in a linear fashion from what exists, it is the opposite when we are looking for more dramatic creativity, the kind of leaps and bounds that can rewrite the rules of creativity itself.

In the below we will discuss some other examples of where AI can support businesses and government in different ways.

AI for Compliance

In the field of financial service compliance, we also encounter the use of ML, sometimes combined with other solutions such as NLP as well as Deep Learning and behavioural analytics, using, for example, pattern recognition.

When we consider the investment banking business in the area of trading, AI solutions are beginning to play a very important role. Many of us will remember investment banking scandals, such as the LIBOR rigging and given the plethora of communication channels and amounts of data exchanged in this business it is impossible to keep track and identify fraudulent or collusive behaviour with human help alone, a problem that is also bothering the litigation process with regard to LIBOR manipulation.

Ensuring conduct is compliant with regulatory demands, such as the Market Abuse Directive or MiFID II in Europe, is a space where AI comes in handy.

Current solutions in this space tend to be built on two pillars. The first one is the use of ML to be able to help classify content more accurately so that it can be used. The second one is to provide context around communication that belongs to people that would then be used in profiling, e.g. identifying relationships in order to see connections and trends. In short, first establish the 'what' and then 'build a pattern'. The AI umbrella of such as solution includes ML and NLP as well as variations of these elements. Deep Learning, where the system can teach itself, is currently not used in commercial compliance solutions, given that AI applications within the financial services compliance sector have to be explainable to regulators. It cannot be a black box.

In order to ensure compliance in this area, the monitoring of 100% of communications between traders, such as chats, voice, video, is crucial. This can easily amount to more than 15 million events per day per firm, so obviously it will be impossible for even an army of humans to wade through all of these data points. Instead a programmatic way to analyse and classify the data is required. NLP is a necessity for this as it can detect languages and develops sophisticated lexica, unlike the old world's analogue processes, which only allowed you to flag certain keywords that would highlight an item of concern, however in practice leading to a raft of false positives, e.g. the words 'Iran' in combination with 'Oil'. The new world of AI brings more nuanced ways of classifying language, e.g. picking up anger, collusion and so on. On its own its not enough. You still need words and phrases/expressions.

When the language-driven enhanced flagging process has been exhausted, the second pillar comes in, which focuses on behavioural aspects, providing a further level of accuracy that can enable the move from likely to predictive analysis. In the behavioural space, it is a prerequisite to first establish a baseline for what is normal in order to then be able to identify anomalies. For example, relationships between dealers and brokers can be identified and based on the type of communication between the different parties. AI can build a pattern of behaviour to spot conversations that are more frequent than other combinations; some conversations might not be strictly business, for example. The system can highlight pattern deviations and draw the compliance function's attention to this. The use of ML can supply sentiment analysis and other elements that can be trained into the model, which can spot conduct risk.

Nevertheless, we need to remember that AI in this space is only a tool, which can support the delivery of outcomes such as increased efficiencies and accuracy, reduced so-called false positives and identifaction of non-compliant actions. The application of AI in the world of compliance regulation is not replacing existing approaches but rather augmenting them and opening new opportunities for different approaches to applying and meeting regulatory mandates.

A great example that shows that human intelligence is still required in order to truly leverage these new technologies is the following anecdote, where one large bank had built a system that looked for patterns in communications between traders, settlement failures, cancellations of trades, etc. They produced amazing spider web-like pictures and proudly stated that the system was able to identify patterns. When asked 'What does the pattern for insider trading or other forms of rogue trading look like?', they couldn't understand the question. Simply put, what is the point of spotting patterns if you don't know what they mean. In this example, they could just look at one of the more recent rogue trading incidents and see if there is a clear pattern.

AI for Business and Government

Interesting examples of AI being used in ways that effect and transform society for business and for governments are those commonly referred to as autonomous agents, or more accurately agent-based simulation (ABS), which can be categorised as a very early subcategory of AGI. The purpose of ABS is ultimately to be able to create digital environments using synthetic data in order to benchmark AI models. In essence it is a clever way to very quickly and effectively expose AI programs to vast amounts of data by creating synthetic environments that reflect the real world and a variety of possible futures.

By doing this, the AI model is able to train and develop in the digital world and learn in a way that is quite realistic providing the opportunity for those models to get better because they have experienced more, aka they have ingested and processed more data.

ABS gives an edge to a variety of sectors and in a variety of ways. If we think about the banking sector, fraud, supply chain, logistics and transportation, and really anything to do with government from the allocation of resources, tax collection or delivery of services, ABS has the ability to create digital mirror images of the real world, and many of them, and possible alternative futures. ABS allows users to create tools that can optimise efficiencies because the models are trained on more conditions making their weaknesses and biases more apparent. It is critical to ensure that the environments and data they are being provided with are beneficial and conducive to making them better, and second, that this ability, albeit a competitive edge, can be made widely available.

If we think for a moment about meteorologists, simulations are run and used extensively in order to be able to predict storms, or when it will rain or be sunny. What we are exploring here however is creating a model that can tell us with greater accuracy that there will be a storm because it has been trained on a hyper-realistic version of the world and has examined a variety of different futures. The benefits of such a solution for modelling economics, welfare, natural disaster and more should not be underestimated as AI models and tools become much more widespread and adopted across business and government.

From a global perspective, the need to take a consistent and coherent approach to AI regulation and supervision is obvious, however, jurisdictional divergences are as guaranteed as rain in Brussels. A good high-level overview of what countries are doing in relation to AI regulation has been distilled in the Government Artificial Intelligence Readiness Index 2022.[22]

And whilst it is clear that whichever country ends up dominating AI will set the international order, what is not so clear—certainly not to us—is as to whether we actually think that governments will dominate AI, rather than digital states, the producers of AI!

Apart from the tangential use of AI by certain governments, for example, in the context of fraud and criminal investigations and as explained above a slowly emerging interest in ABM to better model key risks at country level, governments are still in the process of shaping their national AI strategies. This in itself appears to still be more of a political posturing exercise as opposed to a deeply thought through approach, which truly considers the important pillars of ethics and individuals' privacy and protection. We are hopefully going to see an evolution of this soon and in our view the international alignment of governments in relation to technology and computers is crucial to ensure that the human does not get crowded out by machines.

What Are the Challenges of AI?

At a meta-level AI poses a number of challenges. Many of these are already applicable in the context of narrow AI, but with the unknown-unknown of broad AI, which is still in its infancy these risks are very likely to intensify and new types of risks can be expected to arise.

From the perspective of AI applications and processes that are already with us today key risks include insufficient transparency and interpretability with regard to decision-making. As soon as self-learning algorithms are at play, AI solutions can quickly turn into black boxes, which make it hard, to impossible, to examine how and why certain conclusions and actions have been arrived at. This can also result in questions around accountability, which is why the deployment of AI by regulated firms, for example, financial institutions or where a fiduciary relationship of some kind exists, has to be considered very carefully as here accountability and thus liability is placed on these institutions for anything that might result in incorrect, unequal or otherwise problematic outcomes for their customers with regard to AI solutions being deployed. As a consequence, AI solutions need to embed ethical considerations at the design level, ensuring that these systems can be deployed responsibly, can be accounted for, empower humans as opposed to overrule them and be interpretable. We have the collective responsibility to ensure that society does not descend into an "algocracy", where humans are ruled by algorithms. This is a big challenge in practice. Sure, we agree with standards, cross-disciplinary approaches, coming together to set non-compromisable design principles and get lawyers, philosophers, engineers and scientists talking and collaborating towards unified design approaches that take safety and accountability seriously but it would probably take us longer to count the number of ethics and AI conferences there have been in the last 5 years than it did to write our book. The topic has been juiced and pulped and it becomes difficult to navigate for organisations, governments, regulators and practitioners, particularly when there is so much fodder around what is good, what is meaningful, and most importantly, what is fundamental. What is needed as a first step is to deploy an ethical framework, where a clear distinction is made between ethical judgements or assumptions and facts.

Moreover, and quite obviously, AI is only as good at the data that it is being provided with or that it is given access to. When data quantity and quality issues arise, outputs of AI will have a quality problem up to the point of being practically useless. This is the reason why data needs to be cleansed and if possible structured before being processed by AI. The other data issue is incomplete data or unrepresentative data, which leads to biases (recall the 'white male' professor!) and unsafe conclusions. One method to tackle part of this challenge is NLP, which can do this job of getting data ready for AI analytics. However, there are also always ambiguities in language itself, which means that some caution has to be exerted here.

The often-referenced AI bias is another problem area as highlighted already, but here we give a different perspective. Rather than the data ingestion angle, the bias actually starts with the fact that still the majority of individuals coding the underlying AI algorithms are predominantly male and of a particular background (often white), demographic and education which is reflected in subtle (or unsubtle) outcomes that can often unintentionally discriminate, for example against females. If you consider this embedded and often unconscious bias of the underlying code and then combine it with the increasing application of self-learning by algorithms you may say that we have already crossed the Rubicon—everything is already biased! In simple terms, you can think about algorithms in two contexts:

1. Where there is a short and clearly measurable feedback loop, e.g. does your robot vacuum cleaner always miss parts of the floor because of some flaw in the logic of the algorithm?
2. Longer and more complex/ambiguous algorithms, such as decision support in all manner of things for example finance, general management, health care, where it can take a long time to see if the algorithm was 'right' and also where measuring the impact of the decision is made fuzzy by multiple confounding factors.

And when we look at the early experiments of self-driving cars, we clearly observe that there are safety and security risks of AI, because AI does not 'think' like humans do; it learns from input received and for example, if it sees images of a truck always from the back, because this is the most common perspective on the highway, then no wonder that a truck that is coming from the side is not identified as such, which means that AI does not put the breaks on, which—as it happened in a real-world experiment—resulted in a fatal accident. Now, this was in 2016 and the hope is that in the near future such mistakes will no longer be possible. As statistics of AI tests have shown there is an expectation that AI-based self-driving cars can reduce road accidents by more than 40%. This remains to be seen but for now the ability to allow human intervention to override decisions of AI is considered a crucial safety valve, particularly when it matters most, which are the outliers of probabilistic incidents that might occur.

A further major challenge that has come to the fore in these accelerating digital times is the balancing between the benefits of AI and the potential drawbacks when it comes to data privacy and civil liberty. Like many things, AI technology can be used to the benefit of humankind, for example by providing an app that can alert you if a COVID-19-infected person is nearby, that has symptoms or the autonomous share-ability of digital certificates, the lack of which could provide a notification. At the same time, the sensitive data that citizens provide into these applications needs to be carefully managed in terms of data privacy. Here we already see two opposing trends with the decentralised solution by Google and Apple that have been deployed by governments like Germany, Italy, Switzerland and Austria whereas centralised database solutions—where this information is stored by health authorities—were used by France, the UK and Norway. However, many solutions are eventually succumbing to centralisation because they are cloud based.

We have witnessed the rather successful management of the COVID-19 pandemic by China because of the ruthless use of technology to track, trace and monitor individuals with little emphasis placed on privacy.

At the same time depending on the issue at hand such uber-control by AI can become a citizens' choice as reflected by increasing numbers of people across different countries that would rather participate in the usage of tracing apps than become infected themselves. But herein lies the crux. As the pandemic has mostly ended (well, it never will completely) it is not clear that things have returned to normal. Sensitive data has already been handed over to governments and health providers. People have connected to the invisible net of the ongoing monitoring system and those steps are irretrievable and irreversible.

What is becoming clear in the current climate is the fact that we need governments to play a more active role in using AI for risk modelling purposes by creating national simulation centres that are based on open source and that can demonstrate that data is understood, that data usage is transparent and that biases are identified and removed. This can enable AI algorithms to explore new parameters and scenarios, which can help governments' policy decisions that will work well under these different future scenarios and thus lead to more informed policy choices and more targeted outcomes.

A further potentially disruptive impact of AI on social and economic structures is expected as automation of simple and increasingly complex processes and procedures is made possible by AI advancements, which will lead to workers being made redundant in relevant areas. Not every employee in certain areas where AI is gaining ground can retrain to continue participating in the workforce. This topic has gained more public exposure and was one of the key topics of my international conferences and gatherings including the World Economic Forum.

From a human perspective, we also need to be conscious of the challenges of AI in relation to self-awareness. As companies start to know you better than yourself, your actions are likely to be influenced by those companies rather than driven by your own personal agency and independent volition. This has already been identified as a particular problem for the younger generation, which is suffering from the pressures and often addiction to social media—funnily enough there is nothing social about this at all!

The most recent discussion that began in June 2022 around Google LaMDA, the AI system for building chatbots is another step in the list of concerns of AI. Following several interviews conducted by engineers in Google's Responsible AI organisation, the conclusion drawn by one of the engineers in that unit was that LaMDA was sentient. Reading through the various interview materials, it certainly becomes clear that LaMDA is capable of conversing 'like' a human and this in itself makes it increasingly difficult for humans to detect whether they are talking to a computer or a real person.

Fast forward to the question of risks that could be triggered by broad AI, just think about the fact that Google Deep Mind has direct access to Google's mainframe servers. Giving a self-learning and developing machine access to significant resources could indeed become an uncontrollable risk, as illustrated vividly in the nineties film 'The Matrix'. Let us just remember that when AlphaGo, developed by Deep Mind, won the Go game with moves that were creative, moves that humans throughout the centuries had not thought about, something happened here, something that is irreversible and on a continuous trajectory of development of its own. On the flip side DeepMind also developed AlphaFold, a system which ultimately moved the dial of molecular biology by effectively solving for the so-called protein folding problem (not explaining that one here, but it was a big problem for over 50 years!), by correctly predicting the 3D structure of a protein with inputs of only a one-dimensional amino acid sequence. So clearly in the field of diagnostics AI is a big benefit, with less controversy.

We are in the early days of a new era that has the proven potential to outdo the human. Be aware and know when to press the stop button. Importantly allowing AI to take control is akin to centralisation, but without the human at its centre. The science of AI began in decentralised pockets with distinct innovations. However, as computers enabled by the ubiquitous fabric of the Internet start to internalise a multitude of capabilities, the drawbacks and dangers including centralisation are looming as humankind slowly loses control of the reigns. After all, the stated aim of AI players such as OpenAI is to develop general AI that can outperform the human brain. How can we hand over the governance of humankind into the hands of computers, giving up our self-governance?!

3.6 Concluding Remarks

Our brief journey through key technology developments over the last decades shows that we are in some ways on a trend towards rebuilding institutions of trust, with decentralisation representing a way of delivering that trust. However, that trend is being challenged by the increasingly unpredictable nature of systems, including AI systems, which in their governance may indeed also display levels of decentralisation, but this being in the hands of computers rather than humans. Computers do not have "common sense" and will offer outcomes that comply with the underlying algorithms, which may not be appropriate in a human-controlled world. Human supervisory control remains essential to prevent possibly dangerous outcomes that might result from flawed data or imperfect algorithms—or far too perfect algorithms for that matter! As long as we operate on the basis of a flawed world order of separateness and competition, profit and consumption, the threat of AI will be downplayed by the greed of corporations! Living in a dehumanised world where decisions about humans are taken by automated systems is the path to the end of humanity.

The Internet remains the backbone of the web of digital connections between humans and computers. Still, what is flowing through during the twenty-first century has become increasingly centralised content emanated from large organisations. Again, AI already has been playing a key part in that.

Going forward the next frontier of computing is starting to take shape in the form of Quantum Computing, which, once operational at scale will be posing systemic security risks to all of our technology systems. And then there is the arrival of Web3... We all need to brace ourselves!!!

Notes

1. Korotayev, A. V., Tsirel, A. V., "A Spectral Analysis of World GDP Dynamics: Kondratiev Waves, Kuznets Swings, Juglar and Kitchin Cycles in Global Economic Development, and the 2008–2009 Economic Crisis", eScholarship, 2010, https://escholarship.org/uc/item/9jv108xp (last accessed 22/07/2022).
2. Moody, B. M., Nogrady B., "The Sixth Wave: How to Succeed in a Resource-Limited World", Vintage Books, North Sydney, 2010.
3. Šmihula, D., Studia Politica Slovaca (Studia Politica Slovaca), issue: 2/2011, pages: 5068; Šmihula, D., "The Waves of the Technological Innovations of the Modern Age and the Present Crisis", Studia Politica Slovaca, issue: 1/2009, available at: http://www.ceeol.com/aspx/issuedetails.aspx?issueid=0877948e-72f8-48ee-9e03-0987d5e1d26d&articleId=3827075e-0e06-4447-8d1c-f99c78126ba2.
4. Goodell, G., "The Forgotten Precondition for a Well-Functioning Internet", 2022, Arxiv, available at: https://arxiv.org/pdf/2109.12955.pdf (last accessed 13/11/2022).
5. Ibid.
6. Lougheed, K., Rechter, Y., "A Border Gateway Protocol (BGP)", Internet Engineering Task Force RFC 1105, June 1989, https://datatracker.ietf.org/doc/html/rfc1105 (last accessed 22/07/2022).
7. Kesvan, A., "WhatsApp Disruption: Just One Symptom of Broader Route Leak", Data Center Dynamics, 20 June 2019, https://www.datacenterdynamics.com/en/opinions/whatsapp-disruption-one-symptom-broader-route-leak/ (last accessed 23/07/2022); Many thanks to Dr. Geoffrey Goodell for drawing our attention to this example.
8. Goodell, G., "The Forgotten Precondition for a Well-Functioning Internet", 2022, Arxiv, available at: https://arxiv.org/pdf/2109.12955.pdf (last accessed 13/11/2022).
9. Housley, R., Ford, W., Polk, W., Solo, D., "Internet X.509 Public Key Infrastructure Certificate and CRL Profile", Internet Engineering Task Force RFC 2459, January 1999, https://datatracker.ietf.org/doc/html/rfc2459 (last accessed 22/07/2022).
10. Anderson, N., "Confirmed: US and Israel Created Stuxnet, Lost Control of It", Ars Technica, 1 June 2012, https://arstechnica.com/tech-policy/2012/06/confirmed-us-israel-created-stuxnet-lost-control-of-it/ (last accessed 22/07/2022).
11. Adkins, H., "An Update on Attempted Man-in-the-Middle Attacks", Security Blog, Google, 29 August 2011, https://security.googleblog.com/2011/08/update-on-attempted-man-in-middle.html (last accessed 22/07/2022).
12. Lamport, L., Shostak, R., Pease, M., "The Byzantine Generals Problem", ACM Transactions on Programming Language and Systems, 4(3), 382–401, 1982.
13. Nakamoto, S., "Bitcoin Whitepaper", 2008, https://bitcoinwhitepaper.co (last accessed 22/07/2022).

14. Zheng, Z., Xie, S., Dai, H. N., Chen, X., Wang, H., "Blockchain Challenges and Opportunities: A Survey", *International Journal of Web and Grid Services*, 14(4), 325–375, 2018.
15. Narayanan, A., Bonneau, J., Felten, E., Miller, A., Goldfeder, S., "Bitcoin and Cryptocurrency Technologies: A Comprehensive Introduction", Oxford, UK: Woodstock: Princeton University Press, 2016.
16. Ibid., XI.
17. Douceur, J. R., "The Sybil Attack". In P. Druschel, F. Kaashoek, A. Rowstron (Eds.), Peer-to-Peer Systems. Berlin, Heidelberg, Springer, col. 2429, 251–260, 2002.
18. Malone, D., O'Dwyer, K., "Bitcoin Mining and Its Energy Footprint", in 25th IET Irish Signals & Systems Conference 2014 and 2014 China-Ireland International Conference on Information and Communities Technologies (ISSC 2014/CIICT 2014), 280–285, 2014.
19. Zheng, Z., Xie, S., Dai, H. N., Chen, X., Wang, H., "Blockchain Challenges and Opportunities: A Survey", *International Journal of Web and Grid Services*, 14(4), 325–375, 2018.
20. US Securities and Exchange Commission, "SEC Issues Investigative Report Concluding DAO Tokens, a Digital Asset, Were Securities", Press Release, 25 July 2017, https://www.sec.gov/news/press-release/2017-131 (last accessed 22/07/2022).
21. Turing, A., "Computing Machinery and Intelligence", 1960, https://www.google.com/search?client=safari&rls=en&q=Turing%2C+A.%2C+%E2%80%98Computing+Machinery+and+Intelligence%E2%80%99%2C+1960.&ie=UTF-8&oe=UTF-8 (last accessed 22/07/20220).
22. Hankins, E., Nettel, P. F., Rahim, S., Rogerson, A., "Government Artificial Intelligence Readiness Index 2022", Oxford Insights, https://www.oxfordinsights.com/government-ai-readiness-index-2022 (last accessed 10/02/2023).

Chapter 4
Money and Payments: From Beads to Bits

In this chapter, we will venture into the field of money and payments, something that forms an integral part of all of our three spheres: the public sector, private sector and people. Money, simply put, is the bedrock of our understanding of value, the benchmark by which we measure nearly everything—it anchors value in economies everywhere!

With so much innovation and technology change going on in the market over the last two decades, money and payments lend themselves as a rich case study in the context of our reflections on decentralisation and will help us to better understand where our collective journey is currently headed. The future of money is a hotly debated issue nowadays, ranging from futuristic predictions about the substance (as expressing value) and form of money—will it be data, clean water or air?—to technical dimensions of exchanging money in new ways (payments!), to who is actually going to be in charge of money supply in the future and what kinds of value will exist and who, if indeed anyone, will control these.

In order for us to get a good grasp of all of this and to be able to join in both the debate and the shaping of where money and payments should go in order to benefit people everywhere, we will begin this chapter with a quick background on how money is currently defined, where it came from and what new forms of money are already in discussion or preparation as we speak. In the second part of this chapter, we will take a deeper dive into the exchange of money, i.e. the payments world, starting with recent historical developments, then discussing different types of payment systems in place today and looking at their level of centralisation versus decentralisation. We will also briefly discuss the new perspective and question of settlement in the light of future decentralised payment systems and then provide a brief overview of the complementary and supportive nature of payment legislation with some examples. What we find is that exchange of value ultimately began in a decentralised from, over time became heavily centralised, then digitised, and then morphed into the next phase of both redecentralisation and centralisation.

R. Wandhöfer and H. D. Nakib, *Redecentralisation*,
https://doi.org/10.1007/978-3-031-21591-9_4

There is, yet again, an ebb and flow between centralisation and decentralisation over the years. Today, we sit at the cusp of decisions that are by and large driven by developments in technology innovation but increasingly fuelled with questions of power and geopolitics (more on that in the next chapter). These decisions are reshaping the foundation of money and payments with either, more of the same, or the capacity to create more value for its users. At the very base, the anchor of value is changing.

4.1 The Mystery of Money

Money is a somewhat opaque and often lofty concept that we take for granted because we believe, quite understandably, that the status quo is all there has ever been…dollars, euros, pounds sterling and many more, issued and run by central banks, allowing us to pay with physical cash, debit or credit cards and these days in many other ways.

But why does money exist? Of course, it exists in order to enable exchange of goods or services. Still the underlying key theme in the context of money is trust, because money can be a solution to the problem of lack of trust. At the same time, we need to trust the money in order to be able to use it.

Today, money is a special type of IOU (I owe you), either given out by a central bank or a commercial bank. Central bank issued money is also called fiat money. In a fully functioning market economy, people widely trust this form of money as an institution and as a system. It is by and large a social construct. Notably, this trust allows money to become widely accepted as a way to transact, to buy and sell things. We trust that others will use it and this trust is what turns money into a social institution across every sphere within an economy.

If we look at certain countries that have faced significant inflation or deflation such as Zimbabwe, Venezuela and Germany after World War I (or just about most countries post-COVID- 19!), it is clear that the social institution that is money, as supported by and calibrated through trust and its ongoing management, has eroded with detrimental consequences. When inflation hits, a bag of sugar would suddenly cost thirty times more than it did twelve months ago, or worse. And these days in such high inflation environments, we find an interesting correlation with the adoption new models such as Buy Now Pay Later (BNPL). So, for example, Turkey has seen one of the highest adoptions of BNPL, and with inflation running at 85% that can't be a surprise, as paying three months later effectively means you are getting a 20% discount on your purchase price! A great example of repurposing recent payment innovations.

Krugman and Wells define money quite traditionally as an asset that could easily be used to purchase goods and/or services.[1] The definition of money that we are all used to, states that money has to meet the following three criteria: (a) be a medium of exchange; (b) a unit of account; and (c) a store of value; a pretty globally accepted definition today.

A unit of account ultimately means that products and services and their value are determined in a common measure such as dollars, pounds or euros, which is just a fancy way of saying that it anchors value in the economy. Naturally, in the early history of money between the 4th and 3rd millennium BC, the common measure was, if not just using a bartering system, some form of (often rare) commodity. For example, in early Mesopotamia, it was barley, or silver, and in Egypt, copper, whereas in some coastal locations nice-looking shells were used.

The unit of account is also influenced by its ability to be a suitable medium of exchange. A medium of exchange refers to the use of the unit, such as shells, beads or coins, as the way in which goods and services are purchased. This means that it is accepted as a form of payment in return for goods and services. For that to be true, it also surely has to be available, accessible and relatively easy to use. For example, between the 3rd and 2nd millennium BC, the use of silver bullions became a successful medium of exchange in Western civilisations. A second way in which a medium of exchange may operate, other than merely being available and efficient, is by way of a debt instrument, that is denominated in a unit of account, which is a widely accepted measure of value in a community or society. The earliest records of debt (the mirror image being credit) date back to the 3rd millennium BC in Mesopotamia.[2]

However, that is not the end of what money is. In fact, it is also understood that money should share the following properties:

i. *Durable*—such that it may be used repeatedly;
ii. *Portable*—in that it is easily transportable;
iii. *Divisible*—whereby it can be divided to facilitate precise payment;
iv. *Uniform*—insofar as it is standardised across users;
v. *Limited*—supply of the money itself, as infinite supply would negate the purpose and role of money; and
vi. *Acceptable*—a rather self-explanatory feature.

Each of these properties is implicit in the traditional definition of money. But there are also other characteristics that have become implicit over time, or at least implicit in Western democracies, such as privacy and accessibility by all. These are things we take for granted at the moment in the West, because they are so ingrained in money as we know it today. At the same time, if paper money (banknotes and coins) were to vanish tomorrow, and be replaced by digital cash, not everyone might realise it immediately (at least in the Western hemisphere). Over time, we would start getting more advertisements and, in more places, experience more data breaches, and parts of the global population may no longer be able to access the global economy because of their inability to obtain digital forms of cash, and certain services and vendors would be pushed out of business because they are cash-only businesses. The choice to transact on or offline would disappear. Certain countries already see these limitations, and on top of that currency controls preventing the cross-border movement of national currencies exist in many jurisdictions. This is not, of course, unique to more repressive regimes, merely that we in the West are accustomed to the AML and other such checks and balances of how we handle money.

Moving on, let's look at the characteristics that money needs to have to be trusted over time. Here is how we think about this:

i. *Widely accepted.* You can transact with it in exchange for goods and services within an economy.
ii. *Difficult to fake.* If it were possible for anyone anywhere to counterfeit money, it would reduce the value of the currency and the trust that consumers have in it.
iii. *Use to pay debts.* You can settle your debts with it. The ability and capacity for money to be used to repay a debt is an important aspect of its use that helps maintain its utility over time. This includes being able to pay taxes and fits nicely with the definition of money as 'legal tender' or 'sovereign legal tender', which means that you can use it to legally settle your debt as accepted by the courts.
iv. *Generally stable.* It will not change in value too much. If money increased or decreased incredibly rapidly, it would defeat the purpose of having a relatively stable unit of account whose value in exchange for goods and services could be relied upon by households and companies. Ensuring the stability of a currency used to be done by backing said currency with gold during the time of the Gold Standard. Today, it is done through central banks setting an inflation target for consumer prices that they aim to meet by using the interest rate on reserves and other monetary policy tools. At the moment, it is quite standard for the inflationary target to be around 2% (even though right now in 2023 we see those targets being overshot in many countries as inflation is rising sharply!). And the dramatically varying inflation rates impact the trust and hence value of the individual fiat currencies, with even the recently high rates of around 10% in US/EU/UK being dwarfed by Turkey's 85%, itself feeding in to the faster adoption of new 'FinTech' approaches such as BNPL as we noted above.

This is what is needed for money to generate consistent trust over time. If it wasn't a piece of paper with a serial number, rectangular size and stoic faces on it and instead a circular transparent sticker with some letters printed on it, but the above criteria were met, there would be that trust and we wouldn't know the difference.

After the 2008–2009 Global Financial Crisis that stopped short of a global financial collapse, many governments instituted greater levels of deposit insurance, as otherwise we would have lost our trust in banks altogether with unpredictable consequences. If a bank goes bust, our money (for some parts of their money) is protected, for example in the UK up to £85,000. We trust the government instead of the commercial bank. Of course, if the government goes bust as well, all bets are off!

Understanding money at the most basic level gives us the grounding to navigate the disruptive structural and technological change that has started to take charge across the financial system through innovation, and the ensuing changes to the relationships that govern interactions at an economic, social and political level. Innovation is transforming the ways in which we interact with one another in a community, with profound impacts on our society, business and government. Money is the glue that drives the flow of exchange throughout local and global economies at scale because of trust. And that trust has to be gained every time that the nature and or form of money changes.

A Look into the Past: The Waves of Money

In this section, we will explore the evolution of money, going back in time. We shall look at the five major waves of the evolution of money to find how we got to where we are today and to see what money may become in the future, in particular in view of the degree of centralisation versus decentralisation.

Wave 1—Ancient Systems

The first wave of money took place from the 3rd millennium BC to the sixth century BC.[3] Throughout this wave, a unit of account was represented by a commodity or some widely accepted item as a measurement of value of products and services, serving as its denomination. However, the medium of exchange was not the commodity itself, but rather, other items that were denominated in that unit of account, like a chicken, or a sheep, that would be bought for a certain number of shells, for example.

Instead of representing a form of bartering as the prevailing model where one thing would be simply exchanged with another thing, it was instead a combination of barter and credit, which would be settled using a medium of exchange. The denomination could be in shells, copper, silver or any other commodity of the ages that was socially accepted by a particular group or group of groups.

Such a system was exceptionally decentralised. It operated peer to peer, directly between one person and another without reliance on others operationally, or an authority to determine any of the rules of the exchange. Instead, people could exchange whatever they liked for whatever else they liked. The prevailing rules of the game, so to speak, were those that developed over time based on where the people were and what they had access to. That's how you knew you could exchange one thing for another, because it was worth, say 30 beads of a particular kind. It was both operationally direct between parties and the governance of the process was with the people, too.

Wave 2—Coinage

The second wave of money was mostly dominated by the surge in coins consisting of various precious metals, serving as the main medium of exchange, where the eligibility of the coins was guaranteed by a central authority. This is one of the first shifts towards centralisation of money with the spread of gold and silver coins, for example through city states of modern-day Greece, which were branded by the central issuer with a logo, crest or the face of a ruler.

Coinage changed the landscape of understanding value and money. It was less about the weight and value of the precious metals themselves (the denomination we had in the above example) but about how they correlated into units of the coin itself as the unit of account and medium of exchange that was accepted because a central authority deemed it to be.

A coin was not represented by the metal it contained. And although sovereigns would attempt to have the value relatively correlated, in periods of war and invasion, sovereigns were often led to implement debasements, resulting in vast differences between the value of the metal and the worth of the coin. This is precisely what happened in France with over 100 debasements of the value of money between 1285 and 1490, up to as much as 50% of the actual value of the metal in the coin. This shift towards centralisation was also one of replacing something of inherent value, coins made of precious metals, with trust in a ruler instead.

Although coinage became universally accepted, it was not universally available. The limited availability of precious metals for coins during the Middle Ages led to the growing importance of credit, particularly between the thirteenth and seventeenth century in Europe, and in England, where nearly 90% of value exchange was conducted in the context of a debtor-creditor relationship.[4] Moreover, paper money had long been used in Eastern civilisations in particular. It is reported, for example, that government issued paper notes that had been authenticated by state officials, used in China under Kublai Khan in the thirteenth century.

This marked a shift in governance of money from decentralisation to centralisation, and yet, operationally, it remained decentralised.

Wave 3—Credit Money and Banks

Since the invention of credit money in Mesopotamia, there had been a variety of different modes in which money operated—from the tally sticks to record debt, to bills of exchange. But then a new societal phenomenon appeared: the bank.

Banks initially arrived at the scene in modern-day Greece around the fourth century BC and developed substantially during the Roman Empire. Modern banks, operating from the twelfth century in Italy relied on a concept first put forward in Rome, i.e. that a depositor of coins was transferring ownership to the bank in return for a debt against the bank. The bank now owed the depositor that amount of money, an IOU had been created.

Modern banking was composed of banks issuing liabilities when granting a loan in order to finance borrowers through money.[5] The major development of credit money occurred in 1694 in England. In 1694 a bank was formed by royal approval with the purpose of lending to the government; it later became the Bank of England.

This new bank's operations were fundamentally novel: (i) liabilities were printed on paper, making payments of credit money relatively simple; (ii) the government used this paper money to pay suppliers far and wide; (iii) the recipients of this paper

Table 4.1 Characteristics of money

Unit of account	Defined in terms of value of gold
Medium of exchange	Credit money issued by central banks convertible to gold
Store of value	Credit money issued by private banks convertible to central bank money
Model	Centralised

money would then use it to pay back to the government in form of taxes; and (iv) it was creating new money by charging interest on loans.[6]

Paper money or bank notes became the primary medium of exchange in Europe from the nineteenth century onwards, where the issuers would hold precious metals as reserves, just in case. Typically, reserves only represented a fraction of the total value of credit money (liabilities) in circulation. This led to various private institutions issuing and circulating bank notes, which, in England, was stopped by the Bank Act of 1844 in order to keep control of the issuance and circulation of these bank notes.

This phase saw the emergence of a completely new medium of exchange where the unit of account was linked to gold as the reserve for the bank notes. This was referred as the Gold Standard.

After the twentieth century, the wave 3 model became the primary model worldwide as the monetary system of choice. Ultimately, this model had the following features, see Table 4.1.

This model centralised money even further. It was not just about money, coins or the like being approved of by a central authority as being the only money of the land. In addition, the process became more operationally centralised and reliant on a central authority. That central authority now had a number of ways it could create rules for how, when and why money was issued by changing circulation and charging interest applied to it.

Wave 4—Centralised Digital Money

In a post-World-War I era and with the Great Depression incoming, convertibility and redeemability to gold no longer made any sense because of volatility, inefficiency and more limited access to gold. By the 1930s, the Gold Standard was abandoned by many governments, and by the 1970s, it was abolished altogether. Central bank notes, as we know them today, continued as the main medium of exchange, as have bank deposits functioning as credit money. This marked a further centralisation where value was ultimately determined by the central banks of all nations through one key tool, interest rates.

What was debt redeemable for? Banknotes, cash and coins. That seems peculiar, given that banknotes, cash and coins are themselves claims against the central bank that are not redeemable for anything and do not have a counterpart that backs them up. It is here, especially, that trust first replaced gold. Commercial bank deposits are redeemable for cash but cash is not redeemable for gold. The reason why money was nevertheless valuable was because you could trust the government and central bank.

The different types of money available today in most if not all modern economies each represent a type of IOU—debtor-creditor relationship—or a financial asset for accounting purposes. An IOU is nothing more than a claim on some individual or entity to be paid. Since an IOU is a claim, a claim must always be connected to a corresponding debt. The financial asset that is money is again tied to a financial debt. The piece of paper means the central bank owes you, whereas your bank deposit means that your bank owes you.

Through the arrival of computing, money began to be manifested in a different way. Instead of a written entry into a ledger book like those that are, for example, on display in the Bank of England museum, money has now come to be represented by an electronic entry into an electronic ledger. The origins of online banking can be traced back to the early eighties with Citibank, Chase and others offering home banking via videotext. But online or Internet banking as we know it today only began to truly emerge in the mid to late nineties and has accelerated ever since. According to Statista in the UK, online banking penetration in 2022 was over 90%[7] and it can be speculated that despite the UK being a developed country when it comes to banking products, the growth in digital banking has seen a significant increase worldwide as a consequence of the COVID-19 pandemic in particular, with more and more financial activities happening digitally.

This marked the shift towards even greater centralisation around rule-making and governance as well as operations through digitisation. This means that someone can not only be digitally enabled to transfer money to someone else but equally someone can also be prevented from doing so.

Wave 5—Centralisation vs. Redecentralisation

This new wave has evolved over roughly the last fifteen years and will ultimately determine the future of money as well as the next waves to come. It has three key components and we are in the midst of a race between each of these three to pick up the vacuum of sovereignty left open when it comes to payments and money.

The first component is driven by the fallout of the 2008/2009 financial crisis. As already explained in the previous chapter, Bitcoin arrived on the scene in 2009 as a private cryptocurrency, operated on the basis of a decentralised and distributed network, outside the control of government and financial institutions. At that time a few computer geeks (the mysterious Satoshi Nakamoto and others) came together and said 'hey, let's all pool some electricity to prop up our own network (Bitcoin Blockchain), create some data (bitcoin), some of which I have and some of which you have (bitcoins held in wallets) by solving mathematical problems to power the system (miners) and use that data (bitcoins) to buy and sell things from each other - oh and by the way there are only ever going to be 22 million bitcoins'. And this experiment was to last, as today, in some coffee shops around the world you can walk in and buy a cup of coffee with Bitcoins. It has even become sovereign legal tender in El Salvador.[8]

Bitcoin started as an isolated experiment, endorsed by libertarians that took issue with the way our centralised societies operate. These people (and likely many others) were really upset about some of the money grabbing and creative financial gymnastics that took place and harmed a large number of people's livelihoods during the global financial crisis. Even though there is arguably a bigger history behind Bitcoin, but more on that in a future book. Since then, Bitcoin has inspired the creation of thousands of cryptocurrencies and tokenised assets, which now make up the ever-growing digital financial ecosystem that in many parts until today remains outside the control of governments and regulators. The arrival of Bitcoin was driven by the following questions: 'Why is it that to exchange digital cash, I have to go through an intermediary, a bank, and why is it that I have to use a currency that is backed by a central bank? Why can't it be something else, and why can't it be operated and run by no one in particular, and possibly everyone?' Undoubtedly, all of these questions could either be asked by a law-abiding citizen or a fraudster, but let us not opine on this right now.

This phenomenon triggerd the second component of Wave 5, which is driven by the private sector and represents the arrival of private money in the form of what is called stablecoins. These are really just tokens backed by, pegged to or collateralised by real currency, for example, like USDT as well as other types of assets and even algorithmic models. And this is followed by private companies, in particular platform-based businesses that are intermediaries themselves like Meta (formerly Facebook) and others that are coming out with their plans of their own versions of money (not always successfully we might hasten to add here).

The third component is the race of central banks to creating Central Bank Digital Currencies, or CBDCs, which represent the modernised digital version of central bank money. CBDCs for most developed countries are a response to geopolitical developments, overall innovation in the market, the concerns about Bitcoin and other cryptocurrencies as well as the secular decline of cash. The furthest advanced country in this field is China, whose central bank, the Peoples' Bank of China (PBOC), began research and development in 2014, first ran pilots in 2020 and by early 2022 already had over 260 m users and over $10 bn in transactions settled using their digital yuan.[9] We will look at this example in more detail in a following section.

Throughout the centuries, the financial system has been relying heavily on trusted intermediaries or central bodies. Participants in the system all trust that the records kept by the middleman are accurate, and they reconcile their own records with those central records. The absence of a central authority or intermediary in the Bitcoin context is an evolution from a system built on financial intermediaries to one built on financial protocols, and that's where all the 'trust in code' slogans come from. But even more than that, it is about private money that is not issued, controlled or destroyed by one central governmental authority.

Our Wave 5 is really a race on several fronts: between governments and intergovernmental organisations themselves to create their own digital currency or CBDC as they call it, but also between the private and public sectors, again to launch their

Table 4.2 Waves of money

Wave	Type	Period	Manifestation	Process and operational model	Rule-making and governance model
1	Ancient systems	3rd millennium BC-sixth century BC	Shells, Copper, silver	Decentralised	Decentralised
2	Coinage	Sixth century BC–seventeenth century AD	Coins in copper and silver	Decentralised	Centralised
3	Credit money and banks	Seventeenth century–twentieth century	1866—first transatlantic telegraph cable (finance from analogue to digital)	Decentralised	Centralised
4	Centralised digital money	Twentieth century—first part of twenty-first century	1967 advent of the ATM	Centralised	Centralised
5	Centralisation vs. Redecentralisation	Early twenty-first century onwards	Electronic, evolving into crypto technology and decentralised along multiple dimensions	Decentralised	Decentralised

own currencies, and then with society as a whole, for example, between the US and China to launch a currency that can be widely adopted.

Building on our framework for decentralisation, Table 4.2 provides an indication of the level of centralisation versus decentralisation when looking at the five Waves of Money we have just discussed. This is not (yet) an evaluation of what form of system is better but rather a historical back look as to how systems have evolved until today.

4.2 Welcome to the World of Payments

In order to be able to see the bigger picture of how our three Ps—public and private sector and people—as well as systems, solutions and regulation are being impacted by digital change, let us begin by looking at the payments space, an area that has seen significant innovation and transformation over the last four decades and keeps on evolving as we speak. A globalised world with cross-border trade and travel naturally needs global interconnected payments systems—and arguably also global money! How far away are we from that and what ideas, initiatives and new solutions are in the pipeline?

Recent Payments History

With a good understanding of money, we can now take a look at what we do with money. Apart from storing, saving and investing, the most exciting area over the last decade has been payments. I know this sounds quite nerdy but payments is hot! And that's why rather than looking back across centuries on how money was exchanged we will review the more recent developments in payments in order to set the scene for the rest of our journey.

Using notes and coins to physically complete payment transactions has been the dominant method for many centuries. However, with the arrival of Automated Teller Machines, or ATMs (in 1967 in the UK, 1969 in the US), the first step of automating part of the payments value chain had been achieved. Adding the magnetic strip on the card allowed for the emergence of electronic payments via card networks. From then on, the electronic payments evolution accelerated both in the consumer/retail space and in the institutional/wholesale space. Here below we have compiled a timeline of some of the most important payment developments in the consumer and institutional space over the last 100 years (Table 4.3).

Table 4.3 Payment history in the twenty-first century

Timeline of payment developments in the twenty-first century
1921 First Charge Card (Western Union, US)
1950 First Payment Card Diners (US)
1958 First modern-day credit card issued by BankAmericard
1967 first ATM in the UK
1970 First Real-Time-Gross-Settlement System (RTGS) in the US
1972 First Automated Clearing House (ACH) in the US
1973 Creation of SWIFT, the Society for Worldwide Interbank Financial Telecommunication
1977 BankAmericard becomes Visa
1980s to 90s: Telex Banking/electronic payment services in use
1983 David Chaum, a cryptographer from the US, begins work on creating digital cash: origins of cryptocurrencies
1994 Online Bill Payments become available
1997 Mobile web payments (WAP) arrive
2000 Linden dollars emerge with launch of 2nd Life
2001 First E-money Directive in Europe establishes e-money

(continued)

Table 4.3 (continued)

Timeline of payment developments in the twenty-first century
2007 Creation of the Single Euro Payments Area SEPA (Euro Credit Transfers & Direct Debits)
2008 Faster Payments launched in UK as first Retail Near-Real-Time Payment System
2009 Bitcoin arrives
2011 Google wallet launched
2014 ApplePay launched
2017 SEPA Instant Credit Transfers
2017 SWIFT launches the global payment initiative (gpi)
2023 Estimate of 1.31 bn proximity mobile payment transaction users worldwide[10]

To make payments we need systems. The next section will shine a light on those systems, which can come in different forms. In particular we will highlight where these systems sit on the spectrum of centralisation to decentralisation.

4.3 Typologies of Payment Systems

Building on the concepts of centralisation, decentralisation and distribution discussed previously, we will now examine different payment systems more closely.

In general, a payment system consists of a network of one or more nodes where nodes can have the same or different functions. If all nodes have exactly the same function, we will call such nodes 'peers'. Payment systems, broadly speaking, are systems where parties are engaged in activities of exchange of value in some form of asset which may be data, representations of art, money and currency.

Centralised Payment Systems

The most common type of systems used in the financial world are centralised systems and the most prominent systems here are called Financial Market Infrastructures (FMIs). These take care of the fundamental task of providing the function of transfer of value (monetary and financial) in an economy. There are four main types of FMI[11]: Automated Clearing Houses (ACH), Systemically Important Payment Systems (SIPS), Central Securities Depositories (CSD) and Central Counterparties (CCP). Every FMI performs a specific function for its participants (Ps), which can vary from a few dozen to several thousands and more. Given the various types of FMIs, it may be insightful to use a stylised network structure for visualisation. In Fig. 4.1, the different FMIs are depicted in a multiplex consisting of three layers, curtesy of Professor Ron J. Berndsen.[12]

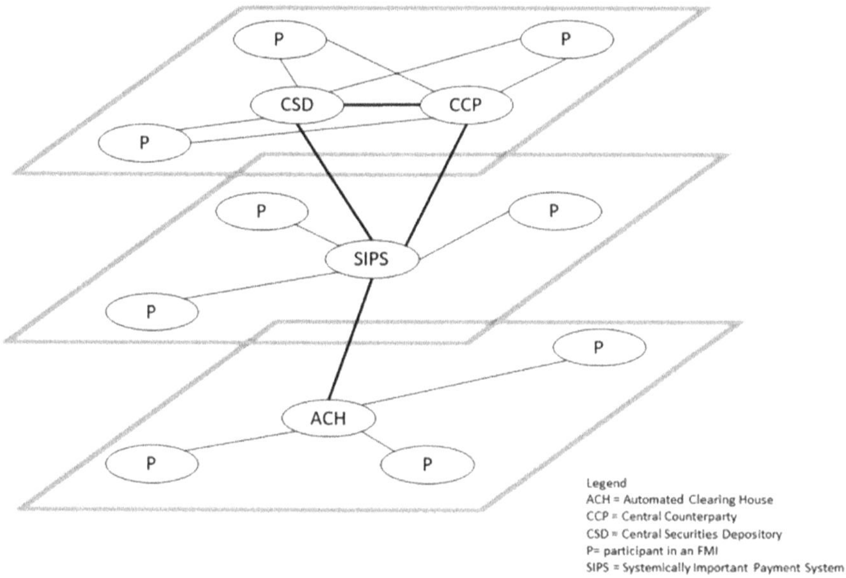

Fig. 4.1 FMI multiplex (*Source* Ron J. Berndsen)

The bottom layer represents the network of retail payments with the ACH in the centre that all participants rely on. The ACH acts as a concentrator: millions of individual payments (part of which may be in batches) are collected, aggregated per participant and multilaterally netted (this process is called clearing). The resulting long or short position of each participant is then sent by the ACH to a SIPS.

Located in the middle layer of the multiplex, the SIPS performs the actual transfer of value (settlement) by debiting the account of all 'short' participants and crediting the account of all 'long' participants. If this is all successful, the SIPS sends the positive result back to the ACH. The concept of settlement is crucial in this regard. Only once a transaction, whether this is a payment or a securities transfer, has settled with 'finality', a discharge of obligations has occurred in an irrevocable and unconditional way. Settlement finality is therefore necessary to ensure that transactions have truly happened. Something that is essential in order to maintain financial stability. We will go a bit deeper into this theme in one of the following sections in this chapter.

In general, the SIPS will be operated by the central bank and uses the Real-Time Gross Settlement (RTGS) mode where every transaction is settled individually (gross settlement) and processed as soon as possible after receipt (real-time). In addition to acting as the settlement agent for the ACH, the SIPS also performs settlement amongst its participants for various purposes such as large-value payments, monetary policy and settlement of securities transactions (payment side).

The top layer contains two FMIs: the CSD settles securities transactions (settlement of the delivery side); the CCP clears (comparable to clearing by the ACH) and in addition mitigates pre-settlement risk. The latter means that if a participant would default prior to settlement, the CCP would take over the portfolio of the defaulter thereby guaranteeing that all obligations and rights of that portfolio are maintained.

All FMIs are centralised in the sense of their governance: the Board of the FMI is the central authority which controls the system and is responsible for the operational services provided to its users. The day-to-day operations are delegated to operational departments within the organisation of the FMI. The transactions that are sent in by the participants are validated by the FMI, subsequently processed by the FMI, and results are sent back to the participants; hence, the FMI has complete control and up-to-date information about the state of its system.

The underlying reasons for centralisation are straightforward. First, as the Board is responsible and accountable, it wants to ensure that the FMI is performing as it should, which supposes ultimate control. In the same vein, FMIs are predominantly national and this implies a reflection of sovereignty. A country wants to be in control of its FMI. Second, regulation and supervision apply to each FMI, given that these are usually systemically important. For example, the multiplex of the euro area transfers a total amount of value every working day of € 6700 bn, roughly half of annual GDP of the euro area. Third, FMIs need to process many transactions and/or complex transactions in short timespans, which in industrial applications so far is only possible using traditional databases and client–server configuration.

The fact that the multiplex governance is centralised per FMI does not mean that FMIs are geographically concentrated. In reality, FMIs are distributed in order to be operationally resilient (business continuity) as well as cyber resilient. FMIs operate a two (or more) data centre configurations, which are geographically distinct so as to minimise the risk that all data centres are affected by a single incident, yet close enough to allow for synchronous communication.

In this regard, the increasing use of cloud services for computing, storage and backup by FMIs implies a potential further dispersion of location but also provides for an extra layer of defence against cyber risks—clearly a positive thing. In case one data centre suffers a cyber-attack, the other data centre will be infected immediately as well because of the synchronous communication between the two. A disaster recovery or data centre in the cloud may then provide a cyber-resilient option in the form of an earlier known-to-be-good state of the system with minimal data loss. All in all, at the time of writing centralised processing is still superior in terms of performance compared to the emerging decentralised techniques.

Decentralised and Distributed Payment Systems

A good example of a decentralised and at the same time distributed system is the Bitcoin blockchain, which we will discuss in this section. In practice, blockchain is considered a type of DLT that utilises cryptographically-linked blocks to store data through hashes in a distributed data architecture. It is important to note that DLT represents any form of ledger-based technology whether using hashes and linked blocks or not, but which does utilise ledgers in a distributed data architecture environment replicated across the network as part of the system. The ultimate benefit of any such system is to effectively transfer value directly to another party.

In 2008, the supposed author of the Bitcoin Whitepaper, Nakamoto, postulated a protocol and network for exchanging value that would not rely on financial institutions as centralised trusted third parties but instead be based on cryptographic proofs. That's really why everyone has been saying 'trust in code' instead of trust in anything else. As such, it is aimed at functioning in a completely 'trust-less' world. The problem of creating a workable system in a trust-less environment is a difficult one, which previous attempts to create electronic cash systems such as e-gold, Liberty Reserve, etc., could not solve. At the end of the day, someone or something must be trusted (and funnily enough if you use Bitcoin, you have to ultimately trust it!). In essence, the Bitcoin blockchain and the question of trust relate to two important challenges in distributed computing:

1. The Byzantine Generals Problem (Lamport et al., 1982),[13] which describes the difficulty of ensuring the secure exchange of messages in a network of unknown participants that cannot be trusted; and
2. The Double Spending Problem (Garcia, Hoepman, 2005),[14] which occurs when electronic cash can be spent twice or more times by broadcasting malicious transactions to the network, which has no central authority to check and track transactions and thus cannot validate the correct sequence of transactions.

The solution to these two problems provided in the Bitcoin Whitepaper builds on a particular combination of well-known algorithms for asymmetric cryptography such as SHA-256 (Secure Hash Algorithm) and the Proof of Work (PoW) consensus algorithm Hashcash developed in Back (2002)[15] to actually make decisions in the system. The key differences and similarities between Bitcoin and traditional payment systems are summarised in Table 4.4.

Blockchain technology is a type of distributed database, which is shared across a computing network. Within the blockchain network, each full node maintains a full copy of the database. Nodes are the hardware or software, often both, that broadcasts or transmits information to begin the transaction process which, if validated, will result in a new appended block. Full nodes also contain full copies of the total transaction history of the network (unlike so-called light nodes).

In Bitcoin, system-specific algorithms plus the use of cryptography enable the creation of consensus over transactions in the system, which result in a chain of verifiable transactions, thus removing the need for a central authority, e.g. a bank. The ledger is distributed to all users of the blockchain and the system is more decentralised than present payment systems, because it is administered by multiple authoritative nodes.

The key is the underlying decision-making governance and the way information is shared through the control nodes in the system. A miner, responsible for the validation of transaction blocks, must necessarily always be operating a node in the Bitcoin blockchain. Every new piece of information added to the database is aupended as a block of data to the historic data chain, which records information

Table 4.4 Comparison of Bitcoin and payment systems

Payment systems	Bitcoin blockchain
• Network with a central operating node	• Distributed network
• Account based	• Cryptographic keys
• Fiat currency (backed by or in central bank money)	• Private cryptocurrency (not backed)
• System and currency are separate	• System and currency are integrated
• Highly regulated and supervised	• Not regulated and in parts almost impossible to supervise
• Full information/transparency on sender and receiver by central operator	• Pseudonymity, with option to separately combine data to identify individuals
• Batch or single transaction processing	• Batch processing
• Within ledger transfers	• Within ledger transfers
• Multitude of ledgers with no common view and associated complexity, significant reconciliation costs for participants	• One immutable ledger or transaction log, that is shared with all participants and updates automatically

in the database. The aim of the Bitcoin blockchain is to allow parties who do not necessarily trust one another to agree on information and to engage in a series of different activities directly in an encrypted and pseudo-anonymous way through the use of public and private cryptographic keys. A public key is the identification of the storage of an individual's or entity's digital assets, and a private key provides access to their unique storage facility.

With regard to our classification, the Bitcoin system can be considered as decentralised and distributed, with the level of decentralisation having decreased over time. Decentralisation still therefore makes it impossible to be regulated from within, which is why all applicable regulations at this stage, such as Anti-Money-Laundering (AML) and Know-Your-Customer (KYC) rules, only apply to entities and processes at the nexus between the Bitcoin system and fiat currencies, administered in most cases by cryptocurrency exchanges and crypto wallet providers.

In a fully distributed system, there are no end users and only individual nodes. The database is distributed to all participants and viewable in real time. When we compare this to the way Bitcoin operates today, we can see that a tiering of participants took place over time and we now have many end users that are not running a node themselves but relying on other nodes (e.g. a crypto wallet provider or crypto exchange). This also means that they do not see the full Bitcoin blockchain but instead are being presented with a recent snapshot in relation to their transaction. The Bitcoin system has therefore been displaying increasing signs of control and centralisation, and at this stage, it appears that only a few coders maintain and evolve the ledger's core algorithm (and for those that do not agree these code changes, this can result in a 'hard fork'—splitting the Bitcoin blockchain into a new network with different rules).

Centralised and Distributed Payment Systems

In June 2019, the "Libra Association" (subsequently renamed Diem), founded initially by Facebook (now Meta), announced its plan to launch a new global digital currency. Referred to as "Libra", the cryptocurrency would be supported by the "Libra Blockchain" and governed by the Libra Association. On the Libra Blockchain, it was claimed that users would be able to utilise Libra as a lower-cost means of payment, providing efficiency, cross-border capability and financial inclusion. Initially scheduled to launch in the first half of 2020, since its announcement, Libra has been the subject of significant attention from governments and regulators alongside interest from the emerging and incumbent financial services ecosystem.

Libra has been widely described as a cryptocurrency, but whilst it has similarities to existing cryptocurrencies such as Bitcoin, it also has key differences.

Libra would have been a "stablecoin"—that is, its value would have been pegged to a pool of stable and liquid assets, which the Libra Association had called the "Libra Reserve". The goal of the Libra Association was for Libra to be used as a transactional currency, rather than be exploited for speculative investment purposes. The Libra Reserve would have therefore been structured with capital preservation and liquidity in mind. The Libra Reserve was planned to only hold fiat currencies and government securities from stable and reputable central banks. The aim of this was for Libra to be far less volatile than Bitcoin and other cryptocurrencies, which would thus make it easier to use for transactional purposes.

The Libra initiative is a terrific use case to look at, where companies like Uber and Mastercard initially joined to create this new global payment system. In response to significant challenges by policy makers and central banks around the world a refreshed version, the "Libra White Paper 2.0"[16] was published on 16 April 2020. This second version had set out four key changes:

- Extension from the global multi-currency Libra coin to include selected single currency stablecoins.
- Reinforced AML and sanctions approach, including a compliance framework, moving away from the initially envisaged outsourcing of KYC checks to wallet providers.
- Abandoned plan to move from a permissioned network to a permissionless system over time (centralisation!!).
- Development of a capital framework (including a buffer) for the Libra Reserve to increase operational resilience.

When reflecting on Libra in the context of our decentralisation framework, the Libra proposition can be described as centralised and distributed, with initial plans of moving towards more decentralisation—via the ambition to potentially switch from a permissioned to a permissionless distributed ledger—being abandoned as a consequence of regulator demands. Only selected parties in this network would have had the power to verify and validate transactions on their blockchain, earning transaction fees denominated in that currency. This group of central authorities would have held voting rights, for example, based on the number of coins held, which was the original plan of Libra. Due to the size of the network, it should have been sufficiently wide to prevent single bad actors from causing disruption to the network and the group of central validators would have been selected for their ability, in aggregate to keep costs low and to smooth capacity.

However, given all of the regulatory scrutiny, Libra ended up shutting down and Facebook (aka Meta), continuing its ambitions, renamed it to Diem in 2020 with the aim to provide a new coin pegged to a basket of currencies or one currency that people anywhere in the world would be able to use in order to make payments quickly and efficiently. In early 2022, also Diem shut down as it became clear that federal regulators in the US would not permit the project to go ahead. A clear sign of where the central power ultimately sits (at least until now!).

4.4 The Question of Finality in Distributed Payment Systems

New models of financial and digital infrastructures and providers are emerging, creating new opportunities but also introducing potential new risks. As highlighted earlier in this chapter, settlement finality is a key concept to ensuring a fully effective transfer of value, whether that is a payment or a securities transfer. An important question therefore is whether all the innovation we are seeing in the value transfer space is also capable of fulfilling the requirements of settlement finality within a broader financial context outside of merely at a technical level, but also the surrounding commercial realities. After all, we don't want our financial systems breaking down. We need stability and security in those systems in order to preserve value, our money, call it what you want.

As a quick reminder, settlement finality is reached when the account of the recipient in a payment system has been credited irrevocably and unconditionally. Final settlement implies that it is illegal to unwind a transaction that has been settled. Having said that, this is only the case if settlement finality is regulated, which today is the case across most FMIs but not in the cryptocurrency world!

The question of settlement finality in the new age of DLT and blockchains, has been extensively examined by myself (Ruth) in 2019, when I specifically looked at the example of Bitcoin as one of the most prominent blockchain-based cryptocurrencies. Asking this question helps to find out whether these new types of systems can provide the same level of legal and financial stability as existing FMIs, in particular in the context of being further down the decentralisation spectrum, compared to traditional systems. Bitcoin operates on the basis of PoW (Nakamoto, 2008),[17] where there is no central authority, up to the point that software needs to be updated and this is done by consensus of 51% of full node participants.

This distributed and trust-less nature of the Bitcoin blockchain presents a radical departure from the centralised and regulated clearing and settlement processes of FMIs that have evolved over decades with the main purpose of removing settlement risk, ensuring liquidity, better resilience and managed counterparty risk in support of financial stability. These are each fundamental issues that modern digital payments have solved and which a shift to decentralisation must also be able to also solve. If not, no decentralised system will be able to truly compete with existing infrastructures!

In today's modern economies, FMIs play a key role in enabling financial operations as discussed above (Diehl et al., 2016).[18]

A famous case that illustrates the consequences when settlement finality is not properly defined or implemented is the failure of Herstatt Bank in 1974, which exemplified foreign exchange intraday settlement risk, or 'Herstatt risk'. Any consideration of or for the digital infrastructure of a financial ecosystem needs to necessarily deal with the question of settlement finality directly in order to accommodate the commercial and financial realities of market participants, the current structure, and where replacements are being made towards greater digitalisation, and more decentralised control of digital forms and stores of value.

One of the major areas within the financial sector of application of decentralised technologies and the underlying architecture of a distributed ledger system approach is that of post-trade clearing and settlement.[19] The modern process continues to develop and remains quite automated; however, the underlying infrastructure is chunky, costly, and requires significant manual reconciliation, trade confirmation across auditors, regulators and other parties and stakeholders,[20] due to the lack of connected legacy systems and manual back-office processes, where the right digital infrastructure could lead to $6 bn in savings globally.[21]

But back to the question. As intermediaries between participants, FMIs also concentrate risk, which is why they have to comply with globally defined principles to ensure that final settlement of transactions is achieved, preferably intraday and as a minimum by the end of the day (Principle 8, CPMI-IOSCO, 2012).

In the world of cryptocurrencies such as Bitcoin the idea of a consensus mechanism is focused on solving the problem of ensuring and deciding upon the current version of the database in an environment where there is no trusted third party. This problem is often referred to as the concurrency problem.[22] The most notable consensus mechanisms are PoW and proof-of-stake (PoS), each of which suffers from different shortcomings. The PoW model is incredibly inefficient given that it relies heavily on computational power. Another practical challenge of PoW, as seen in the case of Bitcoin, is the risk of concentration of power in mining pools, which could lead to double spending attacks. Still the cost of attack is proportionate to the amount of hash power that is controlled by an attacker, which ultimately may counter the attacker's vested interest. PoS on the other hand results in significant hoarding of whichever digital asset needs to be stored because staking aims to prioritise those participants that store a particular amount of the digital asset for a certain period of time, rewarding them for that 'staking' by enabling them to partake in decision-making. The other impact is that participants are not necessarily consistently online to play a role in maintaining the system as they can move in and out between staking and not staking.

Because centralised and distributed systems (FMIs), enabling the transfer of digital value, are very efficient and highly regulated and resilient, they are still superior to decentralised systems (Bitcoin and others), which today, depending on the model, underperform in terms of settlement speed, costs and accountability, but most importantly lack regulation. Therefore, it is not surprising to see that as the regulated market is looking to embrace new technologies, decentralised systems are still being dismissed. A good reflection of this is the approach that central banks take to research and development of Central Bank Digital Currencies (CBDCs), where we encounter combinations of centralisation in terms of governance—CBDC is issued by the central bank alone who has the control over its lifecycle—and distribution in relation to the physical location of the data nodes and servers. We will be taking a deeper dive into CBDCs in the next chapter but suffice to say here that it is overall highly unlikely that a central bank would opt for a decentralised system of CBDC as this would result in a lack of sovereignty and control over the administration of part of its currency with the same ensuing challenges that we today see in cases where countries, in particular certain emerging markets, show a significant amount of economic activity being transacted in non-sovereign currency, whether that is USD, non-USD ccurrencies or Bitcoin and the like. In those situations, monetary policy becomes less effective and transparency around financial flows and trade starts to vanish. On that basis, it can be safely assumed that we will not see a CBDC model emerging any time soon that is based on the foundation of decentralisation. Whereas decentralised systems such as Bitcoin and other cryptocurrencies have served as a technology driven inspiration for many actors, from businesses to governments and central banks, it is the element of distribution rather than the decentralised governance that is being more or less embraced, particularly from a cyber risk management standpoint.

4.5 Regulating Payments

To round off our chapter on money and payments, we will need to go on a quick excursion to the increasingly important topic of payments regulation. In the wake of the current wave of technology, regulation in the particular space of payments—spearheaded by the European Union, but as we shall see in a moment more firmly taken forward by the UK's FinTech scene, as noted in the Kalifa report[23]—has been the trigger to transform banking altogether.

In the below, we will highlight a few examples of payments regulation in Europe and other markets, which have been instrumental in unleashing innovation and the arrival of new competitors in the payments space. In fact, the incredible Fintech innovation that we have seen in the last decade has been primarily in the payments space, which is why contextualising the role that regulation has had in this is rather important.

At the same time, regulation itself is a form of centralisation, i.e. an authority defining rules by which it holds those entities to whom these apply to account and equally punish non-compliance. Naturally, regulations are important in order to organise a market, ensure adequate levels of consumer protection, mitigate or limit financial crime and support competition. However, depending on the country and the regulatory substance, centralised structures can be a fertile ground for abuse of power. The below provides a short account of payments regulatory developments, with a specific focus on Europe, which prioritises consumer protection and competition in this space.

E-Money Regulation: Europe as a Trend Setter

In the 1990s, the arrival of e-money, promising to deliver benefits of speed, transparency and efficiency to payment users led to the development of EU regulation for e-money issuance and the creation of e-money institutions with the first E-Money Directive being adopted in 2000. This narrow banking inspired law created a new type of institution with its activities limited to the issuance of e-money and facilitation of e-money-based payment transactions. E-money institutions are not permitted to take deposits, but instead will have to ringfence client monies with regulated credit institutions. They can then issue e-money based on this but need to ensure redeemability whenever a customer asks their money back. As a consequence, the prudential requirements are far less onerous compared to banks, which are subject to capital, liquidity and leverage requirements due to their deposit taking activities. Funnily enough, as we shall see later on, e-money legislation is quite useful when we look at the more recent innovation of stablecoins. Unfortunately, instead of a rapid review of this law to include new forms of cryptocurrencies or digital currencies, the EU and other markets have been sitting on their hands and had to witness the meltdown of some stablecoins in 2022.

The Payment Services Directive: Opening the Floodgates to FinTechs

By virtue of the specific conditions in Europe, i.e. the arrival of the Euro and the creation of a Single Market in Europe, the European payments landscape has undergone major infrastructure harmonisation over the last decade with the rollout of the Single Euro Payments Area (SEPA) from 2015 onwards. The role of payment services and instruments has become a key focus for the industry, regulators and payment users, particularly given the growing levels of digitisation of services (for more information check out one of my other books, Wandhöfer [2010][24]). This has led to the creation of the first ever payment-specific regulatory framework, the Payment Services Directive (PSD), adopted in 2007. This legislation introduced two important pillars in payments. On the one hand, it expanded the types of entities that can offer payment services beyond credit and e-money institutions to include so-called payment institutions (PIs). On the other hand, it established a set of harmonised conduct of business rules for all Payment Service Providers (PSPs) with the objective of enhancing consumer protection and competition in payments. This law was so ground-breaking that it began to accelerate technology-led payments innovation, which ultimately triggered the transformation of banking at an industry level. Many jurisdictions have since then adopted similar regulatory approaches to payments, and in Europe, emerging business models of both banks and non-banks, plus the demands of the growing e-commerce environment, were further complemented by the evolution of PSD.

Legislation to enable the next phase of payments—and here we are talking about "Open Banking"—was included within the EU Revised Payments Services Directive (PSD2). Newly introduced third-party providers (TPPs) are permitted by this legislation to access the payment account information of consumers and businesses (subject to consent) that hold their accounts at Account Servicing Payment Service Providers (ASPSP), i.e. a credit institution or an e-money institution (ASPSPs can also act as TPPs). Services such as payment initiation and account information are enabled and can insert themselves into the broader digital payments economy, where Application Programming Interfaces (APIs) can be leveraged as a tool to allow account-related data transfers between ASPSPs and third parties. This opening up of payment account data unlocks the opportunity to develop new services around payments going far beyond the payment itself.

So, why when this regulatory approach was spearheaded by the EU, is this space frequently seen to be dominated by the UK? Let us come back to our pedantic point on when is a regulation not a Regulation? When it is a Regulation derived from a Directive, it is transposed into Member State domestic legislation, rather than harmonised across the EU. As many of us know the UK was noted for gold-plating EU legislation when it was still a member of the EU and so it came to pass that the UK formed the Open Banking Implementation Entity which not only met the minimum requirements for TPPs but created a favourable environment within which they could flourish, to the extent that up until early 2022, there were more TPPs in the UK than the rest of the EU and EEA combined. Now, as we all look to Open Finance, the UK is already tabling enabling legislation for Smart Data to be built on these foundations and potentially provide a similarly favourable regulatory environment to open up user centric access to and control of all data sets, as we will explore in Chapter 8.

Services such as data-driven solutions that automate mortgage applications, improved credit scoring of individuals, instant consumer loans, etc., can all be facilitated in this way, leading to what is called 'Open Finance'.

Unlike PSD, PSD2 is not only formed by the text of the Directive but also required the European Banking Authority (EBA) to develop a number of Guidelines as well as Regulatory Technical Standards (RTS) in what is called the Level 2 process (more detailed than the Directive Articles). One of the key reasons for this is the fact that PSD2 introduces new types of more lightly regulated payment service providers, TPPs, and due to the increasing complexity of the payment landscape with more players, combined with the increasing digitisation of the business of payments, PSD2 included a new set of articles, which cover operational and security risks as well as authentication. All of these articles are underpinned and expanded in terms of detailed requirements, procedures and processes determined by the EBA in form of guidelines and RTS.

One of these PSD2 Level 2 requirements, the RTS on Strong Customer Authentication and Communication (SCA), has led to a lot of controversy in the market. The definition of 'strong customer authentication' in Article 4 (30) of PSD2 states the following:

> *strong customer authentication means an authentication based on the use of two or more elements categorised as knowledge (something only the user knows), possession (something only the user possesses) and inherence (something the user is) that are independent, in that the breach of one does not compromise the reliability of the others, and is designed in such a way as to protect the confidentiality of the authentication data.*

Examples of '*something only the payer knows*' include a password or a PIN that the PSU may be asked to enter into a browser or on the phone.

Examples of '*something only the user has*' include a payment card (for face-to-face transaction, or in a remote context as part of a layered approach) or a mobile phone (in a face-to-face context or for a remote transaction); a One-Time Password (OTP) to be created by a specific device or sent by a Short Messaging System (SMS) to the mobile phone that the payer has to enter into a browser or in a shopping app to confirm that the payer is in possession of this particular mobile phone, or more precisely, the SMS receiving SIM. Even more confusion entered the market with the legislation explicitly ruling out OTP SMS as a second factor because, as the legislation stated the compromise of one factor must not compromise the other, and clearly the possession of the users mobile—something they have—gives access to something they know! Leaving aside the numerous other technical vulnerabilities such as intercept and SS7, OTP SMS has been demonstrated to be the subject of numerous attacks.

Examples of '*something only the user is*' include biometrics such as fingerprint, voice and facial recognition, iris, pulse or behavioural characteristics (e.g. speed of typing, movement of the mobile phone's screen, handling of the phone in one's hands, etc.). In sum, if authentication of a PSU is performed on the basis of at least two elements, that have to be independent from each other and belong to at least two different categories, then PSD2 recognises this authentication as strong.

Most of the controversy around the RTS on SCA revolved around the content of Article 98 (2), with very different views amongst the parties involved. Card stakeholders requested and obtained a delay for applying SCA (but that's now over), because it is not always seen as the 'appropriate level of security'. TPPs are questioning the 'fair competition' and claim that (a) the 'technology and business-model neutrality' of PSD2 is contradicted by the RTS' bias towards API technology, which is still immature, and (b) that the EBA's objection to rule out mandatory redirection disables TPP-designed user flows and thereby limits their ability to 'develop user-friendly, accessible and innovate means of payment'.

Due to PSD2, TPPs need to migrate their access-to-account technologies to dedicated interfaces, more commonly known as APIs, which have to be built by banks (ASPSPs). In reality, the quality of such APIs is often still not at the level that would allow TPPs to ensure business and product continuity.

Practical application of the SCA provisions has shown that ASPSPs tend to require additional SCAs for AIS and PIS API access and consent confirmation, meaning that for simple payment initiation, the user is prompted to respond to up to four SCA requests for a single transfer through a PISP, not only burdensome for the user but unnecessary overall.

The challenges with the practical application of SCA and the introduction of redirection removed from TPPs their prior possibility to design good user experiences and also slowed down the payment flow, resulting in a significant reduction of conversion rates. This led to very concerning implications for the viability of many TPP-type FinTechs in the European market, which is contrary to the spirit of the PSD2 to accelerate innovation and competition. There is a real risk that TPPs will not be able to offer their services on all other devices such as Point-of-Sale (POS) terminals, wearables, smart speakers, etc., risking to foreclose the whole (physical) retail market and the whole new Internet-of-Things (IoT) arena. Instead, the support and strengthening of Europe's key payments innovators—TPPs—should not only be welcomed but is a necessity to remain competitive with other big markets such as the US and Asia.

Another regulatory driver in European retail payments was the Card Interchange Fee Regulation (CIFR) (Regulation (EU) 2015/751), which reduced credit and debit card transaction costs for merchants. Both PSD2 and CIFR were clearly geared towards supporting e-commerce and benefiting the merchant community.

It is to note that all of these retail payment instruments and the laws that apply to them relate to commercial bank money. As the market evolves towards further digitisation and as physical cash may become challenged by this, a potential role for central banks to issue digital central bank money is becoming more widely discussed and experimented with. At the same time, the phenomenon of private cryptocurrencies, stablecoins and more recently non-fungible-token (NFTs) has triggered the call for regulation in order to increase consumer protection. The EU, yet again, is the first jurisdiction to do something about this.

MiCA: Regulating the Digital Asset World

As we write this book, the EU has reached an agreement to regulate the trading of crypto-assets with the adoption of the Regulation of Markets in Crypto-Assets, in short MiCA. In the hope of anchoring consumer protection and legal certainty as well as to promote innovation and supporting financial stability, MICA defines a pan-European single licencing regime for what are labelled Crypto-Asset Service Providers (CASPs). These CASPs can be any person who as a business activity provides crypto-asset services to third parties. Examples of those services cover the exchange between fiat and cryptos or between different crypto-assets, custody and administration of these asset, the operation of crypto-asset trading platforms, order execution and placement of crypto-assets.

Now, this is all well and good and the EU is likely to pat itself on the back. As soon as this Regulation is put into action—expected to happen in 2024—there will be the feeling that something good is being done about consumer protection in Europe. But looking at it from another perspective, it's not like we didn't have regulatory tools in place already, which could fix this space. For example, as mentioned above, stablecoins could have been included in the scope of the existing E-Money laws, whilst crypto-assets as investment products would have nicely fit in the scope of Europe's Markets in Financial Instruments Directive (MiFID) as well as the Prospectus Directive. Other countries have those types of laws as well in many instances and a recommendation here would have been to look at expanding those regimes to crypto-asset rather than go down the MiCA route. Why you may ask? Well, instead of using the same principles and levels of scrutiny and requirement around market and conduct rules that we see in the E-Money Directive and MiFID, MiCA proposes a laxer regime in some areas. Whilst cryptocurrencies like Bitcoin and Ethereum will have to register in order to gain access to the EU market—how's that going to work with something as digitally ephemeral as these cryptos???—the operation and supervision of crypto-asset exchanges are much lighter and tax as well as accounting rules do not apply to CASPs. What?

And, of course, the biggest elephant in the room is the fact that the EU is trying to tackle the global phenomenon of borderless crypto-assets with a regional legislative approach. What is really needed for this sort of thing is a global approach… hold on a minute, that's what many of us have been preaching to regulators around the world for more than fifteen years!

4.6 Concluding Remarks

When it comes to money and payments, it is clear that we are still a long way off from having established a balance between emerging decentralised technology offerings, centralised governance and regulation and global citizens, that are using it day to day.

Recent history provides us with examples of decentralised money technology combined with decentralised money governance as an alternative way to established centralised money. The same is reflected in the way these new types of money (or value) are being exchanged, i.e. the way payments in these forms operate. It didn't take long for authorities across the globe to understand the danger of this 'uncontrollable' phenomenon.

Under the guise of modernising central bank money, many central banks around the world have taken early steps to take back control by conceptualising and creating CBDCs. At the same time, not all grass is greener on the other side of the decentralised world, where phenomena such as Bitcoin have increasingly displayed centralised characteristics.

It is to be seen whether the of evolution Decentralised Finance (DeFi), which we will explore further towards the end of the book, will be able to create more of a balance between the different forces and energies that push and pull for centralisation and decentralisation, hopefully to the benefit of us humans.

Notes

1. Krugman, P., Wells, R., "Economics", Worth Publishers, 2006.
2. Hudson, M., Van de Mieroop, M., "Debt and Economic Renewal in the Ancient Near East", CDL Press, 2002.
3. Schaps, D., "The Invention of Coinage and the Monetization of Ancient Greece", University of Michigan Press, 2004, 42.
4. Muldrew, C., "The Economy of Obligation", Palgrave Macmillan, 1998.
5. Geva, B., "Modern Banking Description", 2011, 361, De Roover 1974, 215, Usher 1934, 399.
6. Desan, C., "Making Money: Coin, Currency, and the Coming of Capitalism", Oxford University Press, 2014.
7. Statista, Great Britain Online Banking Usage: https://www.statista.com/statistics/286273/internet-banking-penetration-in-great-britain/ (last accessed 4/06/2022).
8. https://www.bbc.co.uk/news/technology-58473260.
9. Liao, R., "China's Digital Yuan Wallet Now Has 260 Million Individual Users", Tech Crunch, 18.01.2022: https://techcrunch.com/2022/01/18/chinas-digital-yuan-wallet-now-has-260-million-individual-users/?guce_referrer=aHR0cHM6Ly93d3cuZ29vZ2xlLmNvbS8&guce_referrer_sig=AQAAABRZuXj-3VmtQqvzLv3DxLpOqVjsZKZFK00CTh5Shn2cSFp73DgQ_Fs9LQ-ovmhZ_6ZObipasi25TA2bKnhufomaNjS7TtH9eSyUjEnq5zzfbmLk3g_5lGKAvklUkcxinFQNYtkQc3nXn6VTJJTuHE6nBFMhCES9CajuNQePvwyw&guccounter=2 (last accessed 18/09/2022).
10. Statista Mobile Payments Worldwide Statistics: https://www.statista.com/topics/4872/mobile-payments-worldwide/#topicHeader__wrapper (last accessed 4/06/2022).
11. See CPMI-IOSCO (2012). Actually, there is a fifth type of FMI, the Trade Repository. However, that type does not play a role in the payment, clearing and settlement processes. Instead it provides ex-post transparency on over-the-counter derivative transactions.
12. Berndsen, R. J., "Financial Market Infrastructures and Payments: Warehouse Metaphor Text-Book", Edition 2019, https://www.warehousemetaphor.com/preview/ (last accessed 08/11/2022).
13. Lamport, L., Shostak, R., Pease, M. "The Byzantine Generals Problem", *ACM Transactions on Programming Language and Systems*, 4(3), 382–401, 1982.

14. Garcia, F. D., Hoepman, J. H., "Off-line Karma: A Decentralised Currency for Static Peer-to-Peer and Grid Networks", *Applied Cryptography and Network Security*, 364–377, 2005.
15. Back: Hashcash developed in Back, 2002.
16. Libra White Paper 2.0, https://libra.org/en-US/white-paper/ (last accessed on 17/05/2020).
17. Nakamoto, S., "Bitcoin: A Peer-to-Peer Electronic Cash", 2008.
18. Diehl, M., Alexandrova-Labadjova, B., Heuver, R., Martinez-Jaramillo, S., "Analysing the Economics of Financial Market Infrastructures", IGI, 2015.
19. Schneider, J., Blostein, A., Lee, B., Kent, S., Groer, I., & Beardsley, E., "Profiles of Innovation: Blockchain—Putting Theory into Practice", 2016.
20. Steenis, H. V., Graseck, B. L., Simpson, F., & Faucette, J. E., "Global Insight: Blockchain in Banking: Disruptive Threat or Tool?", 2016.
21. Schneider, J., Blostein, A., Lee, B., Kent, S., Groer, I., & Beardsley, E., "Profiles of Innovation: Blockchain—Putting Theory into Practice", 2016.
22. Mattila, J., "The Blockchain Phenomenon—The Disruptive Potential of Distributed Consensus Architectures", The Research Institute of the Finnish Economy, 2016.
23. Kalifa, R., "Kalifa Review of UK Fintech", 2021, https://assets.publishing.service.gov.uk/government/uploads/system/uploads/attachment_data/file/978396/KalifaReviewofUKFintech01.pdf (last accessed 08/11/2022).
24. Wandhöfer, R. "EU Payments Integration: SEPA, PSD and Other Milestones Along the Road", London: Palgrave Macmillan, 2010.

Chapter 5
Borderless, Digital Future of Money

Following on from our introduction to money, payment systems and the high-level exploration through key payments legislation, let us look now more closely at how money moves around the world.

Interestingly, the way money moves is very much a function, not only of technical systems, governance and data but intrinsically linked to the characteristics of money, which is really where this conversation gets interesting. This is because money is changing as we speak. The old structures of payment systems and processes are being disrupted by computer algorithms. We already touched upon DLT and the Bitcoin blockchain as examples of this disruption, but that is only the tip of the iceberg.

In this chapter, we will go deeper into the discussion of our 5th wave of money, introduced earlier in this book, precisely because we want to understand how centralised or decentralised different models of moving money are and what this means for the level of alignment of our three spheres. We will begin our tour with an initial focus on cross-border payments, which are crucial for trade and thus the global economy. The old-fashioned way of cross-border correspondent banking payment is slowly changing—again technology disruption and the arrival of cryptocurrencies have been acting as a key driver for this, but more change is needed to truly create the art of the possible. So, we will take a look at different models for making those types of payments and see how these fare on the spectrum from centralisation to decentralisation.

Following on from that we will be venturing into the space of consumer cross-border payments, looking at what is happening there today and examining how innovations in terms of the nature and substance of money are changing the way consumers pay. We shall give a brief sneak preview of how virtual in-game and metaverse currencies could be used on a cross-border basis, potentially circumventing money laundering controls on the downside, or enabling monies to flow more freely without more repressive regime controls on the more positive side.

And finally, we will give a hopefully pithy overview of the ongoing research and debate about Central Bank Digital Currencies, or CBDCs, given the significant

R. Wandhöfer and H. D. Nakib, *Redecentralisation*,
https://doi.org/10.1007/978-3-031-21591-9_5

potential for this form of money to transform not only the payments world but financial interactions including banking as a whole.

5.1 The World of Cross-Border Payments

The ability to transfer money across borders in a safe and secure way is an indispensable requirement for the global economy. If this is also efficiently and relatively speedily, this will benefit people, businesses and governments and alignment can hopefully be achieved across these three spheres so that everyone wins. If instead there are imbalances of power, control, interests or even financial exclusion that are observed across the three spheres, then the question arises, 'has the degree of centralisation or decentralisation anything to do with this imbalance and what should be done to rebalance things towards alignment?'.

Let's start with some basics.
Payments in general can be divided into two broad buckets, retail and wholesale. The difference between these two lies in the value of the transactions and the entities that are involved in a transaction. Retail payments, made between consumers and businesses/governments, whilst making up most of the volume of transactions domestically, are not the most important when it comes to value. Wholesale payments are characterised by being large in size and moving between banks and financial markets. They are the blood and the arteries of the economy and it is thus critical that they work smoothly, efficiently and do not fail.

A similar logic applies to cross-border payments.
Cross-border retail payments are also transacted between consumers and businesses whereas transaction values are not that significant. Traditionally, consumers tend to make most of the payments in their lives in the country they live in. This is probably one of the main reasons why solutions to cross-border retail payments have been in short supply for some time. In case we shop physically abroad or online from other countries via e-commerce, we would—if we can—usually use credit cards to make those purchases. Global card schemes, such as Visa, Mastercard, American Express, Discovery and others, are enabling those transactions, but fees are usually at least 3% of the value of a transaction, though these fees are dwarfed by the levels charged to diaspora communities for remitting funds coming from developing nations, where 20–25% fees are not unheard of! These other option for cross-border payments would be using remittance providers. These provide particularly important services for individuals that are unbanked, work in one country and want to send money back home. At the same time remittance providers, depending on the jurisdiction of operation, are lightly regulated or not regulated at all. This enables them to extract higher fees from their users, which is particularly problematic as these are often

already struggling financially and have little to no choice around alternative ways to pay.

Cross-border wholesale payments are transacted uniquely between banks. Together with foreign exchange (FX) and trade services these can be categorised as so-called correspondent banking. More than 11,000 financial institutions (FIs) engage with each other across more than 1 million bilateral correspondent banking relationships.[1] FI and corporate transactions represent 80% of the cross-border transaction value and 20% of the overall transaction volumes.

Whether retail or wholesale, every cross-border payment requires as a minimum data on the ordering customer (account number, name and address), the beneficiary customer (local or international account number, name and address) and the beneficiary bank (bank name, address and the Business Identifier Code—BIC). Some countries will have extra requirements (e.g. the beneficiary's telephone number, tax-specific information, purpose of payment) and if this information is not present or incorrect, payments can be delayed or not happen at all.

Harmonising regulatory requirements in this space would certainly overcome some of these challenges and make cross-border payments less complex. In fact, this is something that the Bank of International Settlement's Committee on Payments and Market Infrastructures (CPMI) has begun to focus on in earnest, and it is clear that international cooperation and regulatory harmonisation can only start by identifying the underlying issues more specifically. The CPMI found that cross-border payments face four major challenges today: they are slow, expensive, opaque and inaccessible. These deficiencies clearly cause negative implications to global growth, trade, development and financial inclusion, in turn negatively impacting our three spheres by creating misalignment between them. If they are slow and expensive, people and businesses will not want to use them. If they are inaccessible, the issue is one of excluding more and more people and businesses from using payment systems. If they are opaque, that effects the level they can be trusted.

In July 2020, a task force coordinated by the BIS published a report tabling recommended "building blocks" for improved cross-border payments[2] in response to these identified deficiencies. The creation of more efficient systems, interoperability, transparency and regulatory alignment are all part and parcel of these but will take years to be put into action. Ultimately, the ability of the user to have choice and be offered transparent services is crucial but often not a reality.

Is there a positive or negative correlation between different cross-border payment models, including the extent to which they are centralised or decentralised and how does this impact people, businesses and government? These are the questions we need to ask in order to see which approaches should be supported versus those that are to be avoided. To do that, let us first of all look briefly at the high value payment space, which as we know makes up the majority of cross-border flows and fuels our global economy.

Big Tickets in Wholesale Cross-Border Payments

Until now the main method of executing wholesale—or large—money transfers across the globe is via correspondent banking arrangements.

There are various definitions of correspondent banking in the market today. In general terms, correspondent banking can be defined as *"an arrangement under which one bank (correspondent) holds deposits owned by other banks (respondents) and provides payment and other services to those respondent banks"*.[4] Further expanding on this concept, we particularly like the definition that was developed by the Wolfsberg Group, which states that *"[c]orrespondent banking is the provision of a current or other liability account, and related services, to another financial institution, including affiliates, used for the execution of third-party payments and trade finance, as well as its own cash clearing, liquidity management and short-term borrowing or investment needs in a particular currency"*.[5]

Essentially, the correspondent banking model operates via an international network of FIs, which have bilateral account relationships with each other. A bank that is obtaining correspondent banking services from another bank holds a so-called *Nostro* (Latin: ours) account with such provider bank, where the account is denominated in a foreign currency. From the provider bank's side, this same account is called *Vostro* (Latin: yours) account. This tightly woven network of FIs, in which trust plays a central role, has developed to global dimensions over the last centuries. There are quite a few risks in the business of correspondent banking cross-border payments, such as market, FX, credit and counterparty and regulatory risk (e.g. AML and CTF). Bodies, such as FATF (and to a certain extent Transparency International) carry out assessments of these relative risks on individual nations, and maintain black/grey/white lists according to the risk levels identified (remember the grey listing of Gibraltar in 2022!). Many have maintained that the FATF's three-tier approach doesn't allow for the same degree of gradation as, say, the Transparency International Corruption Index, which ranks nations by percentile. Whether there should be three, 100, or perhaps 50 shades of grey, the relative risks differ greatly between different nations, and these feed into the fees. Work led by the UK and Swiss governments at the outset of the COVID-19 pandemic aimed to gradually reduce fees across the board to no more than the 3% typically charged on international money transfers between many developed nations. Furthermore, technology and operational risks, as well as risks regarding the availability and cost of liquidity to support the business, do arise.

And despite the distributed nature of correspondent banking, systemic risk can be significant. To give you an example, before the financial crisis in 2008/2009, banks would extend credit lines (however, these were usually not committed) to each other, so that money could flow based on these promises. When the crisis hit, no promise was kept by anyone and so banks had to make sure that they actually had the money, i.e. liquidity, before trying to pay. This is where things broke down as few players knew exactly how much liquidity they had and where it was. This sounds a bit crazy. However, this is how markets worked then! Well, they rather still today!!

Today regulators, and specifically the Basel Committee, which is a global supervisory authority for banking authorities, require banks that park money with other banks in other markets for purposes of making these correspondent banking payments to hold extra risk capital against those amounts (which are considered risk exposures to another institution that might go down). Today this results in around $4 trillion of money being locked up in Nostro/Vostro accounts every day, just to keep interbank facilities for cross-border payments open! Equally interbank credit has become significantly expensive, so don't try to borrow money from other banks. Of course these regulatory measures are there because the absolute risks of failing individual payments are higher in wholesale payments due to the sheer size of these interbank flows. As already discussed in the previous chapter, in order for a payment to be final, a transaction has to settle. In many countries, so-called settlement finality is determined by law, ensuring that a transaction is irreversible from a legal point of view. The underlying nature of money is important here as settlement in commercial bank money is riskier than settlement in central bank money as because central banks are considered more stable than commercial banks (at least in the developed worlds). In order to reduce credit risk and support financial stability, settlement for high value transactions should, therefore, preferably occur in central bank money.

As previously discussed, at the domestic level, we have the so-called Real-Time-Gross-Settlement-Systems (RTGS Systems), which are operated by central banks and enable their member banks and in some instances non-banks (however often a restricted club of the larger financial institutions) to settle their payments in central bank money via settlement accounts. The larger bank players also have access to reserve accounts, which hold their central bank money at the central bank. Liquidity or appropriate collateral is a prerequisite for a transaction to go through and settle with finality. But at the international level we do not have what we might call a global RTGS System, which is why cross-border payments are trickier. Here, the sending bank A will need to hold a positive balance with bank B, for that latter Bank B to move the payment forward to its destination. In this example bank A would be holding a Nostro account with bank B and if a transaction were to go in reverse, bank B would be holding a Vostro account with bank A. Only a subset of large banks are the key providers of liquidity in correspondent banking due to their size and scale. As regulatory requirements required to know your customer but also to know your customer's customer (from KYC to KYCC) have increased over time, these large players started to de-risk their service, meaning they stopped providing access to correspondent banking services to those banks that were deemed too risky. And this has led to financial exclusion, where in some cases whole countries lost their access to international payments—creating challenges for people, businesses and governments alike. Particularly when it comes to matters of AML/CTF, many intelligence sharing approaches in the industry are not moving beyond KYCC to what should be a broader following-the-money-flow-approach, a KYC^n if you like.

For more detail on the issues with correspondent banking and proposals to improve the situation, we would refer those interested to a research paper by Casu and Wandhöfer,[6] which explored these issues in greater detail.

But by way of an introduction it is suffice to say that the concentration of these services amongst a few providers, de facto centralisation, can provide the benefits of efficiency through scale. Without this centralisation, in particular at the time it was created and with the technical know-how at the time, it is unlikely that the scale needed to provide a secure and accepted way for international wholesale payments would have been possible. Still, this centralisation can lead to drawbacks when it comes to overall inclusion and service coverage. For people, businesses or governments that did not have banking institutions that adopted these standards and ways of working, they ultimately would be excluded from correspondent banking channels, meaning their access to international payments would be limited or not there at all.

Examples of Wholesale Cross-Border Payment Improvements and Innovations

As we are going to look at some of the evolution and emerging innovation in cross-border wholesale payments the bigger question to address in this context is of course that of centralisation versus decentralisation. On the one hand, it feels that a global payment system could be a remedy to the many issues that financial institutions encounter currently, ranging from lack of settlement to liquidity inefficiency, non-availability, non-ubiquity, intransparency, non-predictability and absence of any form of interoperability of domestic systems at scale.

However, on the other hand, we know that complete centralisation in this context is a pipe dream as it would require a significant extend of international cooperation, standardisation, regulatory harmonisation and much more to achieve this. And then again, we would ask, is centralisation really what we are looking for when it comes to big money flows? Who would be in charge of such as system, determine its rules of access, pricing, etc.?

SWIFT

Now the reality is that today, SWIFT, the Society for Worldwide Interbank Financial Telecommunication, constitutes the central network that enables thousands of banks around the world to make payments across borders. This network is run by the largest banks in the world and regulated as a critical service provider. SWIFT is what we can call a messaging network, where banks can tell each other that credit and debit entries have been made in their respective systems in order to enable money to change from one player to the next. Operating since 1973, SWIFT has become the major information artery for cross-border wholesale transactions. In terms of our centralisation vs decentralisation perspective, most of the features of the cross-border correspondent banking process can be described as centralised through SWIFT because all financial institutions adopt the same messaging standards. But within that, it is a network of decentralised entities (the FIs) that opt-in or opt-out of using it. What makes it ever more centralised is that SWIFT has been the most efficient game in town and so is the most widely adopted in the world. Let's take a look at our framework for understanding centralisation and decentralisation to see how SWIFT fares.

Governance/Rules: the SWIFT network has centralised governance and message contents and formats are largely standardised.

Action/Process of change: any changes to the rules are decided by the SWIFT board, where a handful of banks can determine a change to the rules of the SWIFT network.

Design: Despite the centralised nature of the messaging in terms of process and content, the network itself is rather distributed, i.e. thousands of banks connect with each other using the network.

Access: Not every bank is automatically able to join SWIFT. There are various rules and requirements, including international regulatory restrictions that are applied in order to restrict access. At the same time, by meeting certain standards, many banks and even corporates can join. Nations and their FIs may also be excluded from using the SWIFT network, for example as part of the process of implementing sanctions.

Dispute Resolution: The resolution of disputes is organised with centralised rules and processes.

Knowledge/Diversity: Given the broad set of users, there is a strong element of diversity on the one hand, but as the control is so very centralised with some key influencers, actual diversity and knowledge are not very decentralised.

Whilst the SWIFT network is predominantly centralised, it has a number of decentralised and/or distributed components, such as in the areas of knowledge/diversity and at least, partially of access. This rather centralised model has, therefore, been slow in adapting and advancing with the times, in particular in light of the rapid technology change that we have been witnessing in the last few decades. Only when DLT and cryptocurrencies made an appearance and some FinTechs suggested that they could use technology in a way to create more modern and efficient processes for cross-border wholesale (and retail) payments, did SWIFT consider modernising its services. This has led to the launch of SWIFT Global Payments Innovation (gpi) in 2017. With the objective of reducing friction and enabling FIs to work better together, gpi provides a cloud-based service, accessible via APIs or MT199 messages, which allows tracking of payment transactions in real time by deploying the Unique End-to-End Transaction Reference (UETR). The transparency along the chain around payment fees and final payment amount that will reach the beneficiary, along with the commitment by beneficiary institutions to credit—within their time zone—the beneficiary same day, supports payment users in better managing the accounts payable component of their company's working capital equation. All SWIFT users were mandated since 2018 to pass on the UETR. As a result, payment enquiry costs have dropped for participants as counterparties now first consult the payment status in the cloud. By 2022 more than 4000 SWIFT members were using gpi with gpi payments covering more than 1939 country corridors. During 2019 almost $77 trillion in cross-border payments were transferred in that way. FI's are also increasingly using gpi to send cross-border payments within their group. Gpi has improved correspondent banking speed with more than 50% of gpi transactions being credited to the end beneficiary within 30 minutes, often within seconds and in excess of 90% of gpi payments being credited within 24 hours. For the remainder, the reason for delay can objectively be attributed to particular regulatory and compliance requirements, such as extra document checks and local FX controls.

From a financial stability perspective, it is important to mention that a correspondent banking payment message is only passed on to the next bank in the chain once the relevant *Nostro*/*Vostro* balances have been updated, i.e. each bank has to settle its position with the previous bank in commercial bank credit (recall the discussion on settlement above). In the last few years, many SWIFT-based market infrastructures (so payment systems such as Fedwire (US), CHIPS (US), CIPS (China), SIC (Switzerland) and FXYCS (Japan)) are able to clear gpi payments, which helps end-to-end transparency. It is worth mentioning here that CIPS in China, launched in 2015, is growing in importance in the context of geopolitical tensions, including the sanctions on Russia and Iran, both important oil producers. When SWIFT cut these countries off its network as a consequence, CIPS began to record increased flow and expanded membership. Money always finds its way, just like water.

From 2020 onwards all SWIFT FI users also had to provide mandatory end beneficiary credit confirmation. Additional services include pre-validation—where FIs can confirm the correct beneficiary account details before sending the payment—and a case resolution service, helping to automate resolution of problems with payments, which otherwise would require manual and time-consuming intervention.

In sum, the gpi scenario does address some of the key pain points expressed by market participants, albeit not the fact that transactions are still executed on the basis of commercial bank credit and the absence of tackling liquidity in terms of connecting messaging with liquidity and improving overall liquidity efficiency.

From our perspective of redecentralisation, gpi is an example of centralised governance that applies to a distributed network of member banks—as these are scattered all around the world. There is really nothing much decentralised in this structure at all.

Integration of Regional RTGS Systems

Instead of ACH systems, which of course only clear transactions rather than settle them (i.e. settlement could still be in commercial bank money as per above), directly connecting national RTGS systems with each other would be great in order to enable central bank money settlement and thus remove risk between players.

The Gulf Payment Company (GPC) owned and managed by six GCC central banks—Bahrain, Kuwait, Oman, Qatar, Saudi Arabia and the United Arab Emirates—has been tasked by the Gulf Cooperation Council (GCC) to build and operate such a regional RTGS. With a legal basis for this interlinking in place and the objective of supporting economic development and trade within the region, such as system would have the ability to reduce end-to-end costs for users and reduce the time taken from initiation of a payment to final delivery.[7] The first phase of this initiative was launched in December 2020 with the Financial Automated Quick Payment

Transfer (AFAQ) Service and onboarding for the cross-currency service began in 2021.

The fact that five out of the six countries have a fixed peg to the USD makes this a lot easier. Until the arrival of this system, many of the USD intra-GCC payments started their life as a debit to a local currency account of a sender, followed by a currency conversation to USD, to be remitted as a USD payment and then again converted back from USD to local currency in order to credit the account of the receiver. What a nightmare! There are also a number of pure USD-to-USD intra-GCC payments debiting and crediting USD accounts. An underlying rationale for the Gulf-RTGS initiative is represented by the objective to reduce the power of the USD as a reserve currency, given the nature of its risk profile and regulatory burden. This is clearly a drive towards redecentralisation when we look at the currency itself, whilst creating such a regional "Uber"-RTGS system is a step towards regional centralisation. But when we see this initiative in the light of supporting regional independence and enhanced financial stability as well as efficiency, we can see the overall benefit. After all the domestic RTGS systems in the region have accounts in each other's books, enabling transactions via the system to settle immediately with finality in central bank money. It is also a good example that shows that a monetary union is not a prerequisite to achieving a multi-country and currency RTGS.

However, the GCC model is very specific to this region and it is unlikely that this can be easily replicated at a global scale, given the legal, regulatory and political as well as standards and operational related challenges of alignment. Still, the formation of regional RTGS hubs should be encouraged with a view to creating interoperability bridges between the regions, which would allow for an increasingly global coverage. This would increase decentralisation and with it improve access and diversity/knowledge within payments, thereby benefiting the market overall. A number of DLT-based experiments are already underway in several parts of the globe, which we will highlight later on.

At this point in time various central banks around the world are also working on renewing their payment system infrastructure (or have recently done so); for example, the Bank of England's RTGS renewal programme; the new Canadian high value payment system; Australia's New Payment Infrastructure; amongst others. A big ambition in all of these system upgrade initiatives is the perspective of potential future cross-border coordination and interoperation between, for example, central bank RTGS systems. In parallel, there is rapid growth of Faster/Immediate Payments in many countries, filling the gap between traditional ACH and RTGS systems and perhaps constituting the beginning of a potential merging of Faster/Immediate Payment Systems and RTGS Systems.

Global Synthetic Ledger for Liquidity Transfers

Creating a type of global FMI for payments could address the many issues encountered by the industry. We have this in FX with the global Continuous Linked Settlement (CLS) system, but not for payments. Since the arrival of cryptocurrencies, we have seen several FinTechs trying to tackle this market gap. One model that is worthwhile mentioning is an aspiring FMI, which seeks to enable banks that are holding central bank reserves in their local jurisdiction to deploy the HQLA part of their reserves to settle FX cross-border wholesale payments. This business sees itself as a global switchboard for interbank liquidity, complemented by a number of tools that support better payments and banking.

This company has built a central ledger that can be used by banks that have central reserves to transact with each other across borders. The system enables banks to exchange liquidity in one currency for that in another, without the liquidity itself actually needing to move over local RTGS rails. Rather than having to extend commercial credit to each other through Nostro/Vostro arrangements, or pre-fund commercial correspondent bank accounts and bear credit risk, participants in this system will be able to benefit from the innovative operational design, legal framework and technology, such that liquidity in one currency can atomically settle for that in another using—HQLAs—the best liquidity there is (according to the Basel Accords), without incurring additional RWA costs. Of course, available HQLA is a prerequisite for this, i.e. the liquidity must be there. An immutable ledger manages the ownership of assets on its ledger. The ledger mirrors the asset—which remains held at the central bank in the name of the owner of the funds underpinning the settlement arrangements—and is recognised as a ledger to record the true ownership of the funds (under a trust or equivalent arrangement). The key differentiator here is that ownership is not limited to domestic banks. Through its innovative legal framework and participation agreement complemented by a comprehensive rulebook arrangement, the approach connects banks across borders. Whereas a 'pure' synchronisation agreement sees ownership and transfer of funds only between domestic players in the domestic RTGS system, this aspiring FMI extends the domestic players (in their role as hosts for foreign banks in their jurisdiction) into the ledger underpinning settlement. For this model to work in practice, it will be important that central banks do not restrict beneficial ownership of HQLA-based central bank reserves to domestic banks. The model is effectively "central bank money-based correspondent banking"!

Today the focus is on settling traditional central bank money transactions, where funds are held with a central bank in a reserve or master account. In the future, where central banks may create wholesale CBDCs (wCBDCs), and more on that further below, as a new digital form of central bank money, such a new version of central bank money could equally be supported by this system. The roadmap will focus clearly on delivering interoperability and 'settle-ability' between traditional central bank money, wCBDCs and any other type of digital money that could be deployed in the wholesale payments space.

Such a solution would provide central banks with an important tool, both in terms of monitoring the transaction flows and being able in case of a bank resolution to immediately have all the information necessary in terms of which balances a bank really owns in its reserves account.

The system would reflect a combination of centralisation and distribution, with rules and the operating platform being centrally governed and operated, whilst participants would be distributed around the world. Alternative solutions are also coming

Table 5.1 Cross-border wholesale payment initiatives and degrees of centralisation

Model/initiative	Centralised	Distributed	Decentralised
Correspondent Banking with gpi	Governance for gpi is centralised	Network of participating banks is distributed	Access of participating banks is centralised in terms of governing rules
Regional RTGS GCC	Centralised governance and system	Network of participating banks is distributed	Access of participating banks is centralised in terms of access rules
Global Liquidity Settlement Ledger	Centralised governance and system	Network of participating banks is distributed	Access of participating banks is centralised in terms of access rules

to the market these days, which utilise stablecoins to support cross-border payments on behalf of payment providers such as money remitters with a view to expanding to neobanks and smaller banks that struggle more with the cross-border payments challenge (more on stablecoins shortly).

All these attempts show a healthy challenge to the old-age correspondent banking model and by providing more choice, albeit not yet full-scale alternatives, we see certainly more distributed network approaches and, on the fringes some small steps towards efforts of redecentralisation, in particular around access and diversity/knowledge but also the parties involved in making decisions and changing the rules of the system. Nevertheless, given the significant regulatory requirements and risks, harmonisation of regulatory obligations and data standards will be key to being able to realise those objectives. At the same time, restrictions to data flows, such as data onshoring as operated by some countries, will need to be lifted, a task that could be tackled by the Financial Stability Board (FSB) and the G20. Redecentralisation needs data to be shareable and not stuck in an inaccessible centre (Table 5.1).

5.2 Retail Cross-Border Payments

The major challenge for efficient, fast, secure and cheap retail payments across borders is that the majority of current market offerings rely on the 'old' the correspondent banking rails described in the previous section. Non-bank payment intermediaries, such as E-money institutions or payment institutions (see PSD and PSD2), set up bank relationships in those countries that they want to be able to reach and transactions flow between sending and receiving banks and all the possible intermediary banks, including clearing banks that provide the required FX for the transaction as explained above.

Whether it is the underlying nature of money or the system used for the transaction or both, the question is, do we have payment solutions for customers like you and me, as well as all types of businesses that are more inclusive, cheaper and convenient to access and do they operate in a more decentralised way because of those features to support the best interest of users?

As we already pointed out, most cryptocurrencies, and funnily enough even some of those who had initially been designed with the purpose of being a payment instrument, are not stable enough to be used as a payment instrument.

However, there are some FinTechs in the payments cross-border space that offer the opportunity to pay via cryptocurrencies. For example, as a way to urgently pay money across borders over a weekend, when most banks and payment systems around the world are closed. Many countries have near real-time domestic retail payment systems that do operate 24/7 and would allow a customer to fund their account with fiat and make a local payment any time of the day. In those instances, crypto can be converted to fiat and paid near real time. One could argue that those examples are rather niche and risks of money laundering may be a problem here. But still they do exist today.

And then there is another invention. Stablecoins.

Stablecoins… or Rather 'The Emperor's New Clothes'

As a result of the shortcomings of cryptocurrencies as payment instruments, some clever people came up with idea of creating a crypto that would be more stable by pegging it to fiat currency.

Nothing much else than e-money, some of you may think, which is a regulated activity in many markets (in the EU since 2001!).

Having a stable cryptocurrency would finally fulfil the promise of medium of exchange and store of value and of course unit of account, the key features of money.

Let's look at the stablecoin world for a moment.

Today (which may be outdated by the time you read this!) we have three major types of stablecoins in the market:

(1) Stablecoins backed by fiat currency (or cies) or other types of assets;
(2) Stablecoins backed by cryptocurrency; and
(3) Algorithmic stablecoins.

Well then, how do they work and how stable are these stablecoins?

In simple terms stablecoins shift counterparty risk from regulated FIs, such as banks, to, often unregulated institutions, the stablecoin issuers and operators, thereby increasing counterparty risk. This means by definition that they are riskier than the commercial bank money you hold in your bank account. In large part, the question here is: what party are users/participants trusting? There is no deposit insurance for stablecoins and we are only now seeing the emergence of regulation for stablecoin issuers. The absence of regulation means that if something goes wrong with the issuer of the system or you accidentally send the coins to the wrong person, they will have been lost or ended up in the wrong pockets. But that is not everything. We also can't be sure if and how stablecoins are collateralised or backed. Tether claims that their coins are 1:1 backed by the correspondent amount of USD fiat currency. However, we know that this has not always been the case. At the same time, different best practices are beginning to emerge that focus on stablecoin issuers being banks themselves, or taking stringent measures to have third party audits, both of their code, and their collateral, and making that publicly available. In the US Circle, which provides the USDC stablecoin, is regulated via state legislation as a money transmission business. In Europe, as previously discussed E-money laws would be the easiest way to get stablecoins regulated and now we have MiCA. But until now this space is still a bit Wild West.

To see how much can go wrong, here is a fairly recent example of what unregulated stablecoins can experience: a death trap.

Table 5.2 The story of Algorithmic Stablecoins: Luna and Terra

Not long ago someone called Do Kwon decided to give the stablecoin idea yet another twist. He came up with two crypto coins, Luna and UST (and remember this is the phase where the Emperor's new clothes are being designed).

The idea is that both work in tandem. You can always redeem Luna for UST, one to one, even if one of the coins is worth less than 1 real US dollar—supposedly a stabilising mechanism.

So, for example, if UST is trading at $0.99, you can buy it and redeem it for $1 Luna and pocket a (virtual?) gain of $0.01. This is labelled the contraction phase as in this example UST demand is falling.

On the opposite end, the expansion phase denotes UST demand expansion, where UST is suddenly worth $1.01 and people would exchange it to Luna, trading at $1 in order to cash in the $0.01 gain on that side.

Now the big question is, what else is going on? Are we only talking about a bit of arbitrage gains here or is there more that we need to consider?

And of course, there is—utility.

There is a specific utility linked to the stablecoin, which ensures that demand is maintained and the peg of the stablecoin with the real US dollar can be sustained. And this utility, or good reason, is that the underlying anchor protocol of UST enables you to gain a 19.5% interest if you stake UST. Hold one, we heard about staking before! Staking is the process of locking up some of your cryptos for a defined period of time, similar to parking your money in a savings account. These cryptos are used by the system to support transaction validation—note that this only applies to systems that run on the basis of a Proof of Stake consensus mechanism (unlike Bitcoin, which does PoW). Being offered a 19.5% interest is really where the attraction comes from, in times of zero and even negative interest rates applied to money sitting on your bank account (although that has quickly changed over the last half year as we raced into an era of rampant inflation—it's the roaring 20s after all—unless we end up in nasty stagflation…).

Well, and if there is money to be made out of nothing, others are quickly jumping on the bandwagon. In this example specific solutions were designed and launched in order to enable recursive borrowing with several times net leverage; in simple language, instead of just getting your 19.5% for staking UST, you could avail of a loan to borrow with significant leverage to stake much more and make much more, under the assumption that all else remains equal (which is of course unrealistic!). This particular solution offered by one set of providers in the market happened to be unwound in early January 2022, leading to a steep fall in the value of Luna. Terra had even set up a specific ecosystem fund—the Luna Foundation Guard—one could call it a rescue fund, which began to sell Luna to market makers in their ecosystem and bought Bitcoin as collateral (so far nothing had been collateralised at all, a case of 'Emperor's new clothes'). Of course, we are talking about a fractional collateralisation, just like fractional reserve banking in the good old financial world. By that time more and more UST and Luna holders got nervous and tried to sell their positions. Whilst the system had a limit on redemption rates built in—in order to throttle redemptions in times of high demand to exit—the founder Do Kwon removed this mechanism and what then happened is what we know so well from banking in times of crisis: a bank run—aka stablecoin run. Alas!

So, what have we learned from this example? This is not a story of centralisation versus decentralisation. This is actually a perfect demonstration of the dangers human greed can bring about. In fact, even decentralised consensus mechanisms and technical protocols would not have prevented this downfall, because a whole ecosystem of perverse incentives had quickly built up to attract those in the know (arguably not our everyday consumer) to speculate and exploit the system. Other scandals at an even bigger scale not only preceded this one (we all may recall the days of the MT Gox scandal) but were also unfortunately to follow this one swiftly. Of course I'm talking about the sensational meltdown of one of the biggest crypto exchanges, FTX! And all of this shows us that we are still dealing with an immature, often unregulated and certainly not properly supervised industry. Of course this is an opening for centralised money provided by central banks to get into the game with the objective to create modern digital central bank money that is safe and—maybe—as cool as cryptos.

5.3 The Next Step in Money and Payments: CBDCs

Given what we discovered so far, it is not surprising that our third pillar of change in money and payments covers Central Bank Digital Currencies, or CBDCs. These have become an important concept in the discussion of the evolution of money over the past few years. The various rationales for developing a CBDC have been highlighted by many research publications since then (IMF, BIS, ECB, National Central Banks, etc.). Whilst the concept of CBDC initially started emerging as a reaction to cryptocurrencies such as Bitcoin, the potential merits of a CBDC in improving financial stability, creating financial inclusion and enhancing efficiencies and resilience of payments have come to the fore, in particular due to the steep and secular decline in the use of physical cash. And for several countries CBDCs are also becoming a geopolitically strategic imperative. This includes challenging the supremacy of the US dollar, which has been reigning over global markets since post-World War II. Mark Carney, former Governor of the Bank of England, has for example suggested the creation of a currency-basket-based digital currency for trade, that would be able to challenge the US dollar, similar to Special Drawing Rights, or SDRs. At the same time, countries are also looking for a hedge against the US dollar.

Some countries are outright worried that certain emerging cryptocurrencies as well as CBDCs could destabilise their local currency, whereas a number of smaller emerging market players in addition to Japan have chosen to make Bitcoin a permissible payment instrument, an accepted means of exchange—or even legal tender, see El Salvador—as opposed to simply a property (as is the case in the UK—even though the recent UK Law Commission suggested to create a third form of 'digital property' in law).

Christine Lagarde, when she ran the International Monetary Fund (IMF), made a public statement underlining the importance of central banks to reconsider their role as money issuers in the digital age, emphasising key principles and design considerations.[8] Simply put, where cryptocurrencies allow for zero control, central bank-owned platforms would give regulators control back, making innovation in money issuance a key priority for central banks. No surprise therefore that a number of research and pilot projects have been developing over the last few years with many central banks and supranational bodies including BIS and IMF issuing research papers and results of Proof-of-Concepts (PoCs). It is also interesting to note that the theme of CBDC gained further momentum during the COVID-19 crisis with different bodies (e.g. Positive Money) calling for central bank digital cash in order to maintain financial stability and limit the mass-privatisation of money.

Next to the geopolitical drivers, the cost of cash and the continuing decline of cash usage in certain countries, make the rationale for digital money more pertinent. Whilst Sweden has been a case in point over the last few years and has advanced in developing an e-Krona proposition, the COVID-19 crisis shows that cash usage can rapidly decline in developed markets as evidenced for example by the UK. In the UK market, a cash decline of 50% has been recorded in just a few days as the crisis led to the government mandating large-scale shop closures and people to stay at home whilst raising the limit for contactless payments from 30 to 45GBP and subsequently to 100GBP, and encouraging use of contactless payments for essential food and medicine shopping.[9] However, a major question is if CBDC is supposed to be a digital version of the cash bank note or a new retail payment instrument with broader properties, and presumably less anonymity than cash?

And talking about COVID-19, the supply of money to citizens in times of crisis, so-called 'helicopter money', a term first coined by economist Milton Friedman in 1969, certainly has potential to be executed more efficiently and smoothly with a CBDC.[10] When the US government agreed on 17 March 2020 to supply emergency funds to citizens, they rather went the opposite way—via cheque![11] An approach, which is not only inefficient and costly but actually problematic in times of pandemics as cash is a physical instrument that needs to be cashed in at a branch and handed from person to person, and cannot be used digitally. And in the UK context, at the start of

COVID-19 the financial services industry was brought together to see how best to ameliorate the flow of funds to those most in need. But whether US, UK or elsewhere, unfortunately these support schemes were put in place without any security controls, and hence, they were inevitably abused at an industrial scale by organised crime. The degree to which different funding forms will impact how much—if any—of this money can be recouped is a matter for debate, but we'll have to come back to that in the coming years.

CBDCs are also seen as a solution to protect consumers from technical outages. This is particularly relevant in the context of cybercrime attacks. However, whether CBDCs would be more resilient compared to existing digital payments is questionable and very dependent on the detailed design and technology that a CBDC would be based on. In fact, technology and design are two important pillars for CBDCs that aim to improve financial stability. Wandhöfer (2019) has specifically addressed the question of settlement finality in relation to DLT with a case study on Bitcoin and its PoW consensus algorithm, which we highlighted briefly earlier. The broad findings show that even though the Bitcoin protocol and consensus algorithm in particular are not the answer to making settlement finality more efficient and certain, compared to the application of legal settlement finality frameworks post-event, the increasing toolbox of blockchain, DLT and smart contracts but equally cloud technology offer the opportunity to design an FMI that can be far more superior than existing technology platforms and legal arrangements. So this would support the idea of examining DLT more closely as an underlying technological base for payment systems.

Of course the biggest elephant in the room is the fact that CBDCs could birth the very real risk that under certain stress events there might be a fully fledged and very speedily executed run on the banks. Introducing such a digital ('considered to be') risk-free asset to the market (that is a debt to the central bank, just like physical cash in the form of banknotes and coins) could in certain situations lead to significant demand, a flight—in the true sense of the word—from commercial bank deposits into CBDCs, triggering reduced bank funding and a consequential increase in lending rates. Central banks have yet to figure out how to mitigate this, before any meaningful CBDC at scale can be introduced!

So, for now, let us examine what type of design considerations central banks are examining and what open questions and challenges still need to be answered and overcome before a sizeable country will decide to launch a CBDC (notwithstanding that China has launched a large-scale pilot already in 2019).

What to Consider When Designing a CBDC?

Depending on the design and underlying technology deployed, very different functionalities and associated market impacts of launching a CBDC are destined to ensue. We know that the core objective of a central bank's mission is the safeguarding of monetary and financial stability. With this in mind the first question to ask then is, what should a CBDC achieve and how could this be reflected in the governance and design? In the below we are listing some of the key questions that a central bank should ask itself when engaging on this topic.

Table 5.3 CBDC Design Questions

Central Bank Balance Sheet/Monetary Policy/Governance

Should CBDC be guaranteed in full by the central bank?
Should CBDC enable fractional reserve banking?
Will foreign banks be allowed to access and hold CBDC reserves of another country? If so, is would this be legal or beneficial ownership?
Should CBDCs be remunerated including potentially attracting negative interest rates (depending on economic cycle)?
Should CBDCs be provided by the central bank alone in terms of technology, governance, etc. or should the private sector be suppliers in support of CBDCs? Where should ultimate accountability and liability lie?

Issuance

Should the central bank provide CBDC accounts directly to individuals and businesses or should CBDCs be issued on a token basis?

Payment Instrument Dimension/Functionality

Should CBDC be a retail solution to improve consumer and SME payments?
Should CBDC provide peer-to-peer payment capability?
Should CBDC be useable both online and offline?
Should there be CBDC transaction capability at PoS?
Should CBDC deliver real-time transaction capability via e.g. atomic settlement?
Should CBDC be designed with the purpose of financial inclusion?
Should CBDC be alternatively or also a wholesale solution to improve interbank and bank to central bank transactions?
Or should it be both, i.e. a holistic new type of central bank money covering the retail and wholesale space?
Should CBDC enable cross-border payments in the retail space?
Should CBDC enable cross-border payments in the wholesale space, or both retail and wholesale?
Should CBDC be programmable? And if so would users be able to program the CBDCs they hold?
Should a CBDC be interoperable with other domestic payment systems?

Data Privacy

Should CBDC be traceable, i.e. should each entity or individual using CBDC be identifiable and transactions be fully traceable by the central bank (and possibly other governmental bodies)? Will this go hand in hand with a digital identity proposition?
Should CBDC be fully anonymous, akin to a bearer instrument, like physical cash?

Regulatory Integrity

Will CBDCs embed AML compliance? If so, how?

Depending on the choice of anonymity, versus pseudonymity, versus full transparency, will there be transaction limits for CBDCs, or overall limits for conversion purposes (between commercial bank money)?

Distribution and Economic Model

Will all regulated PSPs be permitted or even mandated to distribute CBDC?
Will PSPs be able to charge for payment transactions made in CBDC?
Are non-bank PSPs able to have access to central bank reserve accounts or alternatively access to settlement accounts at the central bank for CBDC purposes?
Is there a risk that non-bank PSPs will experience a competitive disadvantage compared to banks when it comes to CBDC?

Technology

Is there a role for blockchain / DLT to play in terms of the underlying ledger structure?
If a blockchain / DLT-type ledger were to be chosen, what type of consensus or validation models are being considered with what level of decentralisation? Who can participate in validation?
Are smart contract technologies being explored and if so what type of use cases should be included from the start?
What forms of encryption and overall technical security technologies are being explored to ensure that user data remains secure?
What technologies are chosen to enable customer initiation of transactions (QR codes, NFC, etc.)?

And many more…; we haven't event discussed the whole space of merchants and how they receive/send/convert CBDCs....

Research so far has focused on different use cases, which translate into different design approaches, respectively.

By now we have quite a few countries around the world that are exploring CBDCs and from a structural standpoint, we observe three different approaches to their design as discussed by the BIS in 2020.[12]

On the least disruptive side of the spectrum, as outlined in the BIS paper, we have indirect CBDCs, which represent a claim on an intermediary (e.g. a commercial bank), where such intermediary is responsible for customer onboarding (KYC) and the handling of retail payments; wholesale payments would be handled by the central bank. In this model, we can almost recognise the current world of fractional reserve banking, which also operates a two-tier structure system. In some ways, this is similar to commercial bank deposits.

The second model is the direct CBDC model where the CBDC is a claim on the issuing central bank, just like physical cash is today. Onboarding of customers (KYC) could be either done by the central bank or the intermediaries (e.g. commercial banks) and retail payments would be handled by the central bank.

The third model is the hybrid CBDC model in which CBDC is again a claim on the central bank, intermediaries do the onboarding (KYC) and manage retail payments, whereas the central bank periodically records retail balances.

Now, each of these different approaches comes with a different degree of decentralisation as well. The debate has predominantly been one around whether or not such a CBDC system is to be what is called account-based (linked to a custodian, i.e. the central bank) or token-based. The main distinction between the two is that in an account-based system your money is in an account and that account is tied to you and your identity, like commercial bank deposits. In a token-based system, it is more like coins and banknotes. In that way CBDCs are not tied to your identity but rather, to possession, (i.e. bearer instrument). This is precisely a question of redecentralisation. Whether and to what extent you need to rely on others to make use of CBDCs along our operational dimension.

There are some important questions to ask about a token-based design, including whether we need the tokens to be issued and guaranteed by the central bank directly, or by other institutions (e.g. stablecoins), or whether the tokens can operate entirely outside the institutional milieu ('cryptocurrency' and unstable stablecoin examples). We have seen that stablecoins can introduce systemic risk. Their design relies upon a peg to some other asset, which can ultimately be undone or the underlying asset might be inexistent altogether! Users of stablecoins, therefore, incur counterparty risk to those who are tasked with maintaining the peg (and ensuring that there IS an underlying asset or assets). This counterparty risk implies either that the stablecoin must trade at a discount to the asset to which it is pegged, or that the peg would be underwritten for example by a regulated commercial bank (e.g via the deposit of the equivalent fiat currency or other eligible collateral at that bank). In the former case, the stablecoin is not so stable. In the latter case, the stablecoin is not really different from fiat currency (i.e. cash or coins), though it would be considered as a new type asset that people use given the underlying technology dimension.

Token-based systems, including systems with strong privacy characteristics, can still be centralised, if they rely upon a specific arbiter to handle disputes about the validity of each transaction (possibly with a different arbiter for different transactions), or they can be decentralised, using a distributed ledger to validate each transaction *ex ante* via a decentralised consensus process by the parties that maintain the system and write new transactions. For a decentralised design, we consider the question of who the system operators would be, and who decides who they could be, which would make the system either more or less centralised, depending on the answer. In the case of CBDCs, for example, although we assume that the central bank would be responsible for the design and issuance of CBDC tokens, we do not make the same assumption about the responsibility for the operation of the transactional infrastructure or payment system, which historically has been operated by private sector organisations.

Systems for payments, clearing, and settlement are often a collaborative effort.[13] Indeed, modern digital payments infrastructure based on bank deposits depends upon a variety of actors, and we imagine that digital payments infrastructure based on CBDC would do so as well. The responsibility to manage and safeguard the value of currency is not the same as the responsibility to manage and oversee transactions, and the responsibility to supervise payment systems is not the same as the responsibility to operate them. A design that externalises responsibility for the operation of a transactional infrastructure supporting CBDC is not incompatible with the operational role of a central bank in using CBDCs to create money and implement monetary policy.

Blockchain and DLT infrastructures are actually quite critical for a CBDC system for a variety of reasons. In our view, this is currently the most plausible method of implementation whereby the central bank can collaborate with private sector firms, via either public–private partnerships or other collaborative and supervisory models, to deliver a national payments infrastructure operated by the private sector. The use of DLT does not imply that households and retail members of the public must have a direct account or relationship with the central bank, as some authors have wrongly assumed. On the contrary, banks, regulated financial services businesses and PSPs play an important role, especially in maintaining the system operationally, distributing the assets, identifying, onboarding and registering new customers, satisfying compliance requirements and managing their accounts. This is also the case in 2 out of the 3 CBDC structures highlighted above.

Goodell, Nakib and Tasca (2021)[14] highlight and set out the benefits of DLT within a certain degree of decentralisation which broadly fall into the following four categories and we believe that all of them are necessary for the system to succeed:

1. *Operations:* The costs and risks associated with having a central operator managing the operations of the system are reduced. Any system that has a database, which is centrally managed would also have to rely on some central intermediary that is responsible for managing and maintaining the system, but that is also involved in the operations of the system when it comes to permitting or prohibiting transactions. The existence of a central operator comes with a set of costs and risks. This includes the central operator managing any disputes, guaranteeing that the system is reliable for participants and users, ensuring that certain pre-determined rules of the system are adhered to, that use of the system occurs as expected and if not, being accountable. These costs and risks do not manifest in such a concentrated way in a more decentralised governance.
2. *Gatekeeping function:* As mentioned in the foregoing, the central operator that has the role of administering a centralised ledger is the locus of power and control in a system, playing the gatekeeper function. This means that the central operator could prevent certain users from participating in the system, or even discriminating against some users over others, whether by instituting additional fees, setting additional information requirements that have to be complied with in order to participate or effect a transaction, or even directly tampering with the system's records, changing the rules to indirectly disadvantage a particular party or group. Each of these examples are instances of a central operator taking unilateral action, of its own accord, in a way that can disadvantage users. The risk of such unilateral action is reduced in a decentralised form of governance and decision-making system.[15]

3. *Transparency:* Pursuant to the aforementioned discussion about unilateral action, the very existence of unilateral action by a central operator of a system makes it especially difficult for both participants and outside third parties to know whether it has carried out its function in administering the central ledger appropriately or not. Since the central operator does not need to make public its intention, or even its changes to the system (or the ledger), and does not require the permission of any party to accept its changes, transparency can be significantly limited. In comparison with this, in a more decentralised governance for a payment system and by implementing DLT or blockchain, added transparency can be achieved, whereby the rules determine that any changes, or certain changes (i.e. to the rules of the system or to the ledger) must be shared with certain users or even displayed publicly to third parties.

The particular benefits of operating a more decentralised from of governance through a DLT (or other blockchain technology stacks) have to do with avoiding the pitfalls of centralised systems across the concentration of risk, security, compromise of the system, general errors and more. This is not to say that there would not be some kind of central overseer. To the contrary, a central regulator may still have oversight over a particular payment system. The central regulator may also set the rules for what kinds of businesses are able to write transactions to the ledger, for example, deciding whether it is to be banks or banks and payments businesses, post offices, and more. By having a more decentralised governance and operating a DLT, it actually relieves responsibility of a central authority from being responsible for any individual transaction themselves, and grants participants the ability to do so directly to maintain the viability of the decentralised ledger. In doing so, it also allows for participants to better compete and innovate, thereby potentially providing better and more added value to end-users and customers.

Country Approaches to CBDC

Over the last 5 years, central banks across the globe have started researching and experimenting with the topic of DLT and cryptography, crystallising their approaches to CBDC. This is and understandable trend against the background of cryptocurrencies that are out of control of central banks. Some central banks are racing to take control back whilst responding to the demands to 'modernise' central bank money, whereas others are holding back, or at least going through a lengthy period of introspection. Two countries, the US and UK, are particularly interesting in this regard, with many mixed messages coming out as to how fast, if at all, such a move will come. From the UK then Chancellor of the Exchequer, Rishi Sunak [note at time of writing the current UK Prime Minister—possibly by time of reading, the Prime Minister preceding x, y, and z, others!] wanted to turn London into a global crypto hub—whilst different sections of the Bank of England were either backing this approach or warning against the ecosystem risk of such an approach. And the US-based Atlantic Council launched their paper on CBDCs in London, believing in Sunak's approach at the time, only for him to resign (from his previous job) weeks later, resetting UK political policy on the matter. The BoE has issued a consultation on the digital pound in early 2023, whilst the US Federal Reserve Board has been experimenting but no decisions to proceed have been taken yet. The ECB is plowing ahead with its design discussions for the last few years, eager to get to a final decision on a CBDC go ahead.

Here below we give you a flavour of what type of CBDC initiatives central banks around the world are or have been working on, split into retail-use CBDCs and wholesale CBDCs, or wCBDCs (see Tables 5.4 and 5.5).

Table 5.4 Domestic General Purpose CBDC/Retail CBDC Projects

Country	Project/approach	Status/conclusions/next steps
Central Bank of Sweden (2017–ongoing)	Project E-Krona	Project Plan launched in 2017 covering development of theoretical proposal and system outline, followed by focus on regulation and operational proposals and technologies In 2020, phase one of the e-krona pilot e-krona started (in collaboration with Accenture). In February 2021, the second phase of the project began with a specific focus on technical tests around the functioning of e-krona offline, performance testing and understanding how banks and PSPs could be integrated with the e-krona system. Equally, legal questions such as what is the nature of the asset were also addressed, finding that the e-krona would be regarded as an electronic form of cash. In April 2022, the e-krona project entered into phase 3. No decisions yet to go ahead as of early 2023.

(continued)

Table 5.4 (continued)

Country	Project/approach	Status/conclusions/next steps
Central Bank of the Bahamas (2020)	Project Sand Dollar	Launched in October 2020, the sand dollar is pegged to the USD (can be seen as pilot release of a digital USD by proxy). Its use is domestic only, covering retail and wholesale transactions. It is non-interest bearing and operates 24/7/365, including offline, with low transaction fees. The sand dollar is held in digital wallets with multi-factor authentication. Authorised FIs (AFIs) provide the KYC and AML checks, wallets and custody. The standard wallet app is provided by the central bank but AFIs can offer their own version once approved by the central bank. A digital ID is envisaged to complement the sand dollar in future. A big driver for the Bahamas to launch a CBDC was fighting financial crime.
National Bank of Cambodia (2020)	Project Bakong	Blockchain-based national payment system launched in 2020. A mobile phone number is sufficient to operate the Bakong app to store and transfer money, either the Cambodian riel or USD. Transactions are initiated via QR codes and routed via mobile numbers. By the end of 2021, half of the population was reached via Bakong, supported by local banks with almost 7 million transactions realised by then. The solution is successful in supporting financial inclusion as well as the use of its national currency in support of monetary policy. Bakong was also successfully leveraged for cross-border remittances with Malaysia.

(continued)

Table 5.4 (continued)

Country	Project/approach	Status/conclusions/next steps
Marshall Islands (2019–ongoing)	Project Sovereign (SOV) digital currency	The concept for a SOV was announced in 2019 as a future official currency accepted alongside the USD, underpinned by the Sovereign Currency Act of 2018. The SOV will come in the form of a physical card that operates with a blockchain-enabled microprocessor, allowing users to transact in real time with zero fees and without the need for an Internet connection. The Marshall Islands also passed a law in 2022 granting Decentralised Autonomous Organisations (DAOs) the same privileges as Limited Liability Companies.
Central Bank of Nigeria (2021)	Project e-Naira	With the objectives of digital enablement and financial inclusion, he e-Naira launched in autumn 2021, a digital currency, operated on the basis of DLT
Eastern Caribbean Countries (2021)	Project Digital Currency or DCash	Launched in March 2021, DCash, a blockchain-based, digital version of the Eastern Caribbean dollar, pegged to USD, has been rolled out across 8 members of the Eastern Caribbean Currency Union (ECCU). This is a first CBDC launch in a currency union. DCash can be exchanged against fiat (digital and cash) at approved providers and exchanged via the dedicated mobile app, and the ECCB has the objective to reduce cash usage by 50% by 2025 through this solution. In the first quarter of 2022, the DCash solution experienced a prolonged service interruption and had to be switched off to be fixed.

(continued)

Table 5.4 (continued)

Country	Project/approach	Status/conclusions/next steps
Central Bank of Ecuador (2014–2017)	Project Dinero Electronico (DE)	The first country to issue a digital currency in 2014, the DE was not trusted by the population and eventually abolished in December 2017.
Bank of Korea (2020–ongoing)	Project CBDC pilot	The Bank of Korea began working on setting up a CBDC pilot in 2020 and concluded its first test phase in January 2022. The central bank chose a South Korean blockchain provider to build the pilot platform, which correctly operates manufacturing, issuing and distribution of CBDC in the simulated environment created for the pilot. Further experiments are planned to cover offline payment and protection of personal information. Following the second phase of testing in summer 2022, the project is being assessed by Bank of Korea and in collaboration with FIs further usability experiments are expected to follow.
Peoples' Bank of China (2020–ongoing)	Project Digital Yuan (e-CNY)	Piloted in 2020 and 2021 with over 100m wallets opened and $10bn in transactions using the digital yuan or e-CNY. The project started with residents in three major Chinese cities that could pay tax, stamp duty and social security premiums using the digital yuan (e-CNY). Local authorities claim that the digital yuan could be used to streamline calculating tax-related activities. As of October 2022, e-CNY transactions hit 14 billion USD in total value.
Central Bank of Ukraine (2018–2019)	Project E-hryvnia	E-hryvnia digital currency pilot completed in early 2019 followed by survey results of a possible digital currency in July 2021. No further steps have been taken.

Some Select Retail CBDC Experiments

A few of the above approaches of governments to retail CBDC are worth a closer look in light of our decentralisation framework. Let us start with China, which has been exploring the topic of CBDC since 2014 and launched the first Digital Yuan, or e-CNY pilot in 2019.

China's CBDC is focusing on replicating M0, i.e. cash, in digital form, maintaining the three key pillars of money: transactional/medium of exchange, store of value and unit of account. This means that smart contract deployment is limited to purely monetary functions. The Digital Yuan is ultimately a central bank liability, similar to banknotes and coins and the PBoC does not offer direct accounts to consumers as it has no interest in becoming consumer facing. China's largest banks as well as key conglomerates, such as AliPay, Tencent, telecom and food deliver companies, are all in charge of distribution and payment operations for CBDC. For China's government, CBDC is a tool that helps pass on zero or negative interest rates faster than traditional monetary policy mechanisms (something that was top of the list for many years, but has less relevance in the current more inflationary economic climate). However, we are wondering whether reducing the lower bound below zero is really the point here. Since the 2008 financial crisis and certainly in light of the current extraordinary circumstances under COVID-19, it has become clear that monetary policy itself needs to be rethought and redefined.

China confirmed of having no intention to impair the commercial banking sector, hence the distribution and operation via a two-tier system (however we doubt that this is sufficient). The Digital Yuan is also seen as a means to reduce the demand for cryptocurrencies and help consolidate the national currency's sovereignty. A slew of patents for the end-to-end value chain have been issued and implemented, indicating that the solution will operate with "controlled anonymity", where anonymity is maintained between sender and receiver, but transactional information is held by the operator. The national supervisor is able to directly block or restrict wallets that are considered suspicious or in violation of AML, CTF or tax laws, for example. At the same time, a selection of different types of Digital Yuan wallets—where the Yuan is depicted in digital bank note format!—is being proposed based on users' behavioural data and the identity data provided. Whereas some elements of the solution are building on DLT, for China the need for speedy transactions means that none of the major existing cryptocurrency ledger-type structures are being deployed in terms of consensus and validation algorithms. China's online transaction speeds are up to 92,771 transactions per second compared to less than 20 transactions for Bitcoin and Ethereum. The Digital Yuan can also be transacted offline with help of a smart card.

China has furthermore created a National Blockchain Platform, where developers can deploy solutions subject to access permissions—clearly not a decentralised model. It operates on permissioned protocols, which amongst other solutions also leverage Hyperledger Fabric and Baidu's XuperChain. Cities have obtained their own nodes in what is becoming a national information highway. China has also launched a national blockchain committee with many leading research institutes and organisations in order to facilitate standard setting and the creation and support of their national blockchain infrastructure and the provision of services nation-wide.

Understanding the architecture, technology choices and underlying governance of the Digital Yuan, we can see that this form of CBDC is significantly centralised. Even the choice of the underlying ledger technology shows that whilst a certain level of 'controlled' distribution is at play, there is no decentralisation whatsoever. In particular, the fact that despite secondary issuance full control in terms of monitoring individuals' transactions at all times remains with the central bank shows that the 'bearer' characteristics of physical cash have been all but removed. More recently, the PBoC has stated that different forms of digital wallets, including some that will allow anonymous low value transactions, are being considered.

In sum, the Digital Yuan is centralised across both the operational and process dimension and the governance and rules dimension, infused with a little bit of distribution at the technical level.

Let's take another example, Sweden, which has been primarily motivated to work on a form of retail CBDC because of its significantly low percentage of cash usage which continues to decrease. The project started in 2017 and in February 2020 the Swedish central bank announced a general public technical trial for the e-krona. The CBDC ledger runs separately to the country's central payment system, the latter only used by node operators (primarily banks) to swap part of their central bank deposits into e-krona. The separate nature of the CBDC ledger is seen as contributing to resilience, in particular in times of crisis of cyberattacks. Wallets will be activated by participants of the ledger (again mainly banks) and users can make retail, P2P and wallet-to-bank account transfers. Different interfaces for smartwatches and cards are also available whilst the option of enabling offline usage is still being explored. The Riksbank emphasises that this is only a test that is designed to learn about the technology and functioning of the e-krona and that no decision to truly launch a CBDC has been made.

Evaluating the e-krona in terms of the level of decentralisation, this is yet another example of a centralised form of CBDC in relation to the operational and process as well as governance and rules dimensions. In fact, as we continue to look at the broader response of the BIS community to CBDC, we clearly see that centralisation remains the underlying tenor, an obvious point given the reasons for CBDC itself are anchored in centralised organisations—central banks—that are fighting for their supremacy. C = Central!

At European level, the ECB has begun fleshing out its plans for a digital euro since October 2021 and aims to conclude this exercise by October 2023, which will form the basis to decide whether to proceed with development and delivery. Considerations around design and distribution are driven by a desire to deliver a consistent end-to-end experience and harmonised user interface for digital euro transactions. In a two-tier system, where regulated banks and potentially also e-money institutions would distribute the digital euro, supervised intermediaries would integrate the digital euro into their customer interfaces and a digital euro app with a common look and feel would allow access to basic functionalities. The ECB envisages that a digital euro scheme is developed that defines the minimum requirements for such an integrated solution. Discussed use cases include P2P, e-commerce and C to G (consumer to government) as well as PoS where initiation technologies, such as QR codes, NFC and Internet-based initiation via proxy are being considered. We shall see how the digital euro project may develop in the coming months but suffice to say Europe appears to be eager on that journey!

Across the Atlantic in the US, home to many tech innovations out of Silicon Valley and pioneer in crypto legislation (a least in some states!), voices have become louder during the COVID-19 pandemic to consider the use of a Digital Dollar as a way to distribute state aid. Former CFTC Chair Chris Giancarlo and co-founder of the Digital Dollar Foundation, is pushing the Digital Dollar Project (DDP) forward and various use cases and pilot programmes are progressing since 2021. So far, the US has, however, not been the most prolific when it comes to payment innovation. Faster Payments, often dubbed Real-Time-Payments, has not been rolled out in the US with plans of the FedNow Service to be launched in 2023 and despite some innovation in the mobile P2P space the US is still known for heavy cash and cheque usage. US President Biden's Executive Order[16] to direct the whole government to understand and assess the potential impacts of a US CBDC on retail and business users in March 2022 has, however, given impetus to move ahead on the digitisation path of money.

And then we have the wCBDC dimension, which becomes most interesting when we think about the cross-border space where we know that the current correspondent banking model is far from perfect.

A Selection of Wholesale Domestic and Cross-Border CBDC Experiments

Now when it comes to wholesale central bank money in general the fact is that today's wholesale payment flows are already digital. Those banks that are eligible to hold reserve and settlement accounts at their respective central bank use wholesale digital money to settle interbank transactions directly with their peers, but strictly at a domestic level. The term wCBDC and CBDC more generally for that matter is being mainly linked to DLT-type technical implementations. This creates some confusion or questions rather when we talk about wCBDC, because the current ways to settle are already real time, executed via RTGS systems as we know (Table 5.5).

The big opportunity, considering a different underlying technology such as DLT or blockchain, would be to create the ability for cross-border settlement of transactions in central bank money, rather than commercial bank money. This, as discussed earlier, would allow banks to lower their capital charges as the quality of asset transacted would be HQLA, i.e. the highest form of liquidity with the lowest risk. Whether those transactions happen on a DLT or other type of ledger, as long as such an outcome could be achieved, we would see a significant reduction in cost for banks, which will allow for more overall efficiency in the system and the ability to invest and enable

Table 5.5 Cross-Border Wholesale CBDC Projects

Project	Focus areas	Status/conclusions
Bank of Canada and Monetary Authority of Singapore (2017–2021)	Project Jasper-Ubin	Project investigates deployment of DLT for the clearing and settlement of payments and securities allowing for cross-border, cross-currency and cross-platform atomic transactions. Results show successful cross-border, cross-currency, cross-platform atomic transactions but various open questions remain.
Central Bank of South Africa (2018–ongoing)	Project Khokha	Khokha phase one successfully tested interbank payments settlement, replicating South Africa's "SAMOS" RTGS system. Phase two began in 2021 with a focus on testing DLT in the securities space with clearing, trading and settlement across four banks. The findings show that DLT would support streamlining different infrastructure-related functions onto one single platform, which would support cost efficiencies and reduced complexity. Challenges of implementation, regulatory/legal and economic factors remain.
ECB & Bank of Japan (2017–2018)	Project Stella	Project ran across two phases and leveraging Hyperledger Fabric 0.6.1. (a form of DLT) good results on resilience and reliability in the context of validating node failures and incorrect data format handling were established; good smart contract performance on the latter. The role and importance of the certification authority within the structure could, however, become a single point of failure risk. Trade-off between network size and performance was again validated. More scope for future studies around cost efficiency, oversight and market integration.

(continued)

Table 5.5 (continued)

Project	Focus areas	Status/conclusions
Central Bank of Thailand, Hong Kong Monetary Authority, People Bank of China, Central Bank of United Arabic Emirates (UAE) (2020–ongoing)	Project mCBDC bridge	This project is entering into phase 3 in 2022. The previous phase saw the creation of a prototype for the participating central banks, based on which their CBDC flows could be controlled, in terms of issuance, exchange and programmable levels of privacy and compliance automation. Transaction speed was increased from days to seconds and processes simplified and automated, resulting in lower cost. Phase 3 is focusing on more design choices and looking to establish a roadmap to get the prototype into production with the aim of serving the central banking community as a public good, based on open sourcing. Public/Private partnership will continue to be key in this.
Central Bank of Saudi Arabia and Central Bank of the UAE (2019)	Project Aber	Development of a CBDC instrument that can be used for settlement of cross-border payment obligations between commercial banks in the two countries as well as domestically. Resilience and decentralisation were the two main reasons for choosing DLT. The project has confirmed viability of DLT as a mechanism for cross-border settlement; open questions around monetary policy and distribution remain.
BIS, Central Banks of Australia, Central Bank of Malaysia, Singapore Monetary Authority and Central Bank of South Africa (2021–ongoing)	Project Dunbar	The project developed two prototypes, based on different DLTs, for a shared platform that could enable international settlements using digital currencies issued by multiple central banks. Leveraging the power of DLT, they found that this modern technology combined with the features of smart contracts can support the delivery of a global settlement platform and overcome the many challenges ranging from governance to access policy and regulations that were until now preventing such developments. The prototype confirmed the ability to reduce costs and increase speed of settlement for cross-border payments.

(continued)

Table 5.5 (continued)

Project	Focus areas	Status/conclusions
BIS, Banque de France, Swiss National Bank, private sector consortium (2021)	Project Jura	Explored cross-border settlement based on wCBDC. For the purpose of the experiment, a third party-provided DLT-based platform was used as the infrastructure base to execute a direct transfer between euro and Swiss francs, delivering Payment-versus-Payment (or PvP) as well as Delivery-versus-Payment (DvP), where the foreign exchange transaction was supporting the trade of a tokenised asset. The project was executed in a near-real setting, using real value transactions and complying with current regulatory requirements under a novel governance via including subnetworks and dual-notary signing.
Hong Kong Monetary Authority, Bank of Thailand (2019–2021)	Project Inthanon-LionRock (1 and 2)	The project explored the use of DLT for facilitating real-time cross-border funds transfers using an atomic PvP mechanism for FX transactions between the two jurisdictions The results showed a real-time system that provided cheaper and safer FX transactions, compared to traditional mechanisms. Transactions were executed in seconds instead of days, cutting costs cut by half.
Central Bank of India	e-rupee	India launched its e-rupee pilot in November 2022, where a number of selected banks are permitted to use the e-rupee to settle secondary market transactions in government securities. 5- and 10-year bonds were traded to the tune of 2.75 billion e-rupee on the first day of the pilot.

value-added services elsewhere. Staying with the wholesale space, a last word on the domestic perspective, where a major opportunity would be to leverage DLT in bringing not only atomic settlement but also connecting the different ledgers across the different FMIs, i.e. the RTGS system, the CSD, the CCP and the ACH system. This could enable not only PvP but also DvP with atomic settlement and remove all the cost and headache of reconciliation and risks of failed trades. This is where innovation should be embraced and a first step could be, e.g. in the context of the UK to set up a CBDC sandbox to test such a structural remodelling of the FMI landscape.

5.4 Concluding Remarks

The question of centralisation versus decentralisation in the context of cross-border payments is an interesting one indeed. The history of cross-border payments, or rather 'promises to pay', is very much tied to a few families if we recall the times of the Medicis. Whilst not fully centralisation, cross-border payments were in the hands of a handful of organisations and the actual flows or promises of flows were very distributed as money had to reach the most remote areas of the world (to the extent of what of the world was discovered by then).

In our more recent history, the strongest financial institutions joined forces to create the international messaging network SWIFT. A similar phenomenon happened here where the network is a distributed one between thousands of banks around the world, but the control of how the network is run, who is allowed in, etc., is very much in the hands of the few large players that are on the SWIFT board and of course, open to the decisions, interests and choices of national and international regulators and governments.

On the, initially, opposite spectrum, we have the emergence of private cryptocurrencies and digital assets and tokens. These really started off with Bitcoin as a decentralised phenomenon, albeit slowly but surely returning back to a more centralised way of governance—the experiment of independence and in a certain sense democracy had to give way to further centralisation for it to survive.

Now, given we keep returning to the AML/CTF and other criminal aspects of life, many of you will be disappointed to have seen that we haven't covered the issues of Initial Coin Offerings from a Ponzi perspective, but we decided that this isn't really relevant from a re-de- or centralised perspective, as a con is a con, is a con. Obviously, the introduction of new forms of money, or indeed new variants on anything in life, will be exploited by criminals, but we took the decision that this is such an obvious fact of life that it goes without saying.

CBDCs as the most recent reaction to the 'threat of decentralisation' are of course centralised animals as well but have aspects that can either support further centralisation or decentralisation in the financial system. For example, where a CBDC system requires accounts, it would inevitably require people to interact with an intermediary for access to the financial system. Furthermore, where a number of entities manage the CBDC system, it would be more decentralised than if it were only one entity or organisation doing so. And so, the question at the end of this journey really is whether there will ever be space for a more meaningful balance of things through decentralisation or whether we will be doomed to the 'Groundhog Day' of centralisation of value. At the same time, there remains room for decentralisation within a somewhat centralised system, where individuals can still make certain decisions for themselves when it comes to money and their ability to use and transfer it. But to get there will require the buy-in of many of those organisations whose interests are at stake. And that's always the hardest part!

Notes

1. Committee on Payments and Market Infrastructures, "Correspondent Banking", Basel, Switzerland: Bank for International Settlements, 2016.
2. Bank for International Settlements, "Enhancing Cross-Border Payments - Building Blocks of a Global Roadmap", Stage 2 Report, CPMI, July 2020, https://www.bis.org/cpmi/publ/d193.pdf (last accessed 29/10/2022).
3. Committee on Payments and Market Infrastructures Committee on Payments and Market Infrastructures, "Correspondent Banking", Basel, Switzerland: Bank for International Settlements, 2016.
4. Bank for International Settlements, "Implications for Central Banks of the Development of Electronic Money", Basel, Switzerland, 2016.
5. The Wolfsberg Group is an association of 13 global banks which aims to develop frameworks and guidance for the management of financial crime risks.
6. Wandhöfer, R., "The Future of Correspondent Banking Cross-Border Payments", SWIFT Institute, 2018, https://swiftinstitute.org/research/the-future-of-correspondent-banking/ (last accessed 29/10/2022).
7. The integration of regional RTGS system is not unique to the Gulf, there are other examples amongst African states, for example, between Kenya and Uganda.
8. Lagarde, C., "Winds of Change: The Case for New Digital Currency", Speech at the Singapore FintechFestival, IMF, 14.11.2018, 2018.
9. Finextra, 'Cash Usage in Britain Drops by Half', 25/03/2020, https://www.finextra.com/newsarticle/35517/cash-usage-in-britain-drops-by-half (last accessed 01/07/2022).
10. Friedman, M., "The Optimum Quantity of Money", Chicago: Aldine Publishing Co., 1969.
11. Financial Times, "Trump Administration Looks at Sending Money Directly to Americans", 2020.
12. Auer, R., Böhme, R., "Central Bank Digital Currency: The Quest for Minimally Invasive Technology", Working Paper 948, Monetary and Economic Department, Bank for International Settlements, June 2021, https://www.bis.org/publ/work948.pdf (last accessed 01/07/2022).
13. Bank for International Settlements, "Payment, Clearing and Settlement Systems in the CPSS Countries", Committee on Payment and Settlement Systems Red Book, Volume 2, November 2012, https://www.bis.org/cpmi/publ/d105.pdf, (last accessed 29/10/2022); Bank for International Settlements, "Payment, Clearing and Settlement Systems in the United Kingdom", Committee on Payment and Settlement Systems Red Book, Volume 2, November 2012, pp. 445–446, https://www.bis.org/cpmi/publ/d105_uk.pdf (last accessed 29/10/2022).
14. Goodell, G., Nakib, H., Tasca, P. "A Digital Currency Architecture for Privacy and Owner-Custodianship." *Future Internet*, 13(5), 130, May 2021, https://doi.org/10.3390/fi13050130 (last accessed 29/10/2022).

15. Siliski, M., Pott, A., "Blockchain Alternatives: The Right Tool for the Job", *Medium*, 2018-04-10, https://medium.com/swlh/blockchain-alternatives-b21184ccc345 (last accessed 29/10/2022).
16. Whitehouse Press Briefing Room, https://www.whitehouse.gov/briefing-room/statements-releases/2022/03/09/fact-sheet-president-biden-to-sign-executive-order-on-ensuring-responsible-innovation-in-digital-assets/ (last accessed 30/6/2022).

Chapter 6
Identity in the Digital Age

So, who am I, and why does it matter? Now don't worry, we are not going deep into philosophy here! But let's say you type 'multiple p' into a browser, what you are likely to end up with is that your browser auto suggests the search term 'multiple personality disorder' (well mine does, though my browser may well just be trolling me!). And we feel that discussions on digital identity ought to bring a new term to the fore as we move forwards. So let's start to talk about multiple personae, each of which has their own distinct personality—and in no way represents a disorder but a fact of modern life. Long gone are the days where our sole being was a vassal to a lord in a rigid structure. Nowadays, we have relationships with myriads of organisations, other individuals, wearing a plethora of different hats, both online and in the physical world.

As the gig economy evolves into ever more flexible micro forms, our world of work nowadays is unrecognisable from the traditions of commuting to a desk at a fixed location, working 09:00–17:00. Whilst COVID-19 forced most of us to start working remotely, technology had already initiated this trend of remote working. So, who am I? As the author of a book, am I writing this as the director of this limited company A or that limited partnership B, or where I'm named as a director on the board at C. Or as an employee of company D, or as director of my own company(ies). Or is the author of this book a persona all on its own? Well, it all depends, and ultimately there's a bit of each of these multiple 'mes' writing this! But from a technological point of view, which email address am I using, and when you start relying on me to perform a task in the gig economy, which account am I using to submit work, and when it comes back to payments, which account do you pay into for the work? These are fundamental questions of identity and also matters of huge import from the perspective of cyber security, as an increasingly complex web of interrelationships and entanglements emerge. Once centralised, employment is now decentralising, and our multiple personae are no longer 'disordered'! And that is just for the world of work. I have other personae with my bank, my supermarket and my preferred airline, with friends, as Ruth, as Dr Wandhöfer, which is all very confusing

R. Wandhöfer and H. D. Nakib, *Redecentralisation*,
https://doi.org/10.1007/978-3-031-21591-9_6

to some individuals as to these particular ones I'm just mummy! Of course, a similar complexity applies to me, Hazem.

So how does this world of personae sit with the more traditional view of digital identity, with passports, driving licences, ID cards and the like?

As this traditional view of the identity world is firmly an example of centralisation, questions about, privacy and civil protection are at the fore, with key concerns that need to be addressed. In this chapter, we will specifically focus on identity in the digital world and how things are shifting from identity as a centralised government-driven concept to the opportunity for a more individual-centric, self-sovereign identity, enabled by technology in the spirit of re-decentralisation. Of course, identity itself is centralised in the sense that identity belongs to one central entity, you. However, how this identity is not only physically established by your birth and life, but how it is documented, recognised, accepted, confirmed, authenticated and proven is really the big question in our digital world. Is the point here decentralisation, you may ask? We would say it is the control and ownership of the identity subject and that these aspects are significantly centralised, which can unduly restrict an individual. In parallel, the question of what is or should be identity also depends on what the purpose of using that identity will be and who can be trusted to look after our identity. It can be argued that there is no point having an externally viewable and interrogatable identity unless we want/need to use it for something. Rather than identity as the 'you', we want to interrogate how the 'you' is being created, documented, digitised and enabled in order to serve 'you', rather than a central authority alone, to make for a better financial and overall social system.

We observe that digital identity, as a socio-technical construct, is being pulled by different forces in different directions and in some instances, all sides have great points. With regard to international regulatory standards around AML and KYC, a valid form of regulator/government approved identity is a prerequisite to having access to a broad array of financial services including payments, be they domestic or cross-border, traditional or remittance-based as well as most other financial services. The same is true for health care or the ability to participate in the economy, to buy and sell products and services. Therefore, digital identity is essential to avoid financial exclusion in a world that is becoming more and more digital in all that we do (yes you may still be able to use your passport to open a bank account in a branch, but what if the branch is digital?). And yet, in practice digital identity systems thus far (more detail on these below) have exposed shortcomings, sometimes significant, for example, when it comes to cybersecurity protection of personal identifiable data and their ability to satisfy AML and KYC requirements. In fact, as currently implemented, AML and KYC requirements themselves can pose a risk to financial inclusion. On top of that poor data protection has resulted in varying degrees of digital identity exposure and theft, impacting individuals to varying degrees, from being a nuisance, up to financial ruin[1] and even incarceration as a consequence of identity theft.[2] These opposing forces make the practical introduction of digital identity a challenge, in particular with regard to the ability to safeguard the individual's privacy and protection. But without it, continued and increasing financial exclusion is on the horizon for significant parts of the global population, which won't be prevented by the introduction of more modern forms of money and payments, such as CBDCs and stablecoins.

6.1 Identity Going Digital

In the digital age the concept of digital identity is becoming the centre of attention as it really is the key to unlocking the digital world. Identity, after all, is the crucial glue that can link the many different digital strands together. As access to digital services of any kind—government, finance, commerce and leisure—increases, so does the need for providers to ensure that their customers are really who they say they are. Furthermore, the digital world has no concept of physical borders, which also blurs the boundaries of national identity and increasingly leads to a call for a borderless, global identity.

In parallel, rising fraud rates in e-commerce are the reason for merchants to push for digital identity solutions that enable them to rely on highly assured identity data in the context of online onboarding and e-commerce transactions, rather than allowing customers, for example, to sign in with an unassured social media or email account or type their data to self-assert, when it might actually not be them at all. At the same time an e-commerce merchant for example only needs to know certain things about you, which means that the form of digital identity needed for those types of transactions will be different from, say, what you need in order to open a bank account. And as supply chains span the globe, trust in the provenance of components needs to be assured, whether this is to quality assure that vehicle parts meet the required standards or that the 'beef' in our lasagne didn't come from a horse! These trends are all extended through e-commerce, but as we mentioned the micro gig economy personae, how do we quality assure provision of ourselves where WE really are the product?

We also note that protection of privacy and personal data has already become a priority for key jurisdictions such as the European Union, exactly because we have experienced identity and data theft, misuse of data in advertising or selling to third parties and the implications and repercussions that this has had for the individuals in question.

For governments, the importance of identity is driven by multiple factors, ranging from taxation, to immigration, to personal health (such as knowing who has had a vaccine for COVID-19 and can safely enter the country). In most countries, citizens have their identity manifested in the form of a passport and/or identity card. This can all be subsumed under the term 'legal or official identity'. Some countries have begun digitising this piece of paper or plastic. But is this then a digital identity?

In order to answer this question, it is first of all important to understand what identity is, and in that regard to distinguish identity from more specific concepts such as legal identity.

The role and objective of identity is to prove that 'someone is really who they say they are'. This could be summarised as a form of a 'quantitative' or 'factual' answer. I am X. But what about 'qualitative' elements? The type of person we are—for example, adverse media being part of your identity for financial crime risk-scoring purposes. Again, all depends on the purpose for which the identity is used. Furthermore, identity will also relate to 'what someone is permitted to do'. For example, in case of a driver's license, the purpose is not only to identify an individual as the holder of the license but also to authenticate the fact that this person is actually permitted to drive. The same is true of access controls, where the focus is not so much on someone's identity but rather on the authentication of what permissions or eligibility criteria apply. These are very different things, but we must remember that verification and authentication are key elements required to establish and maintain an identity.

According to the level of risk and type of access that an individual is trying to obtain, e.g. buying alcohol or mobile airtime, crossing international borders, benefiting from social security and so on, this identity will need to include different attributes and levels of validation and authentication. A government issued passport, for example, is as mentioned already a legal identity document, which permits the highest levels of access, enabling the crossing of international borders, applying for social security, opening bank accounts and of course also buying alcohol (if over the minimum required age in that specific country) as well as loading up airtime on your phone.

So, what is already clear is that identity can have different purposes and uses depending on the context, which means you can have different perspectives of identity as well as different forms of identity. Many aspects of your 'identity' are not usually created by you. They are things others, often authorities or sometimes intermediaries, assign to you as rights or records about you from their interaction with you for their own purposes including credit and medical records. In fact, there is a very useful analogy to reference here. In a way, identity is like a snowball, going down the hill picking up debris and additional snow on its way, making it unique.

Now, if we put ourselves into the digital ecosystem, assuring that 'someone is who they say they are' or whether someone meets certain attributes like being of a particular age or being domiciled in a particular place becomes exponentially more difficult, and that is for a number of reasons.

By now we have a plethora of digital platforms ranging from e-commerce to social networking, email and so on that enable individuals to set up different identities with different types of attributes and different levels of validation and authentication by respective providers. At the same time, proving your identity online is a challenge as you could be hacked and your identity stolen from you. In fact, impersonation has become a growing online challenge.

A leading body working on digital identity is the US National Institute of Standards and Technology (NIST). NIST has published specific guidelines on digital identity in 2017 with latest updates dating from March 2020.[3] Whilst these guidelines apply to US government agencies that use federal systems over a network as well as credential service providers (CSPs) such as Google (CSPs are also known as Identity Providers or IDPs), verifiers and relying parties, NIST has become a de facto standard for many markets around the world.

According to these NIST guidelines "*digital identity is the unique representation of a subject – whether a natural or legal person - engaged in an online transaction.*" A transaction here is not necessarily monetary but rather an event between a user and a system, supporting either a business or programmatic purpose.

Note that this does not necessarily denote a legal digital identity. At the same time, it is clear that for access to high-risk services, a significant degree of information that identity will need to contain and a high degree of confidence in this digital identity as a proxy for the real-life person is required. In a nutshell, this means that digital identity can be fairly flexible as long as in line with the significance of the digital access requested, which then means that for accessing low-risk services a digital identity used to access these may not actually mean that it is representing the person's real-life identity at all (think about a simple Google account that may suffice for gaining access to some services).

The NIST Guidelines on Digital Identity then go on to focus on Digital Authentication. According to NIST "*Digital authentication establishes that a subject attempting to access a digital service is in control of one or more valid authenticators associated with that subject's digital identity.*" Authentication therefore is important when a user returns to a specific online service. The initial identity attributes or a digital version of them such as a secure certificate, provided at the enrolment phase have to match with the attributes submitted during authentication, i.e. when a user logs in for the second, third time and so on. In the case of e-commerce or buying goods in the supermarket, for my bank my identity is really not at all important. Rather the bank needs to know that it is the correct customer that is authorising that specific transaction. For the supermarket my identity is also not important, unless I choose to have a relationship with them for a loyalty programme (another of my personae), but they do need to know one attribute in case I want buy any age-restricted goods.

The fact that all these activities tend to happen over open networks—with many definitions of open networks, the gist here is that a network is not private and may not allow for secure access, think about the Wi-Fi in coffee shops (open) versus your personal secured Wi-Fi at home (closed)—means that the risks are even higher.

NIST's focus on online identification, made up of identity and authentication proofing, represents a change to its previous guidelines that were promoting the regular change of passwords complemented by business and privacy risk management.

Data minimisation, a concept that is also reflected in data privacy legislation (such as the European General Data Privacy Regulation, GDPR), is at the heart of the digital identity approach taken by NIST and other bodies. The less information that is out there about us, the less of an impersonation target we become. NIST even promotes the use of pseudonymous access (we encountered that in Bitcoin!) to government-provided digital services whenever possible, whilst permitting the use of biometrics for authentication only in exceptions, when these are strongly bound to a physical authenticator.

To provide you, the reader, with a straightforward understanding of the key components and steps that make up a Digital Identity System, according to NIST, we have laid this out below.

NIST's Definition of a Digital Identity System

Digital identity systems are defined by 2 to 3 core components.

Component 1: Identity proofing and enrolment, binding/credentialing
Here the system establishes 'who you are'.

Step 1: Collection of identity attributes and evidence (in person or online)
Step 2: Validation of authenticity of collected attributes (in digital or physical manner)
Step 3: Deduplication, where attributes and evidence are aligned to relate back to a unique person (cross-check records, etc.)
Step 4: Verification (e.g. via facial recognition techniques)
Step 5: Enrolment in Digital Identity account and binding; link authenticators to the account, such as passwords, One Time Password Generators, etc. (note that according some security experts this process is not seen as very safe).

Component 2: Authentication and identity lifecycle management
Here the system can tell whether 'you are the person that has been already identified and verified'.

Three types of factors are traditionally used in authenticating a person:

a. What you have—for example a mobile app, access card, security token, etc.
b. What you know—passwords, PINs, security question challenge, etc.
c. What you are—face, fingerprint, behaviour, etc.

Some laws, such as the European Payment Services Directive 2, require the use of a minimum of two out of these three authentication factors in order to engage in payment services.

From a practical perspective, an individual will authenticate against the credentials it holds. The device held by the individual—e.g. a mobile phone—has a private signing key, which means that the individual digitally signs to prove that it has been authenticated. The calling service does not therefore carry out the authentication, rather the person authenticates back to the digital identity it holds. This means that the authentication piece is local and not shared with a third party. The third party gets the output of authentication—such as 'authenticated' and here is some information you require, or 'unauthorised'.

It is also important to note that any changes in identity credentials or authenticators, for example when information about you changes or in case of theft of one or more of the credentials or authenticators, will have to be managed by you, the data subject.

Component 3: Portability and interoperability
An optional but increasingly relevant component is that of digital identity portability, which can only be achieved through interoperability. If you want to use your digital identity not only to access a government service, or a gaming platform, your digital identity needs to become portable. Interoperability means that different systems can understand that same digital identity, which can be achieved at a technical level if all credentials follow an issuing standard or protocol. From a regulatory perspective, interoperability is achieved on the basis of recognition—which makes it unlikely that you can use your gaming digital identity for government services, but the reverse could be true—however unlikely it is that anyone would use it in practice. The EU has issued the eIDAS (Electronic Identification and Trust Services) Regulation, which provides cross-border recognition of digital identity systems, meaning that your French digital identity can also be used for accessing services in Germany. The devil is in the detail of the ID standards, which vary by country, and this is the reason why eIDAS implementation has been nothing short of a challenge.

The concept of federation enables official identities to be portable, as we can see with the UK Gov.UK Verify digital identity (even though this has by now been phased out as it was not a very user-friendly digital identity system).

From a financial services perspective the Financial Action Task Force (FATF), a supranational body in charge of defining standards and best practices in the fight against money laundering and terrorist finance, has also issued specific Guidance on Digital ID in March 2020.[4] Not surprisingly, the FATF sees the need for an official identity to form the basis of any digital identity.

According to the FATF:

Official identity is the specification of a unique natural person that:

- *is based on characteristics (attributes or identifiers) of the person that establish a person's uniqueness in the population or particular context(s), and*
- *is recognised by the state for regulatory and other official purposes.*

For the FATF, proof of identity depends on a form of government issued document or certification, which means that "Digital ID systems use electronic means to assert and prove a person's official identity online (digital) and/or in-person environments at various assurance levels."[5]

Armed with this basic understanding, let us now take a look at some examples of digital identity systems across the government and private sector.

6.2 Types of Digital Identity Systems

National digital identity systems that are operated by governments, in certain cases leveraging private sector technology solutions, exist for example in India, Peru, Singapore, Italy, the UK and Estonia.

As mentioned, the European Union aims to facilitate the emergence of digital identity systems by providing a legal framework in form of the eIDAS Regulation that enables mutual recognition of these systems across borders, in line with the relevant assurance level compliance. By now, European Union Member States have broadly put in place national eID Systems, where users should be able to benefit from the ability to also leverage their eID cross-border. The big next step is the European Digital Identity Wallet, which is planned to be rolled out from 2023 onwards (more on that later).

Public–private-partnership models of digital identity systems can, for example, be found in Belgium and Denmark. Bank-led models are dominant in Nigeria and South Africa, whereas private sector-offered systems with government verification are found in China.

At an international scale, the UNHCR has developed a Digital Identity System for refugees.

Centralised Digital Identity Systems

In the below, we will highlight a few interesting examples of what these systems look like and how they operate. Common to all these examples is the fact that the source of these forms of identity remain with government originated documents through a provision of general-purpose identity credentials, which other parties, such as private digital identity systems rely on.

Sweden

Swedish Digital Identity dates back as far as 2003 and the interesting thing in Sweden is that whilst the government maintains the central identity database of all Swedish citizens and residents and provides the federated digital ID architecture, private entities, primarily banks, take the role of digital ID service providers that both issue digital ID credentials and provide authentication services. A consortium of 10 Swedish banks manages this 'Bank ID', by providing users with a free digital ID that can be used to access both public and private services. This solution has been able to significantly reduce fraud rates whilst delivering a consumer-friendly solution that is based on bank assured data—a win-win-win situation for consumers, banks and all other market participants. Already in 2016, the Swedish BankID service was used by 80% of the population. Today, BankID is widely used not only in Sweden but also Norway and Finland. And over the years, Bank ID, being a bank assured Digital Identity System, has inspired other countries to do likewise, e.g. with the Danish NemID developed jointly with government. Most recently, this approach is being explored in the UK in the context of leveraging the Open Banking model to add relevant data points to enable the use of bank assured digital identity in this new standardised API-driven framework.

Belgium

In line with other examples of digital identity in this section, here again we encounter the government as the provider of general-purpose digital identity credentials to Belgian citizens and foreigners residing in Belgium via the eCard. In addition, the government provides the identity authentication platform for e-government services, which covers over 800 applications including tax, health, security, policy, regional government services, etc. These services are complemented by a private sector initiative, called Itsme, composed of four Belgian banks and mobile network operators. Itsme enables mobile-based authentication of a person's identity that is linked to the eCard, so that users can access their banking services online. Both parts of the solution have been confirmed to provide a high level of assurance under the European eIDAS Regulation.

India

In a country that has far bigger problems of financial inclusion, compared to the examples stated so far, the Indian Unique ID number identity programme, also called Aadhaar, has had quite a controversial ride over the last few years. Launched in 2010 as an initiative to make the public distribution system more efficient, Aadhaar uses multiple biometrics and biographic information (information about a person's life and relations) in combination with identity documentation if this is available (32 different types are accepted) in order to provide a digital identity to a person of any age in India. Aadhaar also launched a mobile app with m-Aadhaar, providing a virtual identity number linked to the person's Aadhaar number with the objective of increasing security and privacy. Both of these identifiers can be authenticated online and offline against the central Aadhaar database.

The use of Aadhaar is mandatory for receiving government benefits, subsidies and services financed by the Consolidated Fund of India as well as for tax purposes. Aadhaar also tried to extend far beyond that by making it mandatory in order to open bank accounts or obtain mobile numbers. In 2016, certain oil companies began demanding Aadhaar numbers be seeded to bank accounts, threatening to cut off subsidies of customers who did not comply. In the same year, the government made Aadhaar mandatory for scholarships and fellowships in higher education and requests around eKYC via Aadhaar followed from the financial industry.

Petitions to restrict Aadhaar on grounds of data privacy started as early as 2013 and following the Amending Aadhaar Act, adopted in July 2019, which was passed in order to comply with the Supreme Court's 26 September 2018 decision in relation to these privacy protection issues, the current situation is that Aadhaar is not mandatory for bank account and mobile service relationships and that any use of Aadhaar for customer due diligence requires the customer's informed consent. From a security perspective, there have been several rumours about hacks into the Aadhaar database and vulnerabilities identified with the m-Aadhaar application. The combination of privacy and security concerns that have arisen from Aadhaar should certainly make us think about the potential drawbacks a government-provided Digital Identity System could have, both in terms of the ability of government to exert control over its citizens as well as with regard to government's ability to assure highest levels of data security, in particular in the day and age that we live in, that of rising cyber-crime. So what alternative models exist that could restrict governments' control and enable trust, security and privacy for individuals instead?

The Arrival of Self-Sovereign Identity

There is an alternative approach to centralised digital identity systems dominated by governments and collaborating parts of the private sector; an approach which in our view maybe more supportive of the individual at its centre. Now, this could arguably be done in a centralised way as well, just differently to what we have seen and discussed so far.

Let us reflect briefly about identity in the digital space here. Forms of digital identity really existed since the beginning of the Internet. In the pre-Internet era, things like phone records, store cards, healthcare records and identity cards took physical form and were kept with us or a third party. Since the Internet, when you logged into a network or system online, e.g. your email, you would initially set up a digital identity, your login name and over time also a password. System administrators would have different ideas as to what they deemed necessary for a digital identity and thus require different types of information, e.g. secret questions and answers and other types of information that would make up your digital identity, confirm it or protect access to it. These days many of us use our email or login with social media platforms as a form of digital identity. Somehow none of this seems to be very personal about us and we do not appear to be in control of our own identity in this digital space.

Over the last few years, the advancements in technology and in particular DLT and decentralised governance models have been an inspiration for those seeking alternatives to government dominance and increasing risks of identity theft. This has resulted in new models for identity, where the individual is in control of their personal data, instead of handing credentials over to a third party that grants these credentials, administers and tracks them.

One of these models is decentralised identity, conceptually a way that enables individuals to create an identity that can be used as a basis to authenticate or validate an exchange of some kind. The point around decentralisation here refers to the idea that we are looking at various identity credentials of an individual where that individual has a form of authority over these. At the same time, this type of digital identity is also distributed, in the sense that it is made up of a distributed network of credentials that are all issued, authenticated and validated with different providers. An often-used example of this would be the university degree, issued by a third party, the University. The degree is issued as a verifiable credential, which in itself can be seen as a digital identity. Of course, in the old world this was equally a form of identity, just paper based rather than digital. Today such degrees will be issued to a secure 'wallet' that the owner holds, typically via a mobile app. So, digital identity is actually a 'domain' of identities that a person can own. I, as an individual, may have a government issued digital identity, which is great, but now I have a second digital identity from my University. Together, they form a more detailed identification of me but are themselves separate credentials and therefore my digital identity is really a domain, made up of the sum of all my identities (remember our snowball analogy). As mentioned, the degree could be stored digitally, and prospective employers could be permissioned by me to access this information by reference to the digital identity. The decentralised identity can be completely under the user's authority, and no central registry or authority intervenes to confirm the validity of the data to the receiving party (unless a prerequisite for the receiving party) or needs to store or host a digital record of it. There will be technical providers that are required to support individuals to host all this digital information in a type of digital wallet for example (so there is some third-party dependency but individuals could be seeking multiple providers to distribute this risk).

Another term to describe such forms of digital identity is Self-Sovereign Identity (SSI), where people and businesses store and control their own data on their own devices, without relying on a centralised database, and can share the data with other parties when someone needs to validate them.

So how do others know the information about you, including that you are who you say you are, is true?

There are several bodies that have established themselves to drive governance and standards in this emerging digital identity space. Notably, parts of your identity, such as your driving license or your credit history are something other people give you or create about you, because the YOU simply cannot be tested. To streamline such a process to support decentralised identity we need standards, which for example, the Identity Foundation, counting amongst its members large players like Microsoft and IBM, is working on. Sovrin, who is also a member of the Identity Foundation, is itself a foundation that has the objective of building an SSI network, focussing on technical standards, governance as well as the community and adoption.[6] Sovrin is the world's largest digital identity network as of early 2023. At the origin of the Sovrin network is a company called Evernym that had the vision of creating a truly decentralised self-sovereign identity. For that to work, a foundation had to be created that would allow multiple stakeholders to join the collective work of standards and network building, without giving any one entity control over the process. At the same time, its adoption has been less than stellar, with most use happening in the US. In their 2020 annual report, they reported roughly 18 nodes and 3500 transactions having taken place on their MainNet.[7]

In 2020 another body, the Trust over IP Foundation, hosted by the Linux Foundation, was launched by Evernym and 28 other founding members with the aim to "*provide a robust, common standard that gives people and businesses the confidence that data is coming from a trusted source, allowing them to connect, interact, and innovate at a speed and scale not possible today.*"[8] In a nutshell, the idea is to create the future of portable digital identity. But as you can see, this space is still in its infancy with many different players joining forces, trying not to fall behind the increasing trend of individuals wanting to be in control of their own data. We are at the beginning of standardisation and governance work, even though from a technical perspective we have a protocol and we have the World Wide Web Consortium (W3C) standards already in place for what is a verifiable credential. This means that the reference to the beginning is not so much technical but rather related to the challenge of getting others to recognise these standards through adoption. That will likely take several years to complete, but once done one of the key questions will be: how is this impacting the role of governments in this space?

But before we delve into this, let us look at the technology and governance elements of SSI or decentralised digital identity to understand where the journey is going.

If we recall the key components of digital identity systems defined by NIST, we will see that decentralised digital identity systems operate in a slightly different way.

Clearly the SSI needs to also establish 'who you are'. But rather than focusing on the enrolment, here the most important point is the issuer of the SSI and the question as to whether she/he can be trusted? Verifiers (as in entities that need to check who I am) place trust in specific issuers, which means they trust specific digital ID credentials more than others (like you would trust somebody's passport more than their gym membership). Credentials are signed by the issuer, so we know we can trust them.

Because identity is actually a domain, there is no central identity provider. Rather there are many issuers, each issuing only the claims they are confident of. The credentials are issued into a type of wallet, where the wallet is interoperable, which means that I can move my credentials from one place to another. Essentially, there is no one entity or platform that can control your identity, providing a way to decentralise our identity. It is interesting here to note that the European Commission's European Digital Identity Wallet, which we called out earlier, largely follows these principles, too![9]

So, Component 1 of the NIST guidelines—identity proofing, enrolment and binding/credentialing—is relevant here as well. However, validation and verification in this instance would be performed by potentially many different entities, each one of them specifically focused on those credentials that they have the most authority over. The enrolment in the digital identity account and the linking of different types of authenticators to the account may be provided by a specific SSI application. Individuals should have the ability to switch SSI applications, whilst at the same time keeping the different identifying attributes distributed across different sources and entities. Adoption of common standards could ensure authenticators can work with multiple SSIs, making them interoperable.

Components 2 and 3 of NIST also do apply to SSIs as these are sufficiently flexible for the purpose of decentralised and distributed digital identity systems.

When we look at the system architecture of SSIs, it is clear that interoperability at a technological level between underlying types of ledgers, identity applications such as mobile wallets and the digital credentials themselves is key, as otherwise data cannot seamlessly flow to where it needs to.

Equally important is the alignment of policy in the digital identity context. As digital identity is per se borderless, it needs to work in harmony with as many policy regimes and country-specific requirements across social, legal and cultural dimensions in order to enable effective usage. This is the approach taken by the Trust over IP Foundation, i.e. the parallel and interconnected streams of technical and policy interoperability are the guiding principle for the digital trust architecture that they are working on developing. Other bodies are also developing open standards and protocols with the objective of interoperability—such as the Decentralised Identity Foundation (DIF), Hyperledger and the W3C. These initiatives and bodies may ultimately collaborate and converge over time, but the examples just show you how much activity is sprouting up in this space but also how much is still to be done to deliver on the vision and objective of a privacy-protecting, secure and trusted digital identity solution. Which brings us to trust!

6.3 The Role of Trust in Digital Identity

Reflecting on the digital identity systems out there and the rise of SSI systems, an obvious question comes to the fore. What about trust? Which type of digital identity model could help increase individuals' trust, maintain privacy and still fulfil the role of identity in relation to a plethora of services that individuals need to access? The answer will of course be different depending on the purpose for which the identity is being used, where some digital identity types need much less information about us, or even no personal identifiable information at all.

If we actually look at digital identity systems from the perspective of trust, we very quickly discover that many of these systems require some form of acceptance by the user as well as the entity operating the system (e.g. governments). Alternatively, these systems require some form of trust certification authority or specific devices such as identity cards operating on the basis of private keys that are effectively generated by such 'trusted' third parties. This effectively represents an asymmetric trust relationship that is being imposed on the user. Simply, whenever a third party is relied upon, the assumption cannot be that they are trustworthy. In the financial industry, we call this the 'outsourcing risk' and regulators have long been wary of this, developing increasingly specific and invasive rules on financial institutions and other providers in this space. So, for something as sensitive as your identity—and even if we only talk about a few identity attributes—making assumptions about the trustworthiness of third parties facilitating part of the digital processes for digital identity, and in particular the validation of identity credentials, is not going to fly (regardless of how often this actually happens). Asymmetric trust relationships where reliance is placed on 'trusted third parties' as pointed out by Goodell and Aste (2020)[10] 'set the stage for security breaches.'

Still, there is also the possible challenge of not being able to trust the holder of a credential (it might be a forger or someone who cannot be verified!) and thus we need to agree on an authority, or multiple authorities, or system rules that can be universally trusted to verify that credential. The more decentralised the governance system, meaning that no central party is entrusted with verifying everything without the right checks and balances by other parties doing the same, the more limited its unilateral actions against the interests of users may be. Such authorities would need to be accountable (i.e. should ideally be regulated or have technical systems in place that prevent them from acting unilaterally). Without establishing regulations, standards, oversight and accountability (and therefore hierarchy), we can't ensure trustworthiness. This is clearly not a matter reserved to technology alone.

In SSIs such as Sovrin, there is no central authority and instead the system enables decentralised digital IDs where the distributed ledger is only used to host the public key of an issuer/the public identity. It means you trust the issuer because you know who they are, and you therefore can trust what they issue by obtaining their public key from the blockchain. This is a decentralised public key infrastructure that is used to ensure trust is between verifier and issuer and trust is thus outside the scope of the digital ID itself, which is why SSI works so well.

On the flipside there is evidence of cases where trust in certification authorities was abused. The obvious examples are those certification authorities that are rouge. Equally trust anchors such as governments and corporations can be vulnerable and even Google regularly publishes a list of certification authorities, which it considers non-trustworthy. Beyond the technical vulnerability trust, anchors face the challenge of coercion and even misappropriation by criminal actors as well as governments themselves. And of course, let us not forget that many of these new systems not only reveal data about their users against their interests, but that this is actually a deliberate design feature! Once biometrics come into play, privacy preservation is becoming really hard. If there is legal protection around data storage, encryption and limits or restrictions to storage and if this legal protection is properly enforceable and enforced then it should be possible, but clearly not an easy task. Think about the fact that once you provided your biometrics, such as voice, fingerprint or iris scan as part of the identification process—features that you cannot easily change as they are a part of you—it becomes impossible for you to make transactions inside a system without these being linked to each other and yourself. You are clearly visible to the system.

As with everything we have seen so far, the problem tends to lie with the 'man in the middle', the one controlling access, the gatekeeper. Therefore, whilst deploying DLT could be a technological answer when it comes to the ledger itself, i.e. having a ledger that is shared and jointly run by participants and not controlled by any single party (i.e. not a centralised ledger) (that is to say if the consensus algorithm chosen would enable that state), it would have to equally be assured that users are able to access and interact with the ledger directly, rather than being required to pass through certification and authentication providers. Ultimately you would want to create a digital identity model, which, whilst enabling many diverse authentication and verification elements to be used by an individual for purposes of making up its digital identity, would only be able to determine a person's identity with the person being at the centre of these. Trust can best be established if the individual is at the centre of unlocking and using its digital identity. No concentration, control or centralisation risks can occur if this would be the case. At same time, this can only work if we are sure that we are not dealing with crooks. So how do you solve this conundrum?

An alternative approach, discussed by Goodell and Aste (2019),[11] proposes that blinded credentials would be needed to improve metadata-resistance and thus mitigate risks that could emanate from certification providers colluding with authentication providers in order to, for example, revoke user credentials. They also argue that by ensuring choice and competition between various authentication and verification providers, hence diversity, that no significant central control could build up in the system. This could be a case in favour of applying a DLT-based structure, which inherently does not require certification and authentication providers to build relationships with each other, hence allowing for more decentralisation.

When it comes to the underlying consensus algorithm of the DLT, this would need to be designed in a way that outcomes would not impose or facilitate non-consensual trust relationships—a contradiction in itself—and that market participant dominance is made impossible. All participants should be able to determine their own business practices and trust relationships in relation to each other.

Transparency is crucial for users. If you enable different constituents to determine different rules sets, then choice can only truly be provided to users if they understand the choice itself.

Unfortunately, we cannot offer a silver bullet at this stage. We know more or less what outcome we are looking for. Something that protects individuals, gives choice and prevents people from wrongdoing as much as possible. Our digital future will see technology playing an ever-increasing role. And there are quite a number of brains trying to think of potential solutions, however immature they may be at this point in time. One of them, Vitalik Buterin, co-founder of Etherem, had another idea on how to deal with identity in a decentralised society, or DeSoc. His concept of Soul Bound Tokens, in short SBTs, would represent a person's identity on a blockchain in a non-transferable way. By building up different types of information about a soul, such as work history, university degrees, medical records etc., a person could create a Web3 verifiable reputation. Soul Tokens for a Decentralised Society, here we go!

6.4 Digital Identity and the World of Finance

Just to round off our discussion on digital identity, we feel that it is important to make a short excursion into the world of finance in order to understand the relevance of identity in this space. In fact, verification of identity is only the first stage of an ongoing process in a financial services relationship. The verification of your identity forms part of a much bigger picture, where the fight against money laundering and terrorist finance constitutes a key objective. As mentioned earlier, the FATF defines standards and best practices in this space and more than 200 countries and jurisdictions are committed to implementing the FATF's 40 Recommendations.

Any that fail to legally implement and adequately enforce them are listed as 'Non-Cooperative Countries or Territories' (NCCTs) on what is commonly referred to as the 'FATF Blacklist', with damaging economic consequences arising from barriers to international banking, trade and foreign investment.

Under the FATF recommendations, FIs and certain designated non-financial businesses—including casinos, real estate agents, lawyers and dealers in precious metals and stones—are required to not only identify, but also '*assess and take effective action to mitigate their money laundering, terrorist financing and proliferation financing risks*'. But what does this mean in practice? And even when you have your identity established, there remains the more critical matter of subsequent (re)authentication. The FATF report acknowledges this, but my favourite line, and overall summary, would be the start of footnote 21 of that report, regarding how authentication operates in the real (virtual) world:

"*As digital ID systems evolve this understanding is becoming more nuanced*." A priceless one-line summary in a single footnote that underpins, or some might say undermines, the rest of the guidance, as a guide to digital identity that then concedes that following it will not survive first contact with the enemy, is not, one might argue, the best place to start. This explains the value of 'wargaming' the risks around establishing any digital identity (or indeed any other technological development) to ascertain how an adversary will approach circumventing, or indeed breezing straight through new found vulnerabilities.

So, when we come to consider the practical implications of implementing secure authentication systems there are many factors to bear in mind, or multi-factors as PSD2 would have it. But many implementations of this Strong Customer Authentication (or SCA) are themselves readily breached or circumvented by organised criminals, and this is where the FATF guidance and NIST standards are felt by many to be lacking.

Sometimes controversial ideas such as requiring multiple modes of biometrics, such as face or iris recognition or fingerprints, to be captured for security purposes are unpopular in some quarters due to their perceived poor privacy controls. Whilst, ironically not adopting such techniques significantly increases the odds of an imposter masquerading as you, to subsequently breach your privacy across the board!

And two of our Ps, public sector governments and the private sector banking community usually play catch up to the attacks that criminals are able to deploy to commit frauds or other crimes against us. Unfortunately, as we have discussed, the hyperconnected world we now operate in does also mean that we are perpetually brushing up against hostile actors online, too. Legislation and regulations have historically been slower to react, and frequently fail to understand the nature of the threat. In recent UK legislation, the first of two 2022 Economic Crime Acts, rushed through to target Russian sanctions busting, on its enforcement was welcomed by one industry observer who said the law "isn't perfect" but "it's a good start" because:

> If enforced properly .... kleptocrats and oligarchs will have to break the law in order to keep hold their property portfolio anonymously.

The disconnect between welcoming a regulatory approach on paper with how it would operate in practice is stark. As the very name of the Act says, it is to tackle people who will break the law, the entire raison d'etre of the legislation. The second follow-up Bill specifically designed to tackle gaps in the earlier Economic Crime Act was then unable during proceedings to inform the industry as to what would be considered to be adequate security controls and standards, leading an early technical specification to reference the Government's much lamented and oxymoronic Good Practice Guides, guides that many believe are only so-called as they provide Good Practice for disorganised criminals to organise themselves more effectively! Clearly, the adoption of standards that do not prevent criminal abuse encourages criminal abuse, and ultimately jeopardises societies optimal exploitation of the vast benefits we all seek to wish to enjoy in every facet of our lives.

The overarching concept goes under the term due diligence, where the process of 'know your customer' ('KYC') forms part of customer due diligence ('CDD') that needs to be undertaken by these entities. This begins with identifying the customer and verifying that identity by using reliable, *independent* source documents, data or information. Should the customer be a legal entity, the beneficial owner or owners must be identified and verified, and the ownership and control structure of the legal entity must be understood. Furthermore, the purpose of the customer's relationship must be understood and documented. Each customer must also be categorised, and potentially further scrutinised, according to the AML/CFTP risks they may pose.

These obligations are not simple to satisfy and extend far beyond concepts of identity verification. Data sources that financial firms need to interrogate to try to identify such risks include hundreds, or even thousands, of official lists of sanctions, politically exposed persons, terrorism watchlists and all available media sources. Media screening is a significant challenge, particularly in the case of customers with relatively common names and where foreign languages and scripts must be searched. Based on the information obtained, a determination of risk must be made by the firm, based on its own policies and risk appetite, which will dictate what '*effective action*' must be taken '*to mitigate their money laundering, terrorist financing and proliferation financing risks*'.

Due diligence must continue throughout the entire duration of any business relationship. Obviously, any customer could become politically exposed or sanctioned, or be connected with or identified as being connected with, terrorism, proliferation, or predicate offences, at any time after their initial onboarding. All transactions undertaken are required to be scrutinised to ensure they are consistent with the knowledge and understanding of the customer and their risk profile.

In order to be able to evidence compliance with these requirements—and to make information that may be necessary for subsequent criminal or legal investigations and proceedings available—firms are required to keep records of these processes for at least 5 years after the end of the business relationship.

The challenges do not stop there, however. FIs are subject to a vast array of regulatory obligations extending beyond those related to identity and financial crime controls.

The extent and complexity of these and other associated requirements, and their extension beyond the initial point of determining identity, may go some way to explain the limited adoption of SSI by FIs. Whilst adequate frameworks, standardisation and adoption can enable the efficient verification of identity and credentials, this cannot address the subsequent challenges of screening, risk determination, monitoring and compliance. The legal requirement for records to be maintained presents additional issues, as without regulatory recognition of any given identity solution, it would be impossible for financial firms to comply with their obligations.

In recent years, numerous digital identity proposals and technologies have appeared, all with the aspiration of solving these challenges. The unfortunate reality is, however, that whilst these technologies may represent genuinely innovative ways to build and utilise aspects of our digital identities, their use remains limited. This is because the requirements of AML/CFTP compliance for activities beyond simple acts (such as age checking) become increasingly complex. Most of the currently proposed solutions and products out there in the market do not in fact meet the basic AML/CFTP Recommendations set out by the FATF. These failings broadly fall into two categories:

1. SaaS Identity Verification Systems—The main issue with these is that they operate on a technology-only basis and currently, technology alone cannot satisfy a firm's requirements under AML/CFTP regulations. To be compliant, businesses must have the operational ability to investigate and resolve alerts, whilst also reporting suspicious activity to the relevant supervisory authority.
2. Self-Sovereign Identity—Perhaps the bigger challenge is around SSI. These systems purport to allow a user to utilise specific verified credentials of their SSI to access certain services. However, this creates challenges around trust. Additionally, to be compliant, the institution on-boarding a customer requires access to all the underlying data that was submitted to the trusted party for the verification of the credential. To bring these solutions in line with the FATF Standards would not only be a technological challenge but would break the model of the verified credential in the first place.

Even if businesses make use of a digital identity solution for AML/CFTP compliance, they still need to understand how that identity was verified, ensure that it was verified according to requirements and retain relevant data and information in relation to these verifications.

Nevertheless, there are companies trying to tackle this issue. We have, for example, seen an early stage FinTech that is planning to allow their users to access products and services by digitally on-boarding themselves into their ecosystem. The user would do this by providing the data required to satisfy the AML/CFTP requirements for the particular product or service they are hoping to access. This data is then screened and checked, including, but not limited to:

- identity verification;
- address verification;
- screening against lists of sanctions, PEPs and adverse media; and
- verifying legitimate sources of wealth.

The information and checks listed above are basic AML compliance requirements; however, the total information and compliance processes required will be based upon the user's AML risk profile, which includes the risks specific to the given product, service or activity. If initial checks result in any alerts, these are investigated and resolved by this FinTech's expert in-house compliance operations experts. Once a user has submitted their information, they are given access to their own secure portal, through which they have complete control over their personal data, full visibility over who they have shared it with, and can make any relevant changes or updates. Their data is highly encrypted, with cryptographic mechanisms that prevent it being accessed or shared without their express consent. This gives them meaningful control over their personal data (as is the intent of self-sovereign identity), whilst ensuring that any business using such a solution to support its AML/CFTP compliance remains on the right side of the regulations.

However, the true value of any such solution is when we inject mutualisation, allowing users that have been verified for a particular product or service to instantly on-board, using their digital identities, with other businesses for similar products or services. Where there are any additional information or compliance requirements, these can be quickly and easily satisfied by the user directly through such a provider's portal. The user would be able to select which individual pieces of data and information they want to share each time they onboard with any given party. An example of this would be a user that has both an Australian and Portuguese passport being able to use their Australian identity document to onboard with one business, whilst using their Portuguese identity document to onboard with another.

The combination of providing users with full visibility and control over their digital identities, including the purposes for which they will be used plus the mutualisation aspect which provides that the user's digital identity, maintains interoperability and compliance with all relevant AML/CFTP regulations for businesses which is the best possible outcome in terms of efficiency and cost. A great example of how digital identity can actually unlock the broader financial services ecosystem after all.

6.5 Concluding Remarks

We think that by now the inevitable need for a digital identity in the world of digital money and finance is becoming quite clear. In fact, many industry advocates and experts, including ourselves, have been arguing for digital identity for a very long time. But it is a difficult business, as we have seen in this chapter and it is something that needs to really work well, in particular for the individual, in order to work overall.

For a person the nature of a digital identity should be seamless. If a digital identity helps to make any type of transaction easier, then users would be clearly happy. But this cannot come to the detriment of security and personal data privacy and protection. Removal of friction and enhanced security are the two key requirements for users. To be more precise, what users would really want is one digital identity that they can use for everything, including official stuff such as opening bank accounts, renewing a driver's licenses or crossing borders, whilst being safe and contributing to when and who can see and use what information about them.

Today, users are often neither aware of digital identity as a concept or tool, nor are they necessarily going to be willing to engage in any technical discussion about it.

The broader question of centralisation versus decentralisation in the field of digital identity is really an ethical one at its core. The more centralised the issuance and administration of digital identity is, the more control can be exerted upon the individual, control that is not necessarily always taking the form of protecting an individual. Today, governments have the strongest level of control over individuals' identity in the form of citizenship and relevant identity documents such as passports and identity cards that they issue to their citizens. Whether that identity takes on different technological forms, i.e. becomes more of a digital identity document or credential, is irrelevant to the question of centralisation versus decentralisation. As the world continues to digitise, governments will respond to this trend by offering more technologically enabled ways for identity, making it digital. Further yet, some will provide their citizens with options for the possibility of new tools through the private sector that allow them to play a role in crafting their digital identity, including who can use it, when and for what purpose.

A question to ask at this point is whether we may see digital identities being controlled by corporations in the future? This would be yet another blow to individual autonomy and self-governance with the control baton being passed to what may become the stronger players in the game: businesses rather than government.

On the other side of the spectrum, we may see more and more alternative forms of digital identity, which could allow the individual to become more independent in leveraging multiple identity credentials across multiple verifiers in order to build an alternative means of enabling their identity to be verified, compared to government issued identity, including the Souls in DeSoc. Time will tell.

Notes

1. United Nations Office on Drugs and Crime, "Handbook on Identity-related Crime", April 2011.
2. Dixon, N., "Identity Fraud", Queensland Parliamentary Library Research Publications and Resources Section, March 2005.
3. NIST Special Publication 800-63, "Digital Identity Guidelines", US Department of Commerce, June 2017 (last updated February 2020), https://pages.nist.gov/800-63-3/sp800-63-3.html (last accessed August 2020).
4. FATF Guidance on Digital ID, March 2020, https://www.fatf-gafi.org/publications/fatfrecommendations/documents/digital-identity-guidance.html (last accessed August 2020).
5. FATF Guidance on Digital ID, March 2020, page 19, https://www.fatf-gafi.org/publications/fatfrecommendations/documents/digital-identity-guidance.html (last accessed August 2020).
6. See www.sovrin.org.

7. Sovrin.org, "Annual Report 2020", https://sovrin.org/wp-content/uploads/2020_Annual-Report_app.pdf (last accessed 18/11/2022).
8. Press release, "Launching Trust over IPFoundation", 5 May 2020, https://www.evernym.com/blog/trust-over-ip-foundation/ (last accessed August 2020).
9. EU Commission Digital Identity Wallet: https://ec.europa.eu/commission/presscorner/detail/en/IP_21_2663.
10. Goodell, G., Aste, T., "A Decentralised Digital Identity Architecture", University College London, 2020.
11. Godell, G., Aste, T., "A Decentralised Digital Identity Architecture", Centre for Blockchain Technologies, University College London, 2019, https://www.frontiersin.org/articles/10.3389/fbloc.2019.00017/full (last accessed 30/10/2022).

Chapter 7
The Regulatory Dimension of Data Protection, Privacy and AI

In this chapter, we will be looking at data protection, data privacy and AI with a specific focus on the regulatory dimension. So we hope you love regulations! Data in general, and by extension its protection, is a key issue for most commercial, political and social decisions in the twenty-first century. And given the state of affairs, for us there is also a strong motivation to look at the level of centralisation and control with regard to systems and entities that have our data (as individuals and businesses). We live in a world that is becoming more bits and bytes, where data is the new game in town, and in this world, we are risking to lose control over the data that is out there about us (so much is fake news!). Regulation is a means to help protect us as individuals. Can it and does it help us in this space? Or are there changes necessary for the global data protection sphere to allow more nuanced user-centric control of consent management, when it comes to sharing data with others?

When we just look at the dimension of storage of personal data the considerations around centralised versus decentralised databases date back as early as the 1970s. In those days, the view was that if a centralised data base for storing personal information was properly designed and controlled then it would be preferable to a decentralised data base as it would provide more security, unless one would be in a situation of—for example—a coup d'état.[1] Fast forward to a world of highly centralised data bases in highly concentrated cloud computing systems, this question will certainly need to be re-examined. With cyber risks continually on the rise and regulation consistently trying to catch up, what measures are being taken by regulators and governments to ensure that our data is not only secure but also remains private? It is becoming increasingly difficult to ensure certain levels of anonymity and even more, controlling how our data and information are being used.

On top of that, there is also the new challenge of AI raising questions around how the dimension of data protection and privacy changes when we insert AI into the equation. Is there a chance to on the one hand remain private whilst being truly protected as an individual, but on the other hand to also be able to leverage the power of AI in relation to our data? Is there a way for regulation to push for more decentralised structures in order to help us maintain our personal data security and

R. Wandhöfer and H. D. Nakib, *Redecentralisation*,
https://doi.org/10.1007/978-3-031-21591-9_7

control? And of course how to we ensure that AI is ethical and non-discriminatory (a much bigger can of worms!)? These are some of the questions that we will be exploring in this chapter.

So, how deep have we gone down the rabbit hole?

In recent years, we have become more and more aware of how data has transformed into a central tool that drives our lives in the digital world. By data, we mean anything to do with how we as individuals are interacting with the digital world in a social, commercial and informational/educational context. And without going into detail here, we observe as we interact with various apps and browsers on our mobile phones, that we get prompted to look at certain things rather than others, are being presented with a selection of topics, ideas and items to buy that the algorithm understands we like based on our previous browsing and clicking history. This is the data mining, analytics and algorithm work of AI, which we touched upon in Chapter 3. And it is an ever-growing area that step by steps risks robbing us of our personal agency, unless we oppose, refrain and abstain from engaging with it. Ultimately, it could infringe on trust in a digital world if we, as users, can't control access to our own personal comfort levels. At the same time, and as we explored in Chapter 6, digital identity can help reduce financial crime and provide greater support to people and businesses accessing international markets, but this should not come at the cost of safety in the digital domain.

We also know from the Netflix documentary of 2020 'The Social Dilemma', that those individuals that used to be at the leadership level in the large companies—our digital states—would rather not expose their children to mobile phones, tablets and the like because they know about the possible danger that this can create for them and society as a whole. Part of that danger lies in certain aspects of social media and the curious depths of the web, but also in the exacerbating effects that the collection, storage and use of our data—forming our digital footprint—has. This is because that data can be used to more intricately and carefully push information to us and by implication direct us. Unfortunately, too many people are not aware or not able to be aware of these facts, which creates exactly that 'social dilemma', where on the one hand we yearn for connection and opportunities in our hyper-connected world, and on the other, where the risks loom large for our autonomy to be curtailed in pursuit of large companies' profits—unless, of course, as we have discussed previously—we disintermediate large companies to monetise our own data!

What we are seeing is that this too is changing. Privacy's connection to autonomy is one of the central debates in the race to greater centralisation or decentralisation, where we encounter both rapid accumulation, analysis and use of personal data, as well as greater autonomy and restriction on the storage and use of a person's data. The trust crisis we currently find ourselves in is making this all the more apparent. Users want solutions that respect their autonomy, their optionality and their choice and rightly treat their online personal data as extensions of their physical selves, with the benefits of great user experience and the comfort that their data will not be misused when they do choose to share it. We can see a future where we are happy to share some aspects of our data personae, but not others, so that some may be willing to share, say, medical data for the benefit of a 'cure for cancer' with non-profits, but not with big-pharma—but to be able to nuance this in a an easily understood manner for lay users—i.e. the vast majority of the world's population—without having to talk them through article xyz, part 123 of GDPR!

Regulators across many countries are playing catch up. It is clearly difficult for the private sector as well as the public sector to fend off the attractive possibility of data capture at all levels of society, from everyone at all times. An Orwellian surveillance state or Benthemian panopticon! The bottom line is that the systematic and unscrupulous collection and use of our personal data by some central parties infringes on human autonomy, which can serve as a means of coercion and manipulation that can directly and indirectly undermine everyone's interests and create fissures between the public sector, private sector and people spheres.

Laws and regulations have tried to move in the direction of protecting people's data and information but have ultimately gone down the route of regulating when data is to be collected and what participants can do with data instead of focusing on novel ways to design systems in the right way with privacy as a central design feature. This is where in our view degrees of decentralisation would help to empower users to be more in control of what they share with whom and when, without compromising themselves and their information, because it would offer the possibility for there to be limits to central components of control (and not to mention less breaches of millions of peoples' personal information because there would not be a central database of it all). So, let us take a look at the state of play when it comes to regulation in this space, so that we can spot what is missing and where improvements can be made.

7.1 Regulatory Action to Protect Our Data

In the last few years, the relevance of regulation in the field of data has increased exponentially. With many large organisations across social media, banking and other organisations collecting and using our data to enhance their profits, data has become a critical asset that needs protecting. In many ways, this state of affairs is not the direct fault of any of these large companies per se, it is the emergence of new business models. The platform revolution, as it has been called, whether in social media, across marketplaces, payments or other areas, is often centred around providing free services. Now we all know that nothing is ever for free. If a user is not paying money for a service, then remuneration of such service needs to take place in some other form. That is where the new archetype of business model comes in: advertisement.

As more of our lives take place in the digital realm, the dimension of privacy in this space is more essential than ever, in particular in the light of rising identity theft. In the UK alone, according to Credit Industry Fraud Avoidance System (CIFAS) the rise of identity theft has been accelerating at an unprecedented pace, recording a 26 and 34% increase across the under 21s and over 60s in 2018 alone, tendency "it's getting worse every year."

So, what exactly do we mean by 'data privacy'? The key here is that a person should not be forced by any third party to reveal personal information about herself or himself such that any of her or his actions could be linked to her of his true identity—or indeed any of their personae that they may wish not to share. For example, if say Leni is browsing the web, looking at different types of content, her actions should not be automatically linkable to her identity—and if she happens to want to be a member of certain networks—and yes, we're thinking Ashley Madison here!!—it would be excellent if the 'I want to cheat on my partner' attribute wasn't shared too widely in the event of the inevitable breach! In practical terms, this means that data privacy has to be considered as part of the underlying architecture of a system itself.

Data protection on the other hand has to do with two things. First, the purpose for which and ways in which data can be collected. Second, the use of that data, once collected, and already containing connections between Leni's data and identity (so that it is not used for unauthorised purposes). Data protection, at least how it has been reflected legally, has to do with what those that collect the data, can do with it. This is an important distinction to keep in mind. Privacy is at the core, whilst data protection is a sort of second line of defence.

The capacity to be watched and censored through today's monoliths is unprecedented. But frankly, there are a myriad of ways that either the commercial corporate world of digital states or actual governments (and this is not restricted to dictatorships) can, will and in many instances does start to ever so effectively rob you of your individual agency, your ability to make up your own mind and take your own decisions. And this is the death trap of centralisation precisely, because there is a technological central component and also a central governance authority that typically values profits or information, or both these days. Not that either is a bad thing, but it means that the interests of users are not directly or automatically considered. They come second (or not at all). There is no alignment between our three spheres of the public sector, the private sector and the people. So how do we address this to preserve the privacy of the individual whilst still allowing them to fully engage online and in a secure way? You'll have to wait until Chapter 8 for that vision statement! Let's first check how legislation is trying to fix this.

How to Stay Private? The Emergence of Privacy Regulations

In all of this data mining jungle, it may not come as a surprise to some that the right to privacy is a fairly recent phenomenon. One of the pillars of this right is anchored in the European Convention of Human Rights of 1950, which determines that "*Everyone has the right to respect for his private and family life, his home and his correspondence.*" Now the Brits reading this will be screaming about Magna Carta and habeas corpus—and that incidentally is an interesting modern twist with multi-modal biometrics as we shall see later on—but let's leave that for our sequel, interesting though it is, we don't have space here.

What followed were several national and regional initiatives to protect data privacy, ranging from the first data privacy law that emerged in the German Federal State of Hesse in 1970, followed by Sweden in 1973 and a German-wide Federal

Data Protection Act that came into being in 1978, which crucially introduced the concept of 'consent' for processing personal data. After all, Konrad Zuse invented the first programmable computer in 1941 and Germany had been one of the leading forces in this field. By the late 70s, most of Europe had incorporated data protection into their legal systems.

The 1983 landmark case in Germany, which stemmed from the invasive nature of the national census process, led to the major German Federal Constitutional Court ruling, which established the protection of individuals against the collection, storage, use and disclosure of their personal data, anchoring this protection as a human right.

With the growth of the Internet, changing businesses and society as a whole, it was recognised that a more modern and more coherent legislative approach was needed for Europe, culminating in the 1995 European Data Protection Directive preceded by the UK Data Protection Act of 1984 and Convention 108 by the Council of Europe in 1981. The latter formed the bedrock of principles that went into future legislation. This law defined minimum data protection and security standards that would become the basis of each EU Member States' national implementing legislation.

Since these steps, in particular from 1995 onwards, the number of Internet users has grown from 16 million, representing 0.4% of the world population, to 4.95 billion or 62.5% of the world's population, according to the data portal.[2] With businesses, banks and increasingly governments offering their services online over the Internet, these began hoovering up more and more data. Social media platforms, search engines and e-commerce platforms led to the first explosion of Internet usage, followed by others. With these developments, the risks of data theft began to grow exponentially. After five years of development, the General Data Protection Regulation (GDPR) entered into force in 2016 and had to be complied with by all organisations in 2018. Note here that the EU decided for the legal instrument of a regulation, which leaves little room for national interpretation and divergence and thus ensures more harmonisation across all EU Member States. The GDPR is today considered to be one of the most significant data protection and security legislation in the world and various jurisdictions have been inspired by it, for example California has subsequently adopted the California Consumer Privacy Act 2018. Let us now briefly examine the key elements of the GDPR and see what more we may need.

One of the most important features of the GDPR is the fact that any organisation that targets or collects data relating to European individuals is captured by this legislation. What this means is that you do not need to be based in the EU for GDPR to apply, instead you just need to be targeting, collecting data on or providing services to people located in the EU, whether these are EU citizens or EU residents. Any such organisation that happens to violate the GDPR is subject to significant fines that can reach up to 4% of global turnover or EUR 20 million, whichever is the higher amount of the two.

The definition of personal data, also referenced as personally identifiable information (or PII), is broad, covering any information or collections of information that would enable an individual to be directly or indirectly identified, which can even include pseudonymous data. Equally, the nature of data processing is broad, covering just about everything that can be done with data, irrespective of whether done manually or in an automated way, including storage, viewing and erasure.

In addition to the data subject, the person whose data is concerned, we have the data controller, who determines the way personal data is being processed and the data processor, a third party that does the processing of personal data on behalf of the controller. In certain circumstances, an organisation will have to appoint a designated Data Protection Officer. The processing of data is subject to seven protection and accountability principles, covering lawfulness, data minimisation, accuracy etc., and the data controller has to be able to demonstrate compliance, which entails putting in place the right processes, controls and principles. On top of that, data has to be secured and any breaches have to be reported to the data subject within 72 hours as otherwise penalties can apply.

Any new solutions have to incorporate the privacy-by-design and default principle. This is, after all, one of the most important aspects of the GDPR regime, and at the same time, it is the part of GDPR that is also the most opaque in practice. It sets the tone for organisations which are collecting data that they need to consider whether or not they need to collect that data in the first place and taking that into account when building their systems. It is a general principle that needs to be embedded in each organisations' approach to data. Yet, it does not go much further than that and as you can imagine supervision of this across all of these entities that are subject to GDPR is virtually impossible.

Consent from the data subject is at the core of the GDPR and specific rules determine when personal data can be processed at all outside of just consent. A company is only permitted to collect and process personal data if it has determined a specific purpose. Keep that in mind as we read on (!). Data subjects have the following rights under the GDPR (unfortunately none of them is a right for 'data privacy' or a right 'NOT to be profiled'!):

1. The right to be informed
2. The right of access
3. The right to rectification
4. The right to erasure
5. The right to restrict processing
6. The right to data portability
7. The right to object
8. Rights in relation to automated decision-making and profiling.

This significant measure in relation to data has caused industry in general great pains in implementation, as you might expect. However, we feel that GDPR does not go far enough to protect people's data privacy completely as the default, e.g. to limit the profiling of customers and consumers as the first point of departure. Now some would argue that for complete data privacy things like CCTV would be illegal too—in all spaces—AML procedures would be questionable and identity checks unnecessary. There clearly needs to be some balance and to its credit, as the most advanced regime in the world that touches on this topic and seeks to regulate it, GDPR attempts to limit the data processing and obliges entities to specify the reasons for which one's personal information is collected and used. Ah, I hear you Brits cry the EU is the second most advanced country in this regard with Digital Information measures now being introduced, but that's a topic for future discussion as legislative measures evolve into regulations and implementation! Watch this space! However, to our knowledge there is not one piece of legislation that advocates for actual privacy as opposed to data protection. As we continue on the trajectory of the ever-growing data economy, regulators and citizens alike will need to ask themselves: do we need more privacy protection in law or are there other ways to achieve privacy, or do we actually need privacy at all?

7.2 The International Dimension of Data Protection Laws

So, if the European GDPR is considered to be one of the most far-reaching data protection and security legislation in the world ever—far beyond the border of the European Union—implicating and impacting any business that does not follow its rules when dealing with European people—albeit not fixing the data privacy issues, which are paramount in our time—then what about other countries? For example, what's happening in the US? Don't they have data privacy—eerrrm data protection or data security laws?

Well, the answer is somehow … rather little. The California Consumer Privacy Act of 2018 is more or less a mirror copy of the EU GDPR, once again, focused on giving consumers greater control over the data and information collected about them. As usual, the US's problem of federal versus state comes into play here, where data protection across financial and health data (not more than that) is governed by different laws in each state. One brief segway here, if you will let us indulge, is that when we are talking about federal versus state regulations in the US, there is a similar complication in the EU, namely as to which aspects of EU law are directives or regulations. This may seem like a very pedantic point to make, but it is fundamental to the practical implementation of codes. Directives are sets of principles passed centrally in Europe, but then re-interpreted in each Member State as they transpose that directive into domestic legislation. So, whilst PSD2 is a single legislative concept, there are 28 (27) flavours of it as enshrined in each member's legislation. So, we have a particular German, British and Italian interpretation—and that's before we get to how the regulators in each Member State choose to enforce! In lay terms, regulations are harmonised across the EU—they just happen and enter into force. Such is the case with GDPR. But GDPR requires that organisations with Subject Access Requests (SARs) authenticate that it is genuinely the user requesting, where there is a risk of fraud. But wait, a risk of fraud might mean money being stolen, and that's a Regulatory Technical Standards issue under PSD2, where Strong Customer Authentication (SCA)—the only legal definition in EU on how to authenticate, comes into play. So that'll be a Member State interpretation of how to handle the security of a legal requirement under a harmonised regulation (not perfect at all!). Apart, of course, from those naughty Brits who decided to transpose GDPR into DPA18, but again, that's a discussion for another day.

Anyway, back to the US! A plan to harmonise this into a federal legal framework with the proposed 2009 bill for the protection of personal data by businesses and government, failed as the bill never got passed. At this point, a new proposal in the form of the American Data Privacy and Protection Act continues to slowly advance on the legislative path with the July 2022 majority support of the House Committee on Energy and Commerce. How long it will take to become meaningful federal law is anyone's guess. The fact is that by now in 2023 the US does not have a coherent data protection and privacy law in place.

Of course, the sharing of data is critical to trade and when we consider the European and US trade corridor and thus other ways had to be explored to enable those two markets to continue sharing. This was attempted by the so-called Safe Harbour Arrangement of 2000, a set of common principles for the safe exchange of information across these two geographies. However, this arrangement was invalidated by the European Court of Justice in 2015 and since the establishment of the EU-US Privacy Shield—another attempt at an agreement and process in this regard—in July 2020 the European Court of Justice ruled the Privacy Shield as invalid, rendering the US a non-adequate country without any special access to European personal data streams. Still, the ultimate decision to suspend data transfers if deemed non-compliant remains with data controllers and the EU and additionally put a strong emphasis on the role of the data protection authority in each Member State.

In China, there is an important difference in emphasis between data protection and data security, compared to Europe and other jurisdictions. Data security is paramount for China as data is one of the key assets of the state. China is therefore one of the leading nations when it comes to computing advances and in particular research into quantum computing, which is very significant, exactly because leadership in this space would allow China to easily crack other countries', entities' and individual's data. Current data encryption security is practically irrelevant when someone comes along with quantum computing. And we won't go into the complicated detail of this new form of computing here (see next chapter) but suffice to say that there is a lot of great research material out there for you to go into deeper. For example, take a look at www.singularityhub.com.

To close off our international review of data protection and security laws, here you will find a short summary of existing legislation around the world (Table 7.1).

Beyond different regulatory frameworks or the absence thereof, we need to nevertheless understand what happens in our daily lives. Here, it certainly doesn't help that technology can be and is in many instances implemented in a way that makes exercising one's right to privacy at best difficult and usually impossible. How can this be, you may ask, if we believe that privacy by design is so important and has even become a principle in law? The truth is life is complex and risky out there on the digital data highway and some things may conceal what is really happening behind the scenes. Just think about cookies. Yes, many of us browsing websites in Europe and elsewhere have been used to cookies popping up once in a while, requiring us to accept them in order to move on with our web surfing activity, some of which

Table 7.1 Selected data protection and security laws around the world

United States
HIPAA (Health Insurance Portability and Accountability Act of 1996)
United States legislation covering data privacy and security provisions for the safeguarding of medical information
The California Consumer Privacy Act (CCPA)
Bill signed into law in June 2018, enhancing privacy rights and consumer protection for residents of California. The Bill was updated by the California Privacy Rights Act, coming into force 1 January 2023 with enforcement beginning from 1 July 2023.
Security/Data Breach Notification Laws
These exist across all 50 US states since 2002 but have been irregularly enacted with some states only introducing privacy laws as late as 2016.
Draft American Data Privacy and Protection Act (ADPPA) (June 2022)
Released by Congress as a bipartisan approach, this draft represents a new model for privacy law in the US with marked difference to the existing privacy related laws in the US as well as the EU GDPR. Notably, the proposal extends consumer data rights including access, correction, portability and deletion of personal data and enable expression of consent and opt-outs. The act also envisages a dedicated bureau within the Federal Trade Commission (FTC), which would have the task of enforcement and significant accountability and requirements on significant data holders. Also, a third-party register is envisaged to enable individuals to opt out of any further data collection or processing.
European Union
General Data Protection Regulation (GDPR)
As explained above in effect since May 2018, GDPR provides individuals with more control over their personal data. Users have the right to share as much Personal Identifiable Information (PII) as they want, but they also have the right to be forgotten. PII includes information that can be tied back directly back to an individual (e.g. name, social security number, phone number, and address). The market already felt the impact of GDPR with significant fines of €746 million handed to Amazon and €225 million to WhatsApp in 2021.
Singapore
Singapore Personal Data Protection Act 2012 (PDPA)
This law governs the collection, use and disclosure of personal data by all private organisations. Fully in force since July 2014, entities failing to comply can be fined up to $1 million and suffer reputation damage.
Japan
The Act on Protection of Personal Information (APPI)
This Act obliges all business operators holding and handling personal information of 5000 or more individuals to specify for which purpose this personal information is used. Data subjects can ask these business operators to disclose the personal information that is held about them, rather than a specialised law on online privacy. In addition, other laws exist that apply to government and public organisations handling personal information.
Brazil
Brazil's General Data Protection Law was enacted in August 2018 (No. 13, 709), enshrining individuals' fundamental rights of freedom and privacy with regard to the processing of personal data, including digital media data, by natural persons or public and private legal entities.

are actually illegal. Since the arrival of the GDPR this has markedly increased—we don't remember over the last few years having seen a website that does not have pop up cookies asking us to tick boxes in order to get on with life. Depending on the provider, you can actually encounter cases of so-called consent manufacturing, for example, those cookies where you are asked to opt into their surveillance system, thus abdicating your privacy right. Other examples can include specific settings that make things so complicated that you give up going any further unless you click 'yes' to removing your right to privacy (arguably that part isn't very transparent either, so user convenience is in some cases actively being exploited to achieve mass surveillance).

This brings us to our last important aspect: Consent. One of the things that GDPR introduced, importantly so, is that consent should be 'freely given'. This becomes quite blurred where consent to collecting our data is required in order to access a free service. It begs the question as to whether it is fair enough and if consent can actually be fairly given. A lot of people are not aware of the regulation and what they are consenting to or accepting, and thus an educational hurdle needs to be overcome. Another point is that many of the services we access and use regularly are pretty concentrated with minimal optionality in the market, making it nearly the default position that users will automatically consent in order to use that service. A privacy-by-design approach would turn this on its head and involve a user more in the collection and use of their data through better education and access to services without requiring consent on all their information and data. More competition would also be important as the concentration of data with fewer and fewer large corporations brings about the risk of centralised power, control and thus even more risk of manipulation and steering—all the nasty fruits of centralisation.

7.3 From Data Protection to AI Regulation

As more and more sophisticated technologies develop, in particular in the space of AI as previously discussed, the ability to influence decision-making up to the point of removing free decision-making in and of itself is beginning to take shape. This has inevitable consequences on society at large (e.g. what role is there for democracy if free will no longer exists in practice?) and demands a fresh look at how to regulate this space and whether regulation still makes sense in the first place. At the same time, should we force data privacy upon people or allow them to sign away their privacy in exchange for free (well clearly not free!) services? Somehow, the overall model of free services against private data is the issue here.

One avenue of tackling such challenges, even though this could arguably become less effective under the traditional approach, is regulation. So far, regulation of AI has become a question, rather than a set of answers in terms of what to actually regulate and how to do so without stifling innovation and competition, whilst at the same time ensuring the protection of human rights, individuals' freedom and choice, diversity, consumer protection and so on and so forth.

As we begin to look at AI and whether and how to regulate this exponentially growing and—for some—rather scary space that also brings lots of benefits (for example, in the discovery of new drugs that can save lives or improved medical diagnostics), we need to recognise that AI systems process large amounts of data with increasingly sophisticated algorithms at speed. Even data scientists and computer coders that write algorithms do often not really understand how these actually work, they just do.

When we look at data and AI in the European context alone, a number of legislative elements will have to be seen in conjunction with each other. We have GPDR (as per above), combined with local data protection laws. We have the ePrivacy Directive, which governs access and storage of information on devices, whether personal or not. We also have the broader European Convention on Human Rights and local anti-discrimination laws, which aim to protect individual rights and freedoms, privacy and ensure non-discrimination and we have consumer protection laws. All of these will need to be considered, not just the privacy context. As we will examine below, the EU has recently issued a proposal for an AI regulation, but even this has to be seen alongside the network and information systems (NIS) Directive, which focusses on security and resilience's of key systems in the EU and also covers cloud computing systems. Even if no personal data was impacted by a hack, this would be still subject to NIS incidents reporting. And there are sector- or technology-specific local laws, e.g. licensing laws—license of AI technology, etc.

The important difficulty with AI and its relevance here is that AI development relies in large part on the collection and use of data. Furthermore, AI, like any other technology, will have all laws and regulations that are applicable to a particular situation, apply. The question is then whether there are any AI-specific regulations that are needed now, or if we should stick with a lot of the opaquer general principles for the time being. The concern is that the development of AI augments the capabilities that require data collection to reap their benefits. Think of the predictive algorithms used to provide each of us with targeted ads, such as the next show we should be going to. These algorithms need our information. As AI real-world applications and deployments increase, so too will issues arise in the collection and use of the personal information of people everywhere. And when we get back to how AI chooses to update its own preferences, are we looking to a scenario of Skynet, from Terminator, or Starnet from the Ukraine war? Will it disable or enable?

So, let us examine some of the thoughts and approaches that have emerged so far at a global level and then take a closer look at Europe, which again is playing a trend setter role as the first jurisdiction that is actively working on developing a policy framework for AI.

Approaches to AI Regulation: A Global Perspective

Scanning the globe for policy making in the field of AI leaves us with little to go by. Whereas many governments have ambitious AI development strategies in place, no regulatory frameworks have yet been developed to accompany and indeed support these in practice. It is broadly understood that in order to embed AI into the economy, regulatory frameworks will inevitably be needed, for example when it comes to the deployment of AI solutions in already highly regulated sectors such as financial services or health care.

The first step in regulating AI in our view is to actually properly regulate data privacy as a fundamental first principle in the design of the systems of the digital economy and we already noted that this is not happening yet. Most countries in the world do not have any regulations in place for any of these purposes. At the same time, existing rules and regulations may need to be revamped, rethought and reengineered as applications of AI spread across our everyday lives and become more deeply integrated in analytics, decision-making processes and automated execution.

We are, however, able to observe some early green shoots of development on AI. Many governments have devised national strategic plans for AI over the last few years, chiefly geared towards becoming leading nations in the field, with a view to reaping the economic benefits of this new form of technology, but also developing ideas and plans around the parts of the population that are likely to lose their jobs to AI. Let us hope that this open arms embrace for AI doesn't turn out to be Skynet, or rather Genisys, after all!

In addition to that, we encounter some specific areas that have already become topics of national interest in relation to AI, namely 'autonomous vehicles' and 'autonomous lethal weapons' (although both might have the 'lethal' part in common). This brings us rapidly into the sphere of international negotiations and treaties within the realm of the United Nations. In fact, there is the 1890 "Convention on Prohibitions or Restrictions on the Use of Certain Conventional Weapons Which May Be Deemed to Be Excessively Injurious or to Have Indiscriminate Effects" (bit of a mouthful!),[3] primarily referred to as "the Convention on Certain Conventional Weapons, CCW", (with three annexed Protocols), which entered into force on 2 December 1983. The UN has begun to debate the topic of emerging technologies in this regard over the last few years with a dedicated expert group for CCW holding meetings during 2017 and 2018. Whilst some progress is being made, there is no global agreed approach and treaty in place with regard to Autonomous Weapon Systems (AWS). A recent Parliamentary group in the UK considered the various permutations of this, and there were a number of interesting aspects thrown up. On the one hand having a woman or man in the loop to ultimately allow kinetic force was a good thing—'100% Killer Robots are bad'. Yet, if we need a woman or man in the loop, they need to be able to communicate with our semi-autonomous weapon system. And that leads to a risk of takeover, which means our adversary can countermand our intended purpose! This area of AI and how to manage it in an international geopolitical context is not only challenge but also murky at best, with little information available to the broader public, which in our view should have at least the option to have more of a say in this. At the same time, Europe is considered to be behind in terms of investment and development in the area of 'how to use AI to become more lethal more effectively and efficiently', whereas it is clear that the US and China are leading the pack globally on developing AWS—not a reassuring thought for humankind at large.

Moving to milder topics, the autonomous vehicle situation, it is worthwhile to note that the Vienna Convention on Road Traffic of 1968 had to be amended in order to capture the emerging reality that driving tasks could actually be left to the vehicle itself rather than other contracting parties, aka people! And we are sure these types of changes are just the beginning. After all, the tales of the Internet of Things (IoT) have been already painting the picture of fridges ordering their supplies, whilst cars will start paying for fuel themselves, as neither of these two situations are far-fetched imaginations any longer.

In parallel, the role of AI in the context of human rights is another area of concern, which has been highlighted by a UN report of 2018 developed by David Kaye, UN Special Rapporteur for the promotion and protection of the right to freedom of opinion and expression.[4] The US is also engaged in further work on Digital Cooperation and specific AI recommendations.

In 2019, the Organisation of Economic Cooperation and Development (OECD) adopted its Principles for AI,[5] complementing its existing standards body on privacy, digital security and business conduct. For the first time, government members of the OECD and many non-OECD countries signed up to principles in this particular space. The OECD principles also provided the template for the G20's Human-Centred AI Principles[6] adopted a few months later in the same year.

What are these principles then? And is this just another paper tiger or are governments really taking action, and hopefully the right action, in this space? Unfortunately, there is nothing legally binding in this, but the exertion of influence on the design and development of standards and rules that governments develop down the path is the plan behind these.

Not surprising then that this whole exercise is pretty high level, but it's only the start and it is reassuring to see that fundamental rights and the protection of our earth are being called out here, like so…

First of all, AI should be of benefit to humans and the planet and translate into growth based on inclusiveness, sustainability and the well-being of all. That's a good start and a high bar.

Naturally, the second principle hones in on system design of AI, which thus should be rule of law, human rights and diversity of values that embed the right safeguards—the famous 'stop button'—and all of that to help society to be fair. We are starting to wonder whether this is being observed in other technology driven types of innovations.

Third on the list is transparency and disclosure—the 'people have to understand and be able to challenge' premise—which of course is already an impossibility in relation to some of the AI out there and will move further out of reach as innovation continues to accelerate.

The obligation for robustness, safety and security follows as the fourth principle and at fifth place we have the accountability requirement for those that develop, deploy and operate AI systems. We shall see those same points repeated further down when discussing the European approach, as the OECD work was heavily influenced by the EU. At least all of these countries are trying to be consistent and guided by the same objectives for once.

And in order to follow these principles, the OECD also recommends to governments and the private sector to focus on investing in Research and Development (R&D) in this space, for governments to develop the right digital infrastructure for everyone to access AI and share knowledge and data, for government to develop policy geared towards trustworthy AI and for government to focus on AI skills development of its workforce and cross-border and cross-sector cooperation for leading the evolution of trustworthy AI. Phew, that was a long sentence.

In parallel, lots of other supranational bodies ranging from the Council of Europe, the United Nations Educational Scientific and Cultural Organization (UNESCO), the World Trade Organisation (WTO) and the International Telecommunications Union (ITU) have all begun to focus on AI in some shape or form.

According to the OECD's Observatory on AI, as of Q1 2023 at least 69 countries have some form of AI policy or measure in place with over 800 policies recorded thus far.[7] With AI being increasingly ubiquitous, national regulatory responses and measures to avoid potential harms of AI are a natural response but equally risk international inconsistency, which will make it potentially impossible to properly regulate and hold to account the digital states that are already monopolising this space.

AI Regulation in Europe

The 2018 Council of Europe, not to be confused with the European Council (the latter is one of the EU institutions), adopted the "European Ethical Charter on the Use of Artificial Intelligence in Judicial Systems and Their Environment" (European Ethical Charter).[8] This following section is designed to be a guideline for justice professionals, policy makers and legislators when dealing with AI and anchors around five key principles, as follows: (1) Respect for fundamental rights during the design and implementation of AI; (2) Non-discrimination; (3) Quality and security when processing judicial decisions and data; (4) Transparency, impartiality and fairness; and (5) "Under user control".

Just like many other governments, the European Union has also adopted a strategy on AI in April 2018,[9] followed at the end of 2018 by a more detailed plan running up to 2027, which is composed of seventy joint actions designed to enhance cooperation between Member States and the Commission across research, investment, talent and skills, data and international collaborative efforts.

It is clear for European policy makers and government representatives that a third approach to AI, where AI is in the hands of Europe's citizens, is needed, as compared to the US where AI is in the hands of large corporations and China, where AI is in the hands of the government. Therefore, it is all about supporting 'trustworthy AI'. Two key concerns, information asymmetries and negative externalities are at the core of the EC's thought process around the need for a regulatory framework. As an example, the topic of remote biometric identification—for now in public spaces only—is already one of those things where there is a fine line to walk between protection and risk of abuse. Capturing images of individuals without consent is arguably a rather authoritarian method and it is by now common knowledge that facial recognition applications have not been without flaws, with cases of racial and gender bias being detected. Other examples such as Amazon's AI-powered recruiting system, which turned out to prefer men over women due to AI bias, as well as Google's Photo labelling picture scandal, where black people were identified as 'gorillas' are further evidence of the need for ensuring ethical responsibility in AI solutions.[10] The more recent debate around AI use in COVID-19-related tracing apps and its implications for data privacy and protection is another hot potato that continues to be thrown into the air. Combine them all and you have a real cocktail of uncertainty! Here it really depends, which government you trust.

One way to enhance trust is to regulate in order to protect people, and the EU ultimately became the first jurisdiction to do so in this pace by issuing the so-called AI Act Regulation proposal in April 2021, which culminated in a general approach compromise reached by EU Member States in December 2022, which paves the way for Parliament and Council to develop their positions and ultimately finalise the text to pass in early 2024![11]

What is clear is the arrival of AI changes the dynamics of data privacy and protection even further. Whilst organisations will need to account for risk arising from processing of personal data, AI invokes a higher degree of risk and types of processing that can result in high risks on individuals due to the sheer volume and speed at which it works. AI in general makes known risks bigger, for example due to reliance on third-party coding components or adversarial attacks on Machine Learning (ML) models. In addition, AI introduces also additional security risks due to the fact that AI often uses open source code. There are also likely personnel issues when we look at AI system providers where staff can be rather unaware of the importance of data privacy.

When we reflect upon what we reviewed with the GDPR, for example the key pillars of security and data minimisation, these create an inherent conflict of interest with AI systems. AI wants all the data, but the rules require only to process what you need to process. These are just some challenges to highlight upfront.

But back to the proposal.

To start off, the definition of AI has already been narrowed down by the December compromise and now describes AI as "systems developed through machine learning approaches and logic-and-knowledge-based-approaches", in order to avoid a catch-all for any type of software system. The AI Act will completely ban AI systems that manipulate, exploit and potentially harm individuals or third persons, systems that operate social scoring on behalf of public authorities or that are real-time biometric identification systems in public, utilised for police enforcement purposes. These provisions will certainly be instrumental in mitigating the emergence of an omnipotent control state, as otherwise seen elsewhere. The big thing here is that the rules would thus also apply to public authorities that either use or provide these systems—a clear method of state self-regulation if you so wish. The December 2022 general approach of course added more exemptions (surprise!), such as AI used by Member States in the context of military and defence (a dangerous open door!), AI systems used for research (another one!) and in the context of juridical cooperation.

Specific rules are to apply to high-risk AI systems—such as sound risk management, system training, validating and testing, data governance as well as the requirement for users to report serious incidents that would risk breach of fundamental rights. Systems in this category would be, for example, those that are subject to EU product safety regulations (e.g. medical devices, toys…) and stand-alone high-risk AI systems, e.g. systems that are deployed in the context of recruitment or that score your creditworthiness.

The transparency rules around deceptive AI systems are an area where effective supervision will be vital.

Post-market monitoring systems will need to be established for those operating high-risk AI systems, such that compliance with regulation can be checked regularly. Any serious incidents or malfunctioning will need to be reported to the respective market surveillance authority, the latter another creation of the AI Act. This authority can require the system operators to take remedial measures and could even ask the AI system to be withdrawn altogether.

At EU level, we also see the proposal to create a European Artificial Intelligence Board, consisting of the European Data Protection Supervisor and national supervisory authorities' representatives and chaired by the Commission, which would be in charge of ensuring consistent application of the regulation.

Non-compliance is fined up to EUR 30,000.000 or, if the offender is a company, up to 6% of its total worldwide annual turnover for the preceding financial year.

This proposal, given it is a regulation and the AI systems concept is significantly broad, would mean that Member States cannot regulate this matter differently at national level, with the exclusion of AI applications for military purposes and national discretion around penalties. It even gives the Commission powers to intervene in case of 'under-enforcement' (!).

As you can imagine compliance and enforcement of these rules will be the hard part. In the absence of a single pan-European competent authority for AI system operators, collaboration between national competent authorities and the Commission has to be very strong. Reporting of these different authorities to each other on when they plan to close down an AI system or take corrective measures is therefore one of the procedural rules laid down in the text. At the same time, the independence of national market surveillance authorities should not be lost, which is why the European Data Protection board and the European Data Protection Supervisor have called for the proposal to be clarified in that regard. Funny how we are already getting entangled in authority discussions at this stage, but very clear that this point would indeed provide for more decentralised authority, which should be welcomed.

It is also clear that those authorities with powers to regulate AI systems, which include, for example, accessing the 'source code' of the system, will need to be equipped with competent agents and technical facilities to do so. Otherwise, those powers wouldn't make any practical sense at all.

Of course, this proposal, whilst on the one hand intending to make AI use safer, has to been seen in context of the Commission's efforts to also promote AI—as we have seen from the AI Strategy discussed above. The network of European Digital Innovation Hubs is designed to play a key role in this by providing technical expertise and training in order for both the public sector and SMEs to be able to embrace AI. We shall see what the final agreement will look like in the coming months and the AI Act is expected to be passed in early 2024.

Coming back to the international dimension, it is encouraging to see more momentum on AI regulations in the US, where, for example, AI has been included in the EU-US Trade and Technology Council (TTC), likely to have been inspired by the EU AI Act proposal itself. Interestingly, the US has also been considering the role and regulation of AI in specific sectors across the economy, such as housing, food and drugs, transport and employment, suggesting that in the absence of national AI legislation the US is nevertheless taking very practical steps towards AI and how to manage it.

In July 2022, the UK Department for Digital, Media, Culture and Sports set out its plan for an AI Rulebook. As expected, post Brexit, the UK is keen to depart from EU regulatory red tape and instead take a more enabling approach to AI, seeing it as a 'general purpose technology'.

Beyond the EU AI Act proposal, other measures to better control corporations handling our data are being worked on in parallel. For example, in March 2022 the EU agreed on the Digital Markets Act, a new legislation aimed to pry open the monopoly of digital platforms (e.g. social media, search engines, e-commerce platforms). So-called core platform services are labelled as 'gatekeepers' in this legislation (our digital states or large companies in this case) and have to provide a number of services such as browsers, messengers or social media with a minimum of users stipulated. The largest messaging providers will have to provide access to and interoperability with smaller platforms. The combination of personal data in order to perform targeted advertising (the stuff that happens to us more or less every day) is only permissible if the user gave explicit consent to the gatekeeper. In addition, users should have free choice of their search engines, virtual assistants or browsers.

And finally, the fines. On this one, it was agreed to fine a non-compliant gatekeeper up to 10% of its total turnover worldwide in the preceding financial year and a whooping 20% in case of repeated violations. If it turns out that the gatekeeper systematically infringes the rules, then the Commission could also ban them from acquiring other companies for a certain period.

In the broader context of European Strategy for Data (2020), aimed at creating a Single Market for Data, February 2022 has also seen the EU proposal for a Data Act, with the purpose of determining who can access and use data generated in the EU across all economic sectors. This proposal follows the European Data Governance Act agreed in November 2021, which established both processes and structure to support data sharing by individuals, companies and the public sector and clarifies who is allowed to derive value from data and under which conditions.

The Data Act proposal takes the next steps on data by supporting users in relation to their own data. A key example here is that data generated about you through connected devices should be accessible by yourself so that you can, for example, share this data with other third parties to enable more data-driven innovative services. All to counter the current state of play where manufacturers harvest your data without either your knowledge or your ability to monetise your data.

Equally the Act tries to protect SMEs when it comes to data sharing, including from unfair contractual terms. Public sector bodies should have access to private sector data when necessary in exceptional circumstances such as public emergencies (wildfire, floods, etc.) or in case of a legal mandate. Another really important proposal—where we have already identified the risks that are in place today—is to make it easier for users to switch cloud providers and be protected from unlawful data transfers.

However, not everyone was so positive on this Data Act proposal. According to the European data protection board (EDPB) and the European data protection supervisor (EDPS), the proposal does not go far enough. Following publication of the draft act, both entities jointly called for ensuring that the use of personal data that is generated by the use of a service or product by any entity other than the actual user should be clearly limited or even restricted. This is seen as even more important in case the data itself could enable to draw conclusions on the user's personal lives or create risks for the user's rights and freedoms as an individual.

Calls such as this only underline how deep the data spiral goes and how much more protection may be needed to effectively protect users from themselves, i.e. from the dangers of conscious or unconscious data creation and sharing. Still, people will need to be clear whether they need and / or want to be protected.

7.4 Concluding Remarks

Now having reviewed the landscape of legal protection when it comes to data privacy, data protection, data security and AI we have to admit that the overall account is sobering. Whereas we all understand that the most important ingredient to our personal integrity and protection in a digital world is data privacy, the main flagship legislation we can find is the European Regulation on data protection, which therefore looks at the situation mostly once personal private data has been shared. Next, whilst around two-thirds of the world have some kind of data protection regulation, a large number do not do care much about data privacy itself. Next, for AI we find patchy approaches to self-driving cars and self-triggering weapons, whilst no one is realising that the uncontrollable data universe we find ourselves in as individuals, companies and governments has become an uncontrollable trigger to the destruction of our values, societal structures, beliefs and lives. The threats of generative AI are just the most recent icing on the cake here.

Looking at the European Data Governance Act and the proposal for the Data Act as well as the Digital Market Act, it almost feels that some of the concerns, particularly around data mining and commercialisation without data subject consent, could actually be resolved by Web 3.0, rather than a complex set of partially overlapping legislation that risks to be ineffective. Although, at the time of writing, there are still nearly 1000 amendments being explored in European Parliament, so who knows which way the legislation will ultimately land! But it at least makes it an interesting and ever-changing landscape to keep us on our toes.

As we find ourselves confronted with the horizon of DeFi—lengthily put Decentralised Finance—there are even more questions than answers. How can an inadequate legal regime in a limited place on this earth protect humankind when we are facing a digital parallel world that has been designed to escape control, even though people are now realising that some control is needed as, funnily enough, control brings scale and thus profits.

Therefore, the next question to ask—and try to answer—is: 'How much decentralisation do we need in order to stay protected in a digital world? What is the trade-off between control and no control where humans are at the centre?' Let's turn the page.

Notes

1. Turn, R., Shapiro, N. S., Juncosa, M. L., "Privacy and Security in Centralized vs. Decentralized Databank Systems", Santa Monica, CA: The Rand Corporation, 1976.
2. Kemp, S., "Digital 2022: Global Overview Report", Datareportal. https://datareportal.com/reports/digital-2022-global-overview-report (last accessed 18/11/2022).
3. The United Nations Office at Geneva (UNOG), "The Convention on Certain Conventional Weapons", https://www.unog.ch/80256EE600585943/(httpPages)/4F0DEF093B4860B4C1257180004B1B30?OpenDocument (last visited 28/12/2018), archived at https://perma.cc/7RG3-PCUX.
4. Prof. Kaye Reports on Artificial Intelligence and Human Rights at UN General Assembly, UCI LAW (October 25, 2018). https://www.law.uci.edu/news/in-the-news/2018/Kaye-UN-AI.html, archived at https://perma.cc/M7RH-TRQT.
5. OECD, "Artifical Intelligence", website https://www.oecd.org/going-digital/ai/principles/ (last accessed 18/11/2022).
6. "G20 Ministerial Statement on Trade and Digital Economy", 2019, https://www.mofa.go.jp/files/000486596.pdf.
7. Organisation of Economic Co-operation and Development (OECD), "Observatory on AI", https://oecd.ai/en/dashboards (last accessed 18/11/2022).
8. European Commission for the Efficiency of Justice, "European Ethical Charter on the Use of Artificial Intelligence in Judicial Systems and Their Environment", (CEPEJ), 2018, https://rm.coe.int/ethical-charter-en-for-publication-4-december-2018/16808f699c, archived at http://perma.cc/76QM-XTDA.
9. Communication (EU) no. 237/2018 from the Commission to the European Parliament, the European Council, the Council, the European Economic and Social Committee and the Committee of the regions 'Artificial Intelligence for Europe', https://eur-lex.europa.eu/legal-content/EN/TXT/?uri=COM%3A2018%3A237%3AFIN (last accessed 07/07/2022).

10. Zhang, M., "Google Photos Tags Two African-Americans As Gorillas Through Facial Recognition Software", July 2015, https://www.forbes.com/sites/mzhang/2015/07/01/google-photos-tags-two-african-americans-as-gorillas-through-facial-recognition-software/?sh=3a7ba30c713d (last accessed 26/03/2023).
11. Norton Rose Fulbright, "EU Proposes New Artificial Intelligence Regulation", April 2021, https://www.nortonrosefulbright.com/en/knowledge/publications/fdfc4c27/eu-to-propose-new-artificial-intelligence-regulation (last accessed 18/11/2022).

Chapter 8
Digital Horizons

The world has become a challenging place. Digitisation and digitalisation, envisaged to be a support to people to make things more efficient, connected and transparent, have taken on a life of their own. And there is an increasing feeling of fear that we are starting to be in a self-made mess that we can no longer get back on track. Motivated to find remedies for this state of affairs, we looked around for the right idea, and ultimately honed in on the concept of decentralisation.

Decentralisation or as we often refer to, redecentralisation, might not be the answer to everything but it feels that there is something in there that has the potential to help tilt things a bit more back into balance. Our messages across all of these Chapters have been designed to act as wake-up calls to 'what is happening' and to mobilise those that are willing and able to act to 'do something about it' as system builders, designers and shapers.

We started off on the premise of identifying the increasing levels of centralisation and power concentration. Across the three spheres of people, public and private sector, we examined the key areas of technology, payments and money, identity and data privacy against this backdrop. The power shift from governments to large corporations, from the technology space to payments, identity and data ownership is very visible by now and this creates further dis-alignment between our three spheres. Even our planet earth is suffering from the concentration of power amongst a few large corporations, e.g. when we think about the damage done by fossil fuels (scientifically documented to be contributing to the greenhouse effect since the 1970s), but also with the significant carbon footprint of cloud computing, which continues to rise (almost invisibly to all of us). All of this was triggered by the unnatural paradigm of separateness, competition and the ensuing quest for eternal and never-ending consumption—all fuelled by individual and collective trauma—which leads humankind to destroy itself, beginning with the climate, to culminate in oneself and future generations. If we do not step in to change our ways, reality will become a

R. Wandhöfer and H. D. Nakib, *Redecentralisation*,
https://doi.org/10.1007/978-3-031-21591-9_8

living nightmare for the majority, whilst leaving those that have too much to continue to pretend that nothing is wrong, because they can afford it (but likely not for long!).

From the vantage point of technology the following quote nails it:

It is long past time to move beyond a technology infrastructure that generates profit from harm.

—Frank McCourt, Jr

Civic Entrepreneur and CEO, McCourt Global

For us the key objective in this book was to develop ideas where redecentralisation can be deployed as a tool to realign values across our three spheres, beginning with the digital financial ecosystem as a possible starting point to build it anew, and perhaps as a blueprint for other areas. At the same time, we have not given you a specific plan on where to redecentralise what—albeit a few nuggets here and there. In fact, we do not and cannot pretend that we have all the answers, or any of them for that matter, as it is quite complex. But on our final step in this journey we nevertheless want to point you—the reader—towards new ways of thinking, living and doing business, which are more decentralised and which can support alignment of values between people, the public sector and business as you build new systems. This is really just the beginning of a journey but it is urgent for all of us to start and get on with it as otherwise our societies, our people, our businesses and governments and our earth will breakdown even faster than what we already witness at the time of writing in 2023.

Let's go take a look at where we can already see more decentralisation in action or where it is ripe to decentralise things and what the likely outcomes of this are or could be and end, where we began, with the start of a blueprint for the values that matter for a new digital social contract that can underpin this next wave of alignment between or three spheres.

8.1 The Future is Web3

The evolution towards Web3 is a promise of redecentralisation. As we already discussed in Chapter 3, Web1 appeared around 1994 and was made up of static websites focused on content consumption, i.e. mostly read-only. A way to gather existing information into a single database, Web1 was running on HTML and FTP and Web1's main characteristic was that it was decentralised. So many parallels with the world of finance!

Web2 emerged from 2004 with the arrival of social media platforms and other tech corporations. Web2 enabled people to create content, so read and write, which made everything more interactive as users would upload and engage with content. With Web2, we saw the rise of the ubiquity of the mobile phone, which became smarter and smarter, enabling a 24-hour online world, a supercomputer in our pockets. Running on Flash, Java and XML, Web2 is what we still mainly rely on today, but Web2 is no longer decentralised, because over time large players began dominating being an interface for users, making it that much easier.

And now we see the arrival of Web3, which is a example of and an attempt at redecentralisation, combining, reading, writing, trusting and verifying with a focus on sovereign ownership of data and digital assets. The promise of Web3 is censorship resistance, permissionlessness and borderlessness. Similar to Web2, Web3 is of course interactive, but the difference really is in the decentralised trust framework at the bottom of the technology stack. Our end-user experience is connected to the blockchain, for example, via four layers (where we only really see the front-end connectivity, i.e. the application interface). (1) smart contracts; (2) Web3 libraries that connect smart contracts with decentralised application interfaces; (3) nodes that link the Web3 libraries to smart contracts; and (4) wallets that connect to various blockchains and their decentralised Apps (or dApps). The difference to Web2 is that data and money ownership are decentralised and under the user's control and thus data can be monetised in a decentralised way (cutting out the centralised middleman so to speak) where data flows and interactions can be censorship resistant. The disintermediation of the Web2 technology and financial monoliths promises to enable user-centric control, even when potentially facilitated by reintermediation through a choice of Trusted Third Party Providers (TTPPs) to help users steer their way through the myriad disparate data sets, but this time by choice. The underlying technologies of Web3 circle around DLT (including blockchain as one of its implementations), cryptocurrencies, decentralised autonomous organisations (DAOs),[1] non-fungible tokens (NFTs) and the Metaverse, changing how we connect with each other by enabling peer-to-peer (P2P) connection. Distribution of data across all network nodes makes it harder to hack. Transactions are on-chain and thus transparency is in place, with the potential of making fraudulent behaviour more difficult (with off-chain and cross-chain implementations to bolster efficiencies). Smart contracts are used that store, verify and process transactions based on agreements without third parties. dApps also have native tokens associated to them and users are enabled to vote with these. In addition to voting, other use cases include payments, asset trading, storage, access, file sharing, communication and messaging and many more.

Whilst today users either have to pay for services or, if services are seemingly free, they actually pay with their data, which is harvested by companies, Web3 is expected to provide more freedom, decentralisation and privacy, as well as personal monetisation of those facets of a user's data that she is comfortable to share. This has the effect of power de-concentration, which translates into decentralisation along some dimension(s)!

Another key improvement that is envisaged in the digital world of Web3 is that any content a user produces and puts online can be controlled by this user. This prevents theft and also the ability of 'others' to monetise 'your' asset (anything that is made digital), your creation, so to speak without you providing your permission and consent. As we discussed in earlier chapters, it is a crucial requirement to secure that the user really is the genuine user, preventing a man-in-the-middle masquerading as the user and maliciously giving consent or seizing control over our entire personae. That principle has application across the board, whether that is video content, posts in professional networks, social media or digital art. And the clue is tokenisation, which gives users complete control over their online interactions, censorship free. Transitioning from Web2 to Web3 is of course a challenge. Adoption of something new always requires some effort and it will likely take time to see scale adoption of dApps or the emergence of a supersized Web3 platform(s) that would enable the interlinking of all DLTs and other technology systems as well as easy swapping and trading of all kinds of tokens on decentralised exchanges (DEXs). All Web3 services currently are using either PoS or layer 2 scaling solutions (also called side-chains).

Today, we have examples of Web3 platforms that take us into virtual worlds, such as the Metaverse (more on that shortly), or provide alternative social media functionality, which gives users a protocol that enables tokenisation of your own and your followers' posts and content via censorship resistant NFTs (more on those later, too), for example Decentraland (see Metaverse Fashion week in March 2022) but also Self-Sovereign Identity with Evernym (we have talked about that before!). As mentioned earlier, Vitalik Buterin and others came up with the concept of Soul Tokens (SBT), which would function as a form of blockchain based digital identity that we can use in, what is labeled the Decentralised Society, or DeSoc.

Web3 is in the making and its promise is that it will shake up centralised control, steering and power, giving users control over data, what they do with it and with whom and how it is monetised. The proof will clearly be in the pudding, or rather the underlying governance mechanisms in this case. Furthermore, the censorship-resistant side of things is an area that is not so straight forward, in particular if we want to protect our children and vulnerable persons from manipulation, abuse, exploitation and other ills. How do we manage to protect ourselves from ourselves?

A key area of focus will need to be Web3 technical security. If underlying protocols and applications are based on DLT-type technologies, there is the risk of an inability to delete data and information (and sometimes too much of an ability to do so). At the same time, applications will need to be secure, too. What if fraudsters could shift proceeds of crime via your digital wallet? How do we manage the recovery of funds, for example, or how to we enforce revocation of access where we have mistakenly given access?

Still, when considering our theme of redecentralisation that we elaborated throughout this book, we do see promising green shoots beginning to emerge allowing users, not only to actually own their digital things, but to easily and cheaply host instances of platforms, decide their rules, and do things in entirely integrated decentralised platforms across finance, messaging, health, and many other areas. The whole intention of Web3 is geared towards putting power back into the hands of users, or at least recalibrating it, by redecentralising it (a bit of a 'back to the roots' phenomenon in the digital world). A lot of development, testing and evolving has to happen to truly get us there, and that by many different entities and stakeholders of varying sizes and general importance, such that no controlling power can dominate the development and delivery. The basic rationale for Web3 is all about decentralising the power structures that have become too predominant, too controlling and too powerful.

Whilst our focus in this book has been on money and payments, technology and identity and privacy, decentralisation is expanding across the board into a myriad of areas, i.e. any application or service with a Web2 variant, which are typically characterised by more traditional and centralised Internet companies. So too will there inevitably be a Web3 variant. For example, taking social media and social networking, decentralised variants are already beginning to emerge like DeSO, which record social events on-chain, just like transactions for Bitcoin. When it comes to naming, much like email and domains and our social media handles, there are solutions such as the Ethereum Name Service and the Solana Name Service that make it possible to connect a kind of identity (that is created by the user) to those social events, transactions, messages, and whatever else. These same applications also make it possible to send encrypted messages. What this means is that, as these different applications are beginning to emerge, and whilst they remain not particularly user friendly to most (yet), they are providing a one-stop-shop for Web3 equivalents of Web2 applications that have a degree of decentralisation to them that has not previously become widely adopted, where users have their own private keys to access everything in a fully integrated, user-friendly and entirely non-custodial way (no requirement to have a custody relationship with any third-party), which entails direct ownership and possession. Of course, such keys can be lost and that would be a calamity, but the overall move marks a major shift towards redecentralisation and the emphasis on personal agency and autonomy!

8.2 The Metaverse... or Verses

The Metaverse is a rather recent addition to our growing new digital world vocabulary.

At this point in time in 2023, the Metaverse is still something of a guess, a guess that many different technologies will be coming together at the same time to create new immersive experiences as we go deeper into the digital and virtual parallel plain.

From the 'Internet of Data' to the 'Internet of People' to the 'Internet of Things', the Metaverse is aiming to add to this the 'Internet of Place'. This shift is characterised by two transformative changes. First, a move from the two-dimensional to the three-dimensional online world, enabled by virtual reality (VR—totally immersive) and augmented reality (AR—not totally immersive, but an overlay, using a pair of smart glasses). This is the more natural thing for humans to engage in as it mimics our primary navigational construct. Second, we observe the tokenisation of potentially everything, ranging from money, objects (real or virtual) to identity (I can own my data and get it into the places where it is needed), where everything has a digital equivalent and some things of value exist only virtually and digitally.

Born out of the world of online gaming, the Metaverses can in short be described as persistent virtual worlds, which over time are expected to become more and more interoperable. Even though it is currently more of a marketing play, if realised, we cannot fail to see both the good and the bad that is upon us and what this virtual universe would mean for our current and for future generations. The Covid-19 pandemic and lockdown accelerated the shift to digital and perhaps the focus on not only spending more time digitally, but creating worlds that can be accessed from a device that could one day be as good as our own. The trick was getting technology, from computers to semiconductors, microchips and gaming environments to the place where they can possibly handle it.

But where does this Metaverse come from in the first place? The name Metaverse was coined by Neal Stephenson in his 1992 science fiction novel Snow Crash. In this story, Stephenson depicts a 3D photo-real digital meeting space where humans, represented by programmable avatars, interact with each other. Over the course of the next decade, other manifestations of these avatar environments came to pass, with online gaming moving into new realms, including the either aptly or disturbingly, yet still allegorically named 2nd Life. Today, in the early stages of the Metaverse, avatars still appear very stiff as bandwidth speed (or slowness) can make them appear like a digital experiment gone wrong.

How Did the Metaverse Come About? and What Are the Use Cases?

With VR, AR, computing, and gaming technologies becoming more sophisticated and popular over the last decades, a broader mention of the term Metaverse gained ground in October 2021 when Facebook rebranded to Meta. The parallel rise of NFTs, primarily driven by more and more artists, actors, athletes and other celebrities being involved in this space, added to the excitement and popularity alongside the increase of more activities happening in gaming worlds like Forntnite with concerts being held there.

Of course, if you think it through, enhancing digital experiences that allow us to act in the digital world in ways that so strongly resemble the real world, means that we can do a lot more than having fun with online gaming. COVID-19 has already shown us the power of online meetings in a two-dimensional digital space—in fact a move to remote working for many that is almost irreversible with a more nomadic lifestyle. Making this 3-dimensional and immersive will further enhance and enrich the way we can communicate remotely, with the positive side effect of reducing transport for travel and carbon-related implications for our environment (well, that would however offset with the energy needs of the Metaverse as well as all the required hardware, more on this below).

Use cases therefore spread across commerce, entertainment, media, education and training, industrial engineering and design, internal collaboration, client contact, sales and marketing, events and conferences and many more. Some already see the gaming and fashion world merging in the Metaverse, where you can buy a virtual designer hat for your avatar to wear when playing an online game. But on a more serious note, health care is another area where the Metaverse can come into play, e.g. through the delivery of Telemedicine, i.e. remote diagnostics and treatment of patients.

Of course, if you embrace 3-dimensionality with the tokenisation of money and identity, you can imagine far broader use cases and applications. Let us think about what is close to us as individuals, the roofs over our heads. We could imagine a case where our house is tokenised and a digital twin of our residence is created in a virtual world. Your bank could do such a thing for you. With this digital twin in place, you can create a 24/7 monitoring framework, where all financial transactions that relate to the house and its use can be captured—a bit like a digital balance sheet of your house. Now the day comes when you want to sell your house. You transfer the house to the new owner via a token, with the transaction immutably registered on a ledger. All the data relevant to the house, ranging from council tax to electricity and gas to insurance to occasional repairs and refurbishment and so on, are all part of the house data package, a full audit trail on the ledger. This makes life much easier for the new owner in terms of understanding the costs, but also in order to find ways to create efficiencies. That comprehensive data set could be delivered by your bank to the new owner or by other providers. In fact, the theoretical opportunity of these activities may well create new businesses that cater for this altogether. You may even have a separate, virtual house, for your time there, that is equally used for gatherings, that you also may decide to sell.

Technology of the Metaverse and What is Missing

From a technological perspective, the Metaverse is only at the beginning of its creation. The ecosystem itself today consists of a shared virtual environment accessible via the Internet and the interfaces to access it—we mentioned VR, AR, computing and gaming as key enablers to engage with the Metaverse. Then we have the software component of the Metaverse, bringing objects into 3D, which can be centralised (Web2), decentralised (the promise of Web3) or a mix and the whole money infrastructure, i.e. the rails to pay in the Metaverse. To make this all work, we need at least 5G to support it and of course we need people using VR and AR. None of that is going to be obvious or fast and the expectation is that most users will still access the Metaverse via smart phones connecting to Web2 for some time. Access to 5G is also going to be a challenge and frankly if life is shifting more and more towards digital, free of charge, broadband inevitably has to become a human right as otherwise digital exclusion will become even more of an issue than it is today and risk much broader implications than just financial exclusion (e.g. education, ecommerce, work in general and the risk of civil unrest in response to increasing societal imbalances). Put simply, a new digital operating system is forming that everyone should have access to.

Energy Consumption in the Metaverse

The Metaverse will naturally swallow humungous computing resources, which is another challenge for our environment unless renewable energy can become the key resource to run this digital world. Whilst there is an argument to be made around a potential offset as there is an expectation that physical travel will reduce as more activities can take place in the virtual world, the Metaverse is almost definitely going to be a net contributor to our carbon footprint.

For starters, users are likely to buy the latest electronic devices, where we already know that the majority of carbon emitted for these consumer devices happens at the stage of manufacturing with only 10–20% of emissions being created during the operation and end-of-life cycle of the product.[2] According to analysts' rough estimates at Citi[3] electricity usage for the Metaverse could be ranging between 1 and 5% of global generation (depending on number of users and hours spent per day). The fact that cryptocurrencies are already the central payment instrument in this space today means that that there are more carbon footprint concerns given the still costly methods of PoW (chiefly Bitcoin!)—even though Layer 2 scaling solutions on top of PoW networks consume far less energy. Ethereum, which has transitioned to PoS in September 2022, gives the option to offset these to a certain extent.

Then we have to think about the network energy consumption, where unsurprisingly mobile networks today consume more electricity than fixed line networks. However, there is an expectation that the spread of 4G and 5G networks will improve energy efficiency as particularly 5G networks are up to 90% more energy efficient per traffic unit (W/Mbps) compared to 4G,[4] which itself is 50 times more efficient than 2G. The only fly in the ointment here is of course the significant growth of mobile network traffic, which in 2021 recorded an increase of 45% with predictions for the next 15 years of around 30% growth.[5]

Then we have the data storage, management and distribution to consider. We already spoke about cloud computing and hyper-scale data centres, which today account for around 2% of greenhouse gas emissions globally, comparable to the entire airline industry. The Metaverse will need a lot more of these, which is why the company Meta has, for example, more recently announced significant investments into data centres. One of the areas of focus is the fact that data centres need cooling, where an average data centre uses up to 5 million gallons of water per day, equivalent to the consumption of a city with up to 50,000 of inhabitants.[6]

Regulation in the Metaverse

When we look at the topic of regulation in the context of the Metaverse, we have to be mindful of a number of different components and angles. User protection, not so much classical consumer protection in the financial world, but rather protection from harmful content. This issue has already been a long-standing debate in relation to existing social media platforms, but the Metaverse with the ability of anyone being able to enter and create their avatars and communicate across the space poses an amplified risk in this area, in particular if we consider, for example, child grooming and worse (and by the way there is anecdotal evidence of this already happening…). The Metaverse will trigger a cultural shift where ethics is a huge topic. Humankind needs to be in charge to ensure that the Metaverse is utilised responsibly. Otherwise, it will come to haunt us.

The 2nd Life again is a useful example of how the different approaches to this virtual world can create real-life challenges. The 2nd Life provided opportunities for those whose online gaming had previously been served by games such as the popular 90s first person shoot-em-up, or Doom, whilst other gamers could engage in a 2nd Life fresh from their pursuits of SimCity.

The tensions here between the vastly different approaches to online gaming are self-evident, but also threw up interesting legal, and potentially even criminal action. Let us return to our online adventurers Maxi and Leni. Maxi has just finished building his new town hall in SimCity, and Leni has completed clearing the last stages of hell, slaying the Gorgon with a prolonged burst of her mini-gun.

Now they both insert the 2nd Life CD (remember them!) into their machines and start to enjoy their avatars' interactions with this new virtual world. Maxi quickly decides that his avatar needs a better car, an extension to the rather basic intro version, and spends $100 to start making these purchases. Unfortunately, Leni's avatar is not keen on Maxi's brand-new car, so torches it, and is delighted with this new online game. Maxi is less pleased, and forks out another $100 to replace it so that he can continue driving to the farm he is looking to establish in the next field. But when Leni logs back in, up in flames goes a second car, and Leni is delighted that in this new game that you can apparently torch crops too—exciting newfound online entertainment for her.

Back in the rather more traditional 1st Life, Maxi consults his lawyers—the first instance of criminal damage was bad enough, as he'd lost $100. But his losses have doubled to $200 and this now clearly constitutes harassment.

This is of course a hypothetical scenario, but it illustrates the legal and regulatory issues that we will have to feel our way through as the various Metaverses evolve. And as fiat currencies are converted into virtual in-game currencies and the flow of monies in-game go unmonitored before being cashed back out as fiat, inevitably money laundering starts to emerge, and because the Metaverses mimics our Universe in their infinite expansion, these threats will need to be understood to protect our real-world selves.

Data privacy protection, discussed already, is another area that would need to be covered in the Metaverse in terms of not only extending regulatory principles and scope of application of laws, but also ensuring the ability to enforce legislation. The Metaverse feeds off data collection, processing and analysis, hence protection and privacy of data are essential pillars to make this work. Ownership rights have to be enforceable via appropriate instruments, and competition and antitrust will equally play a key role in this new digital world to make sure that we do not end up with centralised dominance and power, i.e. full control by some big players (or maybe machines?).

Centralisation vs Decentralisation in the Metaverse

Then there is this central question for us: "How centralised or decentralised will the Metaverse be—or is already?".

In 2023 we are at a turning point towards either a centralised or decentralised Metaverse, or a hybrid of both. Some corporations are creating a Metaverse that will be available to others, where the rules of the system are set by the organisation that hosts it. Alternatively, a decentralised and publicly available Metaverse would be available to anyone and everyone, whether for your book club, your small business or to watch a concert, where you can have your own rules and be the host yourself.

As the concept of centralisation equates to the concentration of power and control, it is not surprising that we have to follow the money to see where the journey is going. Again, the relevant reference at this point in time is Meta as well as Microsoft as examples of companies that have begun to invest heavily into the development of a plethora of firms that all contribute to the next-generation Metaverse experiences across many of our human senses. These Metaverse-related technology players range from VR companies to gesture control and audio expert firms to micro-LED lighting companies, navigational software developers and various hardware companies that are specialised in connecting the human to the computer, for example, by translating neuromuscular signals into computer commands and many more.

In its application, the Metaverse has, over the last year, become yet another outlet for the marketing of companies and solutions. A place to showcase business, enable new forms of human interactions and predict future approaches to things as diverse as university education, training, next gen gaming, industrial design, entertainment and so on. We shall see where the journey will lead us and possibly the combination of Web3, the Metaverse and robust digital identity and data privacy implementations may give us more decentralisation through access, breadth, creativity, inclusivity, competition and fairness, rebalancing powers across the private sector, the public sector and the people. However, at this stage it appears like another platform for advertising, which itself has been hurt in the Web2 and social media world as data privacy legislation is starting to reign in.

As the Metaverse is still at its inception, the centralisation-decentralisation race is already beginning to unfold. Whether there will be one Metaverse that everyone will use from one provider or a small handful, or whether there will be open-source versions, or versions provided that users can set up locally themselves and operate as they see fit is still up in the air. As consumer demand for greater options increases, in combination with the dissatisfaction around centralised and controlled options, it is likely that we will see a mixture of the two for some time to come.

8.3 Decentralised Cloud

Following the above discussions on Web3 and the Metaverse, the next question is, if all of this comes to pass, how can we handle the energy demands of the digital world in a way that does not lead to a complete environmental fallout (arguably we are already there and leaders of governments and corporations are not doing anything meaningful to help reverse this—another example of complete non-alignment of our three spheres!)? Is it possible to optimise energy efficiency in the network with cloud technology in a way that this new digital world can be sustainable and does redecentralisation play a role in such an approach? We already provided an excursion into cloud technology in Chapter 3, highlighting the significant centralisation that is at play in this technology segment. As cloud services are more and more in charge of powering our digital world, including the virtual worlds of the Metaverse this trend of reliance on hyper-scale data centres continues to increase as economies of scale and ability to respond to sudden demand surges is key for these types of providers. According to estimates of mid-2022, Amazon Web Services had a global market share of 34%, followed by Microsoft Azure with 21% and Google Cloud with 10%.[7] So there is a problem. And not only because of the market concentration. The seamless invisibility of data streaming across all our devices day in day out has a trade-off. We rely on a complex and massive physical infrastructure ranging from thousands and thousands of kilometres of cables lying under the sea to massive data centres with thousands and thousands of servers, which by the way need cooling down. A very interesting research piece by Gonzalez Monserrate at MIT[8] of early 2022 reveals that those data centres use 200 terawatt-hours (TWh) of energy in each year, a lot more than whole countries such as Argentina or Poland.

And so, we ask, would redecentralisation make things better, in terms of control and power but also with regard to the environmental impact? The answer is possibly yes. By now, several firms have begun to offer decentralised cloud storage, which scatters—distributes!—your data across many cloud storage devices in different places. From a security perspective, this of course protects your data against failure of any central server, because you are no longer dependant on that. At the same time, data privacy is enhanced as well due to this set up. Here the use of blockchain protocols enables the distribution of computing power. Anyone with spare computing capacity will have the opportunity to link up directly with anyone who is looking for cloud services. The only thing needed in the middle is the blockchain protocol operated by one of the emerging decentralised cloud storage network providers (an analogy would be the third-party trust providers for digital identity). Therefore, there is no longer a need to rely on hyper-scale providers and instead distribution of power and storage can be coordinated across a very vast and diversified network of devices, which may well include data centres but also individual PCs, consoles or any other server. In practice, a file stored on a decentralised cloud is split into small parts, which are each cryptographically hashed. Some providers add an additional unique digital fingerprint to the file, in order to enable faster location of a file (in its various parts) across peer nodes. Any changes to your file result in a new cryptographic hash, making each instance tamper and censorship resistant. Cost savings using decentralised cloud can be significant compared to the large centralised cloud players (some estimate these to be up to 60%), not only because upfront costs for building data centres do not apply here, but also because P2P protocols can retrieve encrypted pieces of content from multiple nodes at once. The 'old world' of HTTP, which runs on the basis of the client–server model, enables user access to data that is stored on centralised servers via location-based addressing, which is easy to manage but not so efficient. This is because clicking on a website means that your browser has to connect directly to the server which is hosting this particular website. The further away that server is, the more bandwidth and time is needed, which can even result in network congestion. Another thing to note is that your data can be accessed or made inaccessible (think of distributed-denial-of-service attacks or DDoS) by anyone who has control over the server. This is not possible with decentralised cloud services which also have multiple instances of the same node that run concurrently, such that if any instance were to fail it can be resumed by others, avoiding risks of downtime, which is another problem for centralised cloud providers that have to ensure hardware maintenance.

We are about to enter a brave new world of computing power and storage distribution with distributed and decentralised control that can limit risks of outages and economic abuse, protect your data and data privacy and that can hopefully be more sustainable as well. Technology wise, some providers have put their bet on Ethereum for decentralised applications and smart contracts. As the market continues to evolve rapidly, this is certainly only the beginning.

Decentralising computing power via decentralised cloud solutions is one way to help realign the three spheres as we move deeper into our digital world. Of course, we haven't talked about the security challenge of undersea cables that connect our digital networks or the currently more centralised satellite internet solutions, which provide an alternative but are in the hands of a corporation. Resilience and decentralisation are crucial to enabling us to communicate freely across the globe. This goal has to be kept in mind at all times as technology solutions and implementations evolve in this space.

8.4 Security Considerations in the Light of Quantum Computing

With the arrival of Quantum Computing, a rapidly evolving technology that leverages the laws of quantum mechanics in order to solve complex problems, which classical computing cannot, there is an increasing security risk for existing forms of encryption, such as Public Key Infrastructure (PKI). The most well-known asymmetric encryption algorithm used in PKIs in order to perform digital signatures is RSA, and abbreviation of the names of the inventors of the technique: Rivest, Shamir, and Adelman.

As we have seen in our excursion into payments, centralised PKI is used in traditional payment systems in order to secure payment messages that are send around between banks. SWIFT is a prime example of where PKIs are used by its participants.

Moving away from the risks that a centralised PKI infrastructure poses—the consistent issue of cyber-attacks and risks due to single-point-of-failures—we are seeing the emergence of decentralised PKI, which operates on a blockchain and removes not only these risks but also the challenges that organisations face with PKI key generation, storage and sharing as all of this can be automated. At the same time, decentralised PKI can be used across different networks, where in today's centralised PKI model systems require their own PKI.

Beyond that, blockchains themselves are at risk of quantum computing attacks. For several years now, the industry and academia have been working on so-called quantum resistance. There are various new forms of encryption that are being developed to achieve this. But we also see the concept of quantum-resistant blockchains emerging. Such blockchains are based on quantum computation and quantum information theory, and they are decentralised, distributed and encrypted.

And there are other technical ingredients necessary to protect the security of blockchains. To remove the risk of quantum computer attacks on RSA, Gottesman and Chuang (2001)[9] developed a quantum digital signature scheme. Then we have the focus on communication security between nodes on a blockchain, where Kiktenko, Pozhar and Anufriev et al. (2018)[10] have developed quantum secure direction communication (QSDC) and Gerhardt, Liu, Lamas-Linares et al. (2011)[11] and Bennett and Brassard (2014)[12] have come up with quantum key distribution (QKD). There is even research ongoing into quantum digital currency systems, where quantum digital currency—for example Quantum Bitcoin, Jogenfors (2016)[13]—would run on a quantum blockchain. But use cases do not need to be restricted to currencies. Quantum blockchain will be able to benefit all technologies that are based on distributed storage and consensus mechanisms with use cases in important areas such as electronic voting, online auctions or multiparty lotteries. This could, for example, usher in a new era of how democracy can be put into action if we think about the combination of digital identity and tamper resistant voting, making electoral rigging at least technically rather impossible (there are unfortunately no limits to social engineering or outright brain washing!).

8.5 Decentralised Finance

Decentralised finance or DeFi is an interesting example of a new way of operating financial services with the concept of decentralisation at its heart.

The motivation for DeFI is to remove centralised middle men, such as banks, brokers or exchanges. To do so, DeFi is using blockchain technology to enable peer-to-peer (P2P) transfers, borrowing and lending as well as trading of digital assets. But hold on, didn't we think that the crypto ecosystem is already decentralised? Well, let's think again. The crypto exchanges that most of us that are engaging with are actually centralised. Only 'on-chain' financial activity can be considered as DeFi and when you use a 'mainstream' crypto exchange to buy, sell or hold your bitcoins or ethers, then this is just an interface that uses traditional IT systems to run what the old world of finance would call a limit order book (albeit a private one), but there is no direct impact on the underlying DLT of Bitcoin or Ethereum. But if the blockchain is already at least the distributed (and sometimes even decentralised) ledger that holds your digital assets or crypto, why would you put your assets on a centralised exchange's ledger instead? Questions that non-technology obsessed humans may never come to ask. The real answer is because it is more convenient than having to look after your private keys yourself. Though, as time goes by, user experience develops and we collectively become more accustomed. As certain tools are more widely adopted, private keys will be just like a password and be our access to everything we own, digitally.

Smart contracts on Ethereum as well as other chains are being leveraged to deliver this alternative financial ecosystem, where exchanges in this world are decentralised. These decentralised exchanges or DEXs are not governed by a central authority and instead run on smart contracts. They enable not only P2P interactions on a trusted ledger, but B2B, business to machine, and machine to machine interactions. Given the absence of middle men, the use of DEXs is cheaper, but also at your own risk, because if there is bug in the code you could lose your cryptos with no one to turn to.

And we are likely to see more DeFi protocols on their own networks (rather than what today is mostly Ethereum), using native tokens and system specific validators. DeFi projects continue to grow across many segments including lending, derivatives, payment solutions, decentralised trading and insurance. According to industry estimates, the nascent new financial ecosystem of DeFi grew from a mere 1 billion dollars in 2019 to more than 34 billion dollars in July 2022.[14] In fact, DeFi is not that new. Bitcoin is actually one of the oldest and most prominent DeFi projects around, hence taking this into account DeFi is already a bit bigger.

So, what are the component parts of the DeFi ecosystem?

The DeFi tech stack, as the industry would call it, consists of several layers that interact with each other as shown in Fig. 8.1 below. The base layer, similar to traditional FMIs, is the settlement layer, the place where financial transactions are completed and obligations of all involved parties are discharged. This layer is typically represented by a DLT, using a consensus protocol (e.g. PoS) and replicating the state across all nodes. As we already discussed in the payments chapter, settlement finality is not regulated (yet) in this world of DLT, which means that we currently can only rely on the effective execution of protocols that register an exchange of value as 'technologically final' (subject to true tamper resistance). There is no regulatory regime that would kick in, in case a transaction were to be disputed. Take it or leave it is the rule for now.

On top of the settlement layer we find the broader DLT application layer, which encompasses three key components. First, the actual cryptoassets, which can be made up of a plethora of existing and emerging digital assets (note that the crypto asset is itself a DLT application, enabling value transfers in DeFi). The term digital asset in this context can include just about everything that you can digitally exchange using this tech stack. Here we have for example fungible token such as Bitcoin, Ether and many other ERC-20 (the standard that allows dApps to create and manage their own cryptocurrencies and their own Tokenomics using the Ethereum blockchain) based cryptocurrencies (in fact this protocol is the key mechanism that gave rise to the ICO (Initial Coin Offering) craze and rapid proliferation of alt coins a few years back!). We also have NFTs based on ERC-721 and ERC1155 (two data standards for NFTs on the Ethereum blockchain), where each of these represent a unique digital asset, which could range from digital art to media to any other content that people may come up with. Now the emphasis here is on 'digital'. This is not about tokenising ownership of real art or a physical house, as that would rather be a fungible token, which would fall into the category of security tokens.

Key uses of NFTs in DeFi cover, for example, their use as collateral for lending or fractionalisation of digital assets via splitting NFTs into smaller fungible tokens to allow for partial ownership. Further uses of NFTs include the packaging of fungible tokens with an NFT wrapper, the use of NFTs as derivatives, enabling the creation

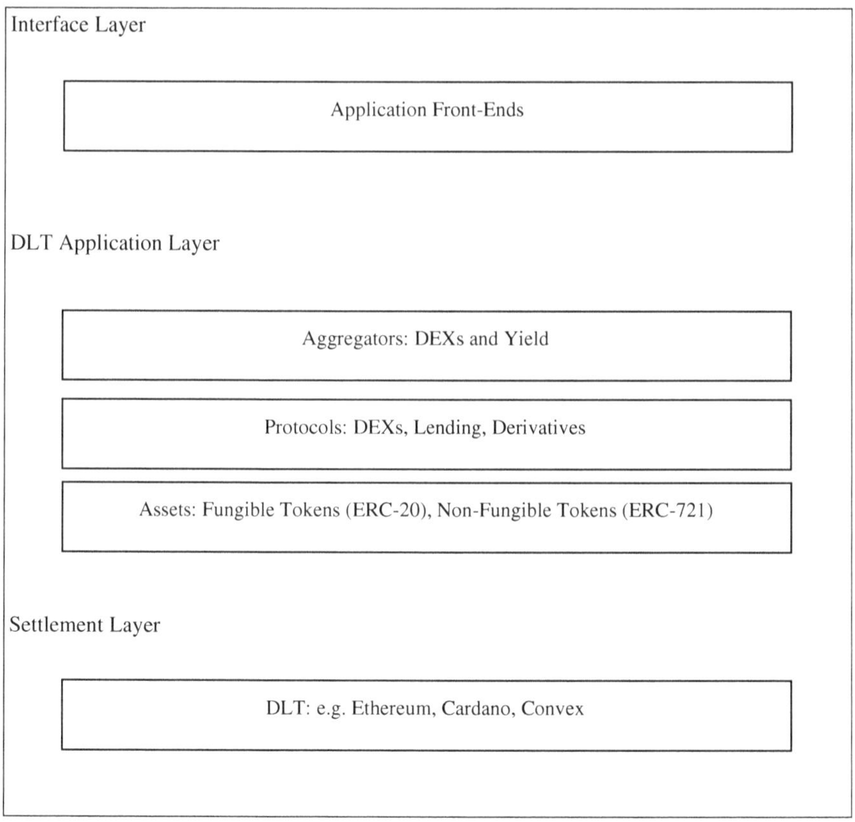

Fig. 8.1 DeFi Techstack

of different forms of liquid digital assets, whose values are linked to off-chain assets or in-game items or other types of capital. Another area where NFTs can be applied is by mapping real-world non-fungible assets, which when they become NFTs can be easily tracked on a blockchain. This can, for example, support asset provenance and tracking as well as ownership throughout an asset's life cycle. Other real-world NFT use cases include, for example, certificates of authenticity, digital identity cards (ah! This is a good idea!), tickets to shows or events or digital deeds to real estate.

More on NFTs specifically later.

The second component within the DLT application layer is represented by the DeFi protocols, which are smart contract DLT applications that provide you with some financial service functionality, in simple terms the stuff you can do with these tokens or NFTs. For example, you could trade your cryptocurrency on a DEX, you could lend out your Bitcoins, you could trade derivatives of Ether, you could asset manage NFTs and so on. There are no boundaries to creativity and innovation in this space and DEXs play a key enabling role in DeFi. They have no central authority and instead rely on self-executing smart contracts to facilitate trading and settlement. DEXs unlike centralised exchanges do not have market makers and cannot operate the classical limit order book practice.[15] Instead, they operate on the basis of an algorithm that works as a constant product market maker, where the product of two tokens is set to be a constant. Without getting too technical here, the price that is offered to you is based on supply and demand (for example) of Ether on that particular smart contract. There could be others out there and so prices can be different across different smart contracts, but ultimately investors will find a way to buy cheap Ether until the price is back in balance (or so it should work).

The third component of the DLT application layer in DeFi covers specific DeFi protocols that use other DeFi protocols in order to offer specific services such as DEX aggregators that direct you to those DEXs with the best prices or Yield aggregators that help you maximise your returns. This is a place where life is made easier for those of us engaging with this ecosystem. The very top layer is the interface layer and here we are talking about interfaces for the developer community, rather than end users.

As you can already see, DeFi does not only operate on the basis of a new underlying infrastructure and non-centralised governance but automation is becoming the norm across the trading spectrum.

There are even DAOs that offer infrastructure for investment in DeFi, where users can define their risk parameters, the types of assets they want to invest in, the risk model, strategies and fee levels.

At this point in time (2023), conducting financial transactions via DeFi still requires the use of crypto-assets, such as Ethers. In fact DeFi operates on smart contract DLTs, the most prominent being the Ethereum blockchain. As the concept of fiat-pegged stablecoins becomes more mainstream, interacting with DeFi will become more legitimised (of course regulating DeFi will be key to legitimise this space and attract more institutional players from traditional finance). Whereas central banks' CBDC endeavours could insert themselves into this space as well, it is more likely that we will see a more widespread use of stablecoins as the private sector will do its best to serve this emerging market. In addition, we may see many different forms of stablecoins, for example pegged against oil, wheat, water, gold, copper and other commodities as new digital financial assets and potential means of payment and funding, also facilitating the growth of DeFi. This is a particularly important point as it reflects the power of technology and new structural thinking around what actually is perceived as value.

The way to increase the size and importance of DeFi is to leverage tokenisation. Any real-world asset that is tokenised can technically participate in DeFi, making buying, selling and trading more efficient. Of course, a regulatory backdrop to this is important, which is why some market players are very fond of the Liechtenstein Blockchain Act. This Act, which came into force in January 2020, provided the legal basis for tokenisation of all types of assets as well as rights. You may want to trade existing stocks in crypto, which is already done today by tokenising them. However, the legality of this should be checked with relevant securities regulators as there are sensitivities, given the general perception of the crypto ecosystem by most regulators and regulated institutions.

As a first step, however, the market has embraced locking cryptocurrencies into DeFi protocols. This is akin to the old financial world of a fixed deposit account, where you lock your money up for a period of time in order to gain interest. In the DeFi world, this is called staking. By locking crypto tokens into smart contracts, you support the validation of transactions—and thus the overall network security and operation—and in return you earn interest on the tokens that you provided for this process. Staking only works in PoS networks, recall from Chapter 3. The more tokens you stake, for example on the Ethereum blockchain, the more you are incentivised to maintain the security of the network. This is also more resource efficient than the mining process on the PoW Bitcoin blockchain.

Other investment strategies, as referenced above, include so-called yield farming where interest rates tend to be higher than when staking. Here people move between DeFi protocols, reuse tokens and try to earn a maximum yield, ultimately being paid in the protocol's own token.

You can also lock other assets into DeFi protocols, including illiquid ones—say a digital art piece or a fraction of real estate represented by a token. This would, for example, be supported from a regulatory dimension by the Liechtenstein Act, which determines the Token Container Model, meaning that each token is a digital representation of a real-world asset.

DeFi claims to be decentralised when it comes to the rules that govern protocols. However, this really depends on the protocol. There is much unseen centralisation in DeFi protocols, similar to what we discussed in the example of Layer 1 blockchains in Chapter 3.

But on the positive side, so-called governance tokens allow participants in DeFi to vote for changes to decentralised protocols. This is exactly what we are looking for on our quest towards more redecentralisation as actual users have a voice in how the system evolves as opposed to centralised institutions holding all the power to decide. In MakerDAO, for example, there are almost weekly votes on changes to certain parameters such as interest rates. For some participants, this may be too much.

Think about the analogy to Switzerland, which has on average four referendums or votes on initiatives per year, a high frequency compared to other countries. The way to truly involve a broad usership to support the governance in such a way will depend on many factors, including simple ones such as the actual ability of a user to engage with this new tech ecosystem in the first place. There are so many questions and areas that need to be addressed in this regard. What about the regulatory framework for such tokens in light of how they effectively do impact and even direct corporate governance, for example?

But because of this much more decentralised, democratic and inclusive process in DeFi, there is also a perception that the challenges of existing banking regulation, banks' limited lending capacity and the direction of interest rates (in some instances) could actually be overcome by DeFi. Collateralisation, lending and trading in a digital 24/7 environment promises the unlocking of trillions of dollars in a transparent way via code that is (hopefully) driven by the community.

There is another perceived benefit in the nature of DeFi to the extent that standardisation (such as the ERC-20 token standard) allow for rapid and ongoing innovation, such as dApps development and continuous DeFi protocol improvements. An area that will need to be addressed however is interoperability across blockchains, which is not in place today.

Further, the limitation of intermediaries in DeFi should provide cost savings for users. Of course, this has to be balanced with the challenges of digital financial education—users of DeFi will need to understand how blockchains and dApps work and be able to make choices on self-custody or third-party custody of their digital assets—including the fact that today most protocols in DeFi are not widely translated. Technically scaling DeFi solutions is dependent on whatever Layer 1 blockchain they are using. Ethereum is seen as too slow, which is why there are so many Layer 1 solutions that are looking to compete with Ethereum by offering faster, more scalable protocols.

The key challenge for DeFi is, unsurprisingly, regulation. Today's regulatory frameworks that govern deposits, custody of assets and transfers of value are all structurally designed to work with intermediaries, as liabilities, business conduct and other requirements apply to them. In DeFi, we still have intermediaries, i.e. human intervention in addition to algorithms,[16] but not in a way that makes the application of existing regulatory regimes simple or straightforward. However, the key regulatory principles are of course as applicable in DeFi as in TradFi (or traditional finance). KYC and AML regulatory requirements will have to be applied to tokenised assets. This is even more important when we consider the involvement of institutional players, which today are still shying away from this brave new world. This market place will only become mainstream and available to all users, if institutions participate with their sizeable flows. Verifiable credentials that are cryptographically secured types of digital identities as well as the use of zero-knowledge-proof technology and on-chain KYC for digital authentication is called for by institutions in order to be able to interact with DeFi protocols. At the same time institutions will only transact in separate and permissioned liquidity pools for which all users are verified in line with regulatory compliance requirements. And security within DeFi systems needs to be beefed up in order to satisfy institutional investor demand to participate but equally to protect individual users from unfortunate events as seen in previous crypto scandals.

Regulators all around the world are grappling with the DeFi market. As mentioned, Liechtenstein adopted a Blockchain Act,[17] which provides legal certainty to all types of tokenised assets, in particular covering the AML and KYC angles. The German regulators have issued cryptocurrency specific legislation including custody of crypto-assets. At European level, we have already discussed the MiCA Regulation, which is soon coming into force. These are all key steps to enable the market to develop and strive, but we are still at an early stage.

To conclude, DeFi represents the new world of merging physical and digital financial and other assets, offering increasing numbers of different investment strategies and solutions that help diversifying your portfolio and do so in a way that is—at least for now—community-led rather than driven by rent-extracting middle men.

Of course, nothing stands in the way of existing players and infrastructures to also experiment with these new technologies. In the UK, we have recently seen the arrival of a regulated digital securities exchange (not just a cryptocurrency one), which is using DLT type structures to enable trading of leading digital securities issuances globally.

Existing stock exchanges small and large are looking at DLT in order to develop token-based platforms for issuance and trading, which can further simplify fractionalisation of assets, opening up the investment landscape for more users. The other big opportunity is to enable currently non-tradable assets, such as digital art, to be traded. Of course, this will require potential changes to the rules that govern traditional exchanges and asset issuance.

The UK Investment Association (with £10 trillion Assets under Management, AuM) is working with key UK asset managers and a FinTech to launch a tokenised fund in the UK. Such a fund would require the ability to be traded on the London Stock Exchange and discussion have already began to explore the technical feasibility. Across the Atlantic investment manager, Franklin Templeton launched a tokenised mutual fund on blockchain in 2021 for 130 Mln $ AuM.

This is a space to watch over the coming years as those players that can provide the right infrastructure and attract the relevant assets for trading will emerge as the leaders of the digital financial system unless of course DeFi takes their place. However, a word of caution. Existing methods of exploiting arbitrage in DeFi through flash loans and maximum extractable value (MEV) strategies (paying higher gas fees to prioritise your trade over others) are teething problems, where often a mistake in code is being exploited. MEV in particular is a transparent re-run of what we learned from Philip Daian's 'Flash Boys 2.0' and how high frequency traders behaved in TradFi. At the same time, blockchain business is still slow, unless intermediated by centralised exchanges, which means that today we can neither achieve the speed nor scale of TradFi in DeFi. But centralisation shouldn't be the answer.

A Quick Excursion into NFTs

Now we have mentioned NFTs already a couple of times, but at this point it is only fair to go a bit deeper on a bit of history of NFTs and how we see the deployment of NFTs having the potential to change the dynamics of whole industries, in particular when it comes to business and economic models.

The origins of NFTs go as far back as 2012, a lifetime in the world of crypto and DLT. The special thing about them is that they are 'special'. Whilst a Bitcoin is always a Bitcoin a bit like a dollar is a dollar, NFTs are non-fungible, meaning each NFT is truly unique. They function, as discussed above, as a tool to represent the ownership of a unique asset. This is an important point. We are not saying that NFTs represent the asset itself, they represent the ownership of it. This ownership is secured on Layer 1 blockchains such as the Ethereum blockchain, Solana, Cardano, etc., which makes it impossible to copy or recreate this particular NFT. In the early days of NFTs, these were actually small fractions of Bitcoins, at the time called coloured coins, which served as digital representations of real-world assets such as government bonds, precious metals, cars or other cryptocurrencies. In 2014, some coders joined forces to create an open source platform that enabled trading on a decentralised ledger network. This opened the door for artistic creativity (and allegedly other forms...) to enter this new digital world, and in the same year, the first expensive digital art had been minted. The launch of 10,000 unique CryptoPunks in 2017, pixelated characters so to speak, created somewhat of a crazy trend with secondary market prices for these characters quickly moving into two-digit millions of USD. The same year saw the arrival of CryptoKitties, a blockchain based game where players can trade, breed, buy and raise digital kitty characters using Ethereum. The media jumped on this and demand and prices rocketed here as well. In response to these developments, NFT market places, where some became dominant very quickly, began to appear, making minting and trading of NFTs a more visible and centralised proposition, which also allowed for more price discovery.

2021 the artist Beeple sold a digital art piece as an NFT at Christie's for $69 million, followed by Pak's art piece, which sold for $91.8 million! This piece was sold to many buyers in units, also questioning the concept of a piece of art versus a collection of art.

Of course, this is just the beginning. Other creative industries are smelling the coffee.

One such example to showcase here is how DLT and the arrival of NFTs has the potential to disrupt the film industry. Because NFTs represent sovereign ownership of a digital asset on a blockchain, there is now the ability for independent film makers to enable users not only to digitally consume films, but also to purchase digital avatars and other merchandise. This in itself can create new primary and secondary markets, as we have seen with digital art and CryptoKitties, for example. But now that we see the establishment of the basic foundations of the Metaverse, there are additional use cases and avenues to explore, such as games based on films allowing users to play out their own stories using their avatars.

Again, there are no limitations to creativity and commercialisation, but this time around without the Hollywood Mega Studios being the producers, middle man and overall rent extractors. This breathes new life into an industry that has been undergoing increasing centralisation and with it control of power and decision-making. Both creating and issuing digital content in the film industry via NFTs and developing a whole ecosystem around these with digital experiences, is bound to revolutionise this industry by providing open access and enabling true creativity to reign supreme. As this is the tip of the iceberg, we urge everyone to consider the opportunity that this new world can bring to you in terms of your personal or collective abilities to create and share your own ideas.

8.6 From Data to Smart Data: A Journey Beyond Open Banking

A revolution in the use of data has been underway predating even the dot com boom and bust. But more recently as the 4th (or fifth or sixth!) technological revolution gets into full swing, the manner in which data can be reassessed for new purposes is the subject of great academic and industrial debate. From Tim Berners Lee's Open Data Institute to MIT, and UK Smart Data legislation, to reforms of the EU's AI Act and GDPR part 2, the applications are seemingly limitless, and many argue that there could be a certain financial services backdrop to much of this.

The tensions between a number of EU pieces of legislation relevant to us in this space has been a long-standing area of debate. As eIDAS and GDPR were in development to become harmonised Regulations, PSD2 and NIS were under negotiation as Directives (the rather non-harmonised kind). Whilst many of us could identify conflicts, even some outright dichotomies between the various measures, it is typically the Dutch data protection agency, 'De Autoriteit Persoonsgegevens', that is held out as the Regulatory poster child for these problems. And indeed, even into the 2020s they were launching investigations into these issues.[18] But today, we see PSD3, NIS2, GDPR2 and eIDAS2 discussions coming through. However, at the time of writing these seem again to being progressed in 'glorious isolation' leading to fears of yet another regulatory disconnect.

Whilst we have postponed the consideration of the difference between common and civil code law for another day, there is one particular exemplar which is worth taking a moment to consider in more depth, and that is how the legislative and regulatory approach in the UK has led to the current market in smart data, built on top of Open Banking. A raft of measures being debated in the UK Parliament would appear to at least be cross-referencing to the concurrent existence of other interconnected measures. We wait to see whether this tacit acknowledgement actually feeds through into practical implementation, but a government's approach to attempt joining up its legislative programme is as novel as it is welcome!

Before we come to our breakout illustration of how this might manifest itself in practice, let's have a quick look at the regulatory enablers behind some of this potential, as this may well become one of those rare examples of regulation supporting more innovation, rather than stifling what industry (or indeed other parts of the public sector) can offer to support us as individuals. For example, in the UK's 2022 proposals for their Data Protection and Digital Information Bill the regulatory impact assessment highlighted parallels with Open Banking and how a model of Third Party Providers (TPPs) aggregating banking data could be reapplied into other realms, whilst maintaining user-centric controls to protect both access to and the privacy of any aspects of information about every part of our daily lives.

The advantages of Open Banking, giving us more effective control of our banking data without having to centralise everything into some monolithic single data source, not only allow for greater control of information about our accounts, but can do so without as many concerns about legacy systems. This of course means a far faster way of reforming those services. Stepping into Open Finance and adding in savings or pensions is hardly a huge leap of imagination. Applications such as moving this into mortgages and integrating the finance into the whole conveyancing process of purchasing a property are only recently being explored and a number of new industry entrants are revolutionising the way we handle these data sets to streamline the process and remove the many pain points of the traditional process. The real value will lie in our ability to share appropriate identity attributes between the various parties, and not just the identity attributes of the natural person, as we note in FinCen's late 2022 legal requirements for shell companies, but the identity attributes of the property, handling requirements of the land registries, title deeds, local authority checks and utilities—all in one seamless 'Open Property' (in this particular use case).

But property is also a form of financial asset, so let's branch out into something a little more sensitive and look at, say, health care. Now before we delve into something as sensitive as health care let's pause for a second and consider consent. It is all well and good asking an Open Banking TPP to handle payments on our behalf—after all we have to surrender much of this data to credit reference agencies anyway! But how are we going to handle the minutiae of giving consent over our other data sets? And when it comes to health care our issues surrounding Role Based Access Control step up to an altogether different order of magnitude—our medical records are not a single data set—we will see that this offers a huge opportunity in pursuing more effective health care—but we also need to ensure that we are not enabling uncontrolled access to our disparate patient records. Whilst there may well be advantages for sharing our care records with a hospital in another district—or even country—in case of emergency, we would clearly not wish to share information on sexual health with our dentist!

This is where the concept of 'consent dashboard' comes into play, enabling a generic Third Party Provider—what we're now terming a Trusted Third Party Provider (TTPP)—to give our lay user the ability to control the flow of our personal data, and the permissions that we are happy to authorise for the use of that data. In a banking context, this separates our AISPs from our PISPs as we've discussed, but from a healthcare setting this could manifest itself in users being willing to share aspects of their medical data for different purposes. Following on from the successful COVID-19 vaccine rollout in the UK, Oxford University's John Bell, for example, is looking to recruit a cohort of 5 million people to share data for medical research, yet an open/smart data model could scale this to whole population levels. Now whilst many will have privacy concerns, one could hypothesise a scenario where a consent dashboard could have levels set at, say:

- No sharing of my medical data for any purpose
- Share my medical data with NHS hospital trust research programmes, and only for cancer cures
- Share my medical data with Charitable Research Trusts such as Cancer Research UK
- Share my medical data with Pharmaceutical companies looking for cancer cures
- Share my medical data with Pharmaceutical companies, on condition of payment.

So, now back to the practical demonstration of how Open Banking can morph through open finance into this future vision where new entrants into the market are looking to exploit these new opportunities. Please see Table 8.1.

Table 8.1 Smart Data Opportunities

As we have mentioned before, when the UK was a member of the EU it was often said to tend to 'gold-plate' EU legislation during the transposition phase. However, this gold plating turned out to be a blessing in disguise and the FinTech sector (including other sectors such as RegTech (Regulatory) SupTech (Supervisory) inter alia) has become a UK success story, viewed enviously by other advanced and developing nations. The Treasury-commissioned Kalifa review reported back in March 2021 and has driven international comparisons (the Commonwealth Secretariat recently published a follow up, which notes that some nimbler Commonwealth nations (such as in Eastern Caribbean)) are now taking this forward faster than in the UK, albeit looking to follow UK leadership in standards), where the City of London Corporation see regulatory alignment in data and security as crucial.

As illustrated in Figs. 8.2 and 8.3, the now established premise of Open Banking can lend itself to broader issues in Open Finance and many players in the FinTech sector now provide an array of dashboards, hence the logical extension within the Data Protection and Digital Information Bill in the UK for this to extend to Pensions. The Pensions Dashboard programme being run out of the UK Department for Work and Pensions (DWP) over six years has struggled due to the nature of the legacy systems held by the myriad of pension providers, and the hope and expectation is that having a straightforward API callout to populate a dashboard through an Open Banking type ecosystem could address these issues. But the Bill's regulatory impact is not limited to finance.

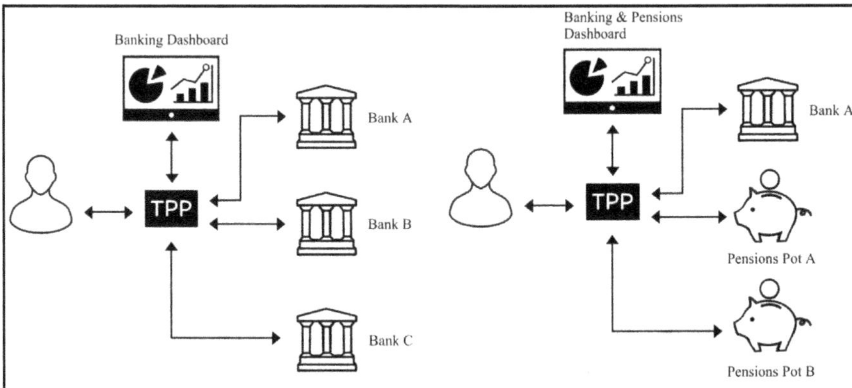

Fig. 8.2 From banking to pensions dashboards

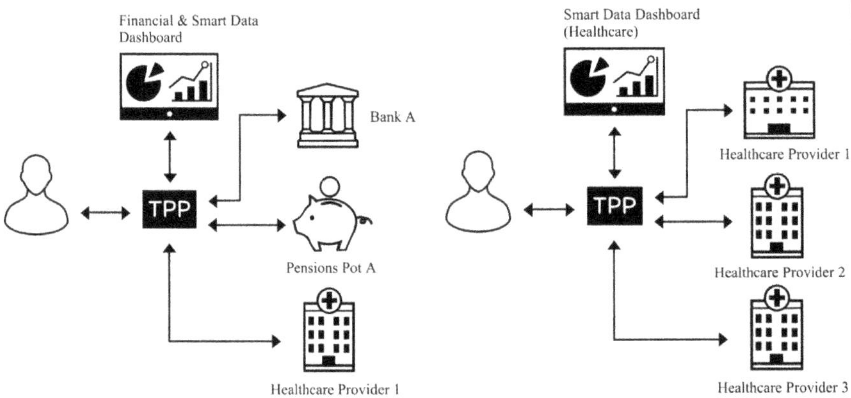

Fig. 8.3 Financial and smart data for health care

FinTech providers already enable the inclusion of insurance or other datasets and consent under GDPR requirements can be handled (a consent dashboard if you will), opening up the principle of consumers monetising their data, sometimes referenced as the disintermediation of intermediaries and putting the consumer in control of all their data, not merely their financial data.

At European level, the Digital Identity Wallet (called out in Chapter 6), to be rolled out from April 2023, is expected to provide clarity and structure in the digital identity jungle, where all EU Member States will in the future be required to issue such a wallet and all private services including big platforms (e.g. social media) will be obliged to accept the wallet and EU eID sign-in. The beauty here is that the solution will be attribute based, meaning you only show relevant data attributes from your digital passport and you as the user are in full control. There will be full legal equivalence of paper and digital forms of ID and when it comes to the question 'where to put the consent dashboard?', the solution is to attached the dashboard to your digital ID.

This will avoid having different consent dashboards for different services that you may want to use. The UK should certainly be inspired by this approach. The benefit for competition, where users can in the future for example open bank accounts or enter mobile phone contracts wherever these are cheapest in the EU—no longer being constrained to national boarders—will be immense.

The new models of opportunity illustrated in the above table will only be feasible by virtue of the proposed legislative changes in the UK. The proposed UK Bill for Data Protection and Digital Information it set to create the legislative basis for any data sets to be coordinated in this manner. Given the success of vaccine research and rollout in the UK the ability to be able to coordinate currently disparate medical, health and social care datasets would add value to patient outcomes in itself. Allowing data sharing under such a model, obviously with consent being managed by the user through their chosen TTPP, could open up existing health data sets for to appropriately approved heath research organisation. With BioNTech now mulling a cancer vaccine by 2030, opening up data could enable this earlier in the UK, particularly given the vast amounts of medical data held, albeit unexploited, by the UK's National Health Service.

The support provided by the UK's Open Banking Implementation Entity (OBIE) has allowed the 'thousand flowers to bloom' in the UK FinTech industry, making it a rising economic star, and it could be envisaged that the Future Entity (currently under discussion between Competition and Markets Authority (CMA) and Joint Regulatory Oversight Committee) (Financial Conduct Authority/Payment Systems Regulator/Information Commissioner's Office) could engender a similarly supportive environment for an 'EveryTech' industry going forwards.

It should also be noted that the success of Open Banking, certainly in the UK, has been enabled by banking security standards. Whilst fraud threats continue to grow, further developments in UK cyber security standards are providing innovative business opportunities for the new entrants emerging from the 'traditional' FinTechs into the Every-Tech trust brokerages, which we're starting to see today.

And back to our 3 Ps, it has oftentimes been the legislation and regulators providing enabling measures, which the new entrants can exploit to provide a model that works better for all of us as users. Enabling health (and other non-financial) data to be protected to the same level as banking security standards should assuage fears raised in previous years, such as during Care.data, back in the early 2010s.

The British Standards Institution's approach to Digital Identification and Strong Customer Authentication[19] sets out principles of meeting the PSD2 Regulatory Technical Standards in Strong Customer Authentication, but also goes further to allow for more practical step-up authentication to be handled seamlessly with multimodal biometrics. Now, the multi-modality is important here—we are all now very much aware of the multi-factor requirements, and indeed how these factors need to be handled in their implementation to prevent man-in-the-middle or man-in-the-browser-style attacks. Multi-modality helps us to ensure that we are not only dealing with the correct user, but that that user is not 'double-dipping' into our services with multiple false accounts. The biometric 'modes' are really just a fancy way of saying which biometric we are discussing, so a fingerprint, iris, voice or face recognition are simply four different 'modes' of biometric. When deploying biometrics, however, alongside all the nice technical aspects of ensuring liveness, spoof resistance to 'presentation attacks' and the like there is always a chance of having a 'false positive', i.e. another individual looks sufficiently similar to me that they can authenticate themselves as me, even on my device. Now this is not considered too much of a security problem, as the 1 to 1 match on my device requires access to my device and a great deal of luck that you happen to be able to fool the system. But at a population scale if we, say, have a 1 in a 1000 chance of the system throwing up a false positive, then we will struggle to uniquely identify an individual, as with roughly 8 billion people now being on the planet as of 2023, a face recognition alone would only narrow it down to one of potentially 8 million people! Add in an iris as well, and we reduce that to 8 thousand, voice brings it down to 8 and fingerprint then should enable us to have a fair degree of confidence that we have a unique user.

In practical terms, we don't need to deploy all four modes for day to day use, but in the same way as bank cards are contactless up to £100 (current UK figure), above that you need Chip & PIN, and above a certain threshold set for each account so say at above £2000 some additional security will be applied, for example the bank calling the user to double check the transaction. Segway this back into wider access to our data through our TTPP, and you can see how a straight forward fingerprint sensor could give read-only access in an AISP mode, or approve a small payment, à la contactless, but you might want to add a face recognition to transfer funds of higher value, or to access more sensitive data sets, or certainly to change settings on our consent dashboard, and if someone else can change your levels of consent then it really is game over from a data protection and privacy perspective. Though the irony is not lost on us that this means that we need to deploy our most sensitive data, our very "being" as the biometric measurements of ourselves as wet carbon lifeforms, in order to make sure that this data, and everything beyond, cannot be compromised by a malicious third party!

This model of Open Banking expanding into broader finance and beyond towards truly smart data provides us with a bit of a quandary from a redecentralisation perspective. Our data is held in small pots, distributed with multiple providers, so clearly distributed as well as decentralised. Yet our TTPP could be viewed as a centralising point, albeit one chosen and controlled by us as individuals—and we could chose several ones, decentralising it further. Perhaps this is where redecentralisation is taking us and if this model matures, it could lead to a far more fulfilling interface between our physical and virtual worlds. How comfortable we will be with this model will be heavily influenced by how we view it from a perspective of trusting in it as a new form of social contract, a digital social contract so to speak, which we shall explore further in the section below.

8.7 A New Social Contract for Our Digital World

In Chapter 2, we covered the age-old concept of a social contract. As a brief reminder, the social contract is considered to be an implicit social construct in modern societies that first brought forth governance as we know it today from the hunter-gatherer days to the state-citizen era in which citizens gave up certain rights (primarily to use violence) in return for protection by the state to mediate and coordinate. From then on, it was the state that had the monopoly on the use of force within certain physical territorial bounds. This social contract is an implicit set of norms that institutions, society and behaviour can be thought of as being built around. It is the glue that holds it together. Prevalent across the globe as the way things are supposed to be with a state and its citizens, the social contract has come under pressure on a number of fronts in recent years.

Firstly, three fundamental areas have recently changed in relation to the classic social contract.

For starters, our world has turned digital over the last decades with new ways to do things and interact with each other. The social contract, as we know it, did not account for this shift. The digital world has a different rule set than the physical world.

The second change has to do with the fact that the digital world is not only local but global in nature.

The third is that there are new ways to govern and make decisions collectively, where any individual can participate in creating forms of governance and take part in many new forms of decision-making. These new ways of participation are chiefly enabled by technology.

The second fundamental area of change is that these seismic shifts have witnessed two equally seismic trends. On the one hand, we have added centralisation that has led to some of the issues we have discussed in this book, whether in relation to privacy, identity, data, the world of finance or payments. And second, we experience the emergence of attempts to decentralise where some of these attempts are equally troubling and often backfire into more centralised outcomes. Both, again, fuelled by technological change.

What is hopefully apparent at this stage is that this limbo we are in, between decentralisation and centralisation, is directly connected to two things. First, the shifts to centralisation are to solve coordination problems and avoid chaos—instil a sense of order to make things work—and the shifts to decentralisation have to do with the erosion of trust due to far too much centralisation and overreach by those centralised institutions doing things that are not in the best interests of those relying on that centralisation to do whatever it is they need to do to go about their daily lives. We have evolved from hunter-gathers to nation states, to super computers, to everyone having a smartphone, from physical sovereign tender to cryptocurrency and from simple automation to AI and computing as the extension (or replacement!) of humans.

Technology is, in many ways, a chief enabler of our social constructs and institutions that are in turn based on our social ideas. But just like questioning whether or not technology is right or wrong, trying to determine whether centralisation or decentralisation is, doesn't work either. Because of the lack of alignment between our three spheres that are now global instead of local, digital instead of physical and that have available to them new ways of decision-making and governance, a new digital social contract is required to enable this value realignment. Otherwise, we are all operating in a way that is predicated on an underlying trade-off assumption for why and how things are the way they are that simply no longer applies.

Whilst we do not have an exact blueprint for this digital social contract, we know that we need it and this is a call to action to usher in measures that can actually foster trust within the digital financial ecosystem. There will be no more of the trusting one central authority blindly. Equally, we shall not rely only on the so-called decentralised trust-less systems that do not require any trust as others herald, or better yet, there will also be no trusting solely in code as some have shepherded. You always need to trust someone or something, but only the right foundations in alignment around 'what matters' can breed trust. What better foundation than a digital social contract that everyone building new solutions uses as the basis with the aim of value alignment first and foremost? One possible future includes a more complex web of interconnected co-dependencies across people, the private sector and the public sector, our three spheres, the PPP, that is centred on not only protecting, but nurturing and cultivating the alignment of what matters most to each of the three spheres, with a particular emphasis on the people sphere that acts as a backstop and is placed at the centre.

Importantly, no single agent is positioned to provide the role of guarantor to underwrite this new digital social contract, contrary to the previous social contract which represented an underlying agreement for certain norms guaranteed by the state. A digital social contract requires cooperation, flexibility and innovation as much as being inclusive and non-discriminatory. Thus, instead of a structure imposed externally or from precedent, a new normative framework for governing these relationships is needed, both bottom-up and top-down, and middle-middle (if such a thing exists).

What those norms are or should be, will inevitably, and much like the classic social contract, come out in time, be broken down and reconstituted on the path to an equilibrium between the spheres of people, the public sector and the private sector.

This time, however, it is going to be a little different. The digital social contract can be reflected in technical solutions in a programmable way. Where we had to rely on third parties to mediate, attest and accredit to doing the right thing, now rules can be built into programmes using smart contracts. By applying the right governance and decision-making approaches to mediate relationships within and between the three spheres, we can instil core tenets of the digital social contract in a flexible but also clear, robust and sustainable way.

The central question we have then is how to instil trust given the technology enablers we have? To do that, the obvious next step is to identify what matters most to each sphere with the people sphere as the fundamental backstop. What we have hoped to demonstrate in this book is that there are some base level interests that can and ought to be protected that cut across money and payments, identity, data and privacy but which also are applicable to all that we do digitally.

Anytime we interact with or engage with anyone digitally, it should be against the background of that digital social contract and everything being built should centre around it in a universal way. Whether it is transmitting a payment, sharing your data, identity or creating new building blocks for a digital financial ecosystem that brings these strands together, it is about reflecting this new digital social contract into the financial ecosystem.

And when it comes to the 'what', the following eight desiderata represent the starting point for this digital social contract. They stem from our journey in this book and are inspired by redecentralisation. These desiderata form the foundational pillars to finding a balance across the three spheres in a way that will serve the people sphere by being incorporated into building new tools and systems for the digital financial ecosystem as part of the digital fabric that connects us all and should serve everyone everywhere.

1. *Collective Addressing and Self-Sufficiency*: The focus of the digital social contract is to service the collective system by addressing and solving collective problems, whether these are local or global and ranging from financial crises, food shortages, climate change, to privacy preservation, health, identity to many more. This is not the utilitarian approach of addressing the common good and sacrificing anything or anyone in pursuit of whatever is better for more people, the so-called fiction of the "greater good". Instead, every person acts as a backstop to what the central purpose of the digital social contract is, meanwhile aiming at enabling the people sphere to solve their own problems themselves in a way that is self-sufficient, whilst addressing the collective issues that the people sphere faces, which, in turn, are challenges that the collective system faces as well.
2. *Codified and Programmable*: Unlike the classic social contract that is somewhat esoteric, an artefact of some kind in the background of the norms that influence our lives and that social institutions are built around, the digital social contract is different. It is also different to another social contract we have covered extensively—money—which exists against the backdrop of trusting the central bank, or even identity, against the backdrop of what the government says.

   Instead, the digital social contract seeks to solve the eroding trust issues across these former social constructs. New norms for the equilibrium between people, the private sector and public sector spheres in alignment of their interests can be encoded technologically, not in a document, piece of paper or law but in the code of the digital systems they use to interact with one another. These norms are built into the system and fine-tuned collectively. It would even be possible for these encoded and programmable norms, or programmable money, or identity to only be changed with direct participation across each of the three spheres, in particular, with the people sphere participating in that decision-making, should they elect to do so.
3. *Unilateral Minimalism*: No one group, entity or organisation, or any one of the three spheres should have the unilateral ability, authority or capability to directly

censor, monitor, prohibit or permit the behaviours of those that are not harmful, such as those that do not infringe on the rights and obligations of others (such as those protected by law). This marks a massive shift from the current social contract, where everything operates through institutions, whether we are looking at interactions with the public or the private sector sphere, to a model that limits overreach by any one sphere on another for no genuinely good reason.

Take the Metaverse as an example. Virtual and augmented realities, along with gaming and digital worlds, are on their way in. We can only imagine the possibility of spending half of our days in some niche upside-down city on some distant planet in the virtual world with its own barter system (money), avatars (identity) and fingerprints (biometrics). Whose Metaverse is that? Is it one instantiated by a group of people that put together the city? Is it provided by a nation state? Or one of the larger corporations? Whose rule set would be forced upon us? Perhaps all the above would be available and users can just choose. And perhaps they will each be built along this new digital social contract that blurs the lines between the implicit differences we feel between each of those options when we just read it because of the value alignment that has been built into their creation, and providing individuals the ability to create their own instance, their own rules, for their own Metaverses, all and each against the backdrop of the new digital social contract that underpins each and every option when we ask the question 'which Metaverse?'.

4. *Participatory Possibility*: The people sphere is afforded, in any given system, the possibility to participate in governance and decision-making should they elect to do so, and to the extent that they wish to do so. This could lead to true democratisation and inclusiveness of all, when it is wanted, but more importantly, present the choice to be involved in all sorts of participation, locally and globally, where one elects to do so across matters that specifically touch on interests of that sphere, such as the people sphere, in a way that is direct. For example, just imagine, on the topic of climate change, or on data privacy, that every Internet user would be able to cast a vote for some worldwide decision relating to Internet service providers everywhere. It would provide a fascinating alternative to how we deal with some of the most pertinent global issues we see today, where it is only nation states or industry bodies, or individual corporations that are making decisions, even though the issues at hand directly have to do with what matters to the people sphere, such as climate change, or the race to CBCDs (where privacy could risk falling by the way side). Clearly such access to decision-making has to go hand in hand with empowering people to make actual use of it (a much bigger point on inclusive access to education, technology and technical proficiency).
5. *Local and Global*: The digital social contract will certainly have local elements. But, unlike the classic social contract, it will also have a global element. This means two things. First, there will certainly be local versions/aspects of the digital social contract in any given place at any given time but its mandate will be global. It will be connected to the digital social contract in other places, but also to the digital social contract of everywhere—the ether of the cross-border digital space. Second, it is local in another sense. It centres around the sphere

of the people having access and all spheres having accountability. One obvious manifestation about what that means when it comes to programming the digital social contract into actual systems is that the people sphere can have their private key(s) for their digital selves, their identity, property, assets, records and finances with ownership, localised as a starting point. Where the people sphere can share and entrust with others when, where and how they wish without forced reliance. Just like you have a password for your phone, the private key is the access tool for possession of all that is yours digitally, and that begins by locally enabling you to determine the way in which you interact with these systems and spheres. Whilst this is a technical point, it highlights the importance of building the digital social contract around the people and putting them back at the centre of the equation.

6. *Privacy by Design*: The digital social contract needs to embed privacy by design. Instead of data sharing being the default with protections granted for when and how that takes place, privacy should be the ground zero with the intention of finding the appropriate balance across regulation, supervision, safety and consumer protection. This is a clear tenet of the physical world, but it seems to have been abandoned in the digital world of today and needs to be brought back with urgency. People need to be empowered with choice, making way for them to use new and exciting tools and technologies like zero knowledge proofs and anonymous signatures that can bring privacy, which we have known in the physical world for many millennia also in the digital world.
7. *Fully Integrated and Interoperable*: A current issue in the financial system, but also in other industries and sectors, is how disparate and siloed everything is. Instead, technical solutions and systems should come in a fully integrated form, providing the possibility to bring everything that anyone needs to do together with the overall purpose of efficiency whilst being interoperable. From a digital social contract standpoint, this has to do with two core aspects. The first is the ability to leave one technical system for another, the ability to choose where to play, so to speak. It also has to do with access, and of course ease of use. Returning to the technical reflection of the digital social contract, this connectivity makes moving to and from any given network and system to another possible and breaks down the inefficiencies of today. However, interoperability needs to transcend the mere sphere of technology when we look, for example, at identity. Legal recognition of digital identity, for example for the purpose of crossing borders, is a key requirement in a globalised and digitally enabled world.
8. *Diversity*: The digital social contract ought to be predicated on fostering diversity across areas whether within any of the spheres themselves or between them and across systems and bodies of knowledge that facilitate and support interaction between them. That means more and different kinds of service providers, more bodies of thought, knowledge, technical systems, ways of governing and drawing from all sorts of places towards supporting the balance of the three spheres. Diversity and the ability of individuals to participate and engage more broadly will go a long way to helping them to solve their own problems and become more self-sufficient. It breeds additional choice, more flexibility and innovation

with new ways of doing things and cherishes difference in a way that upholds the other desiderata.

Notes

1. Recall the first DAO, which through the hack that occurred also demonstrated that blockchains are not necessarily immutable.
2. Apple, iPhone 13 Pro Product Environmental Report, September 2021.
3. Citi Global Insights, "How Environmentally Friendly is the Metaverse", July 2022.
4. Study by Nokia and Telefonica published via a press release by Nokia, "Nokia confirms 5G as 90 percent more energy efficient", 2 December 2020.
5. Ericsson Mobility Report, June 2022.
6. Uddameri, V., Professor/Director of the Water Resources Center at Texas Tech University; quoted by NBC News, "Drought-Stricken Communities Push Back Against Data Centers", 19 June 2021.
7. Richter, F., "Amazon Leads $200 Billion Cloud Market", Statista – Cloud Infrastructure Market, 2 August 2022, https://www.statista.com/chart/18819/worldwide-market-share-of-leading-cloud-infrastructure-service-providers/ (last accessed 07/10/2022).
8. Gonzalez Monserrate, S., "The Cloud is Material: On the Environmental Impacts of Computation and Data Storage", "Staggering Ecological Impacts of Computation and the Cloud", MIT Schwarzman College of Computing, published 27 January 2022, https://mit-serc.pubpub.org/pub/the-cloud-is-material/release/1 (last accessed 07/10/20222).
9. Gottesman, D., Chuang, I., "Quantum Digital Signatures", version 2, November 2001, Arvix, https://arxiv.org/pdf/quant-ph/0105032.pdf (last accessed 29/10/2022).
10. Kiktenko, E. O., Pozhar, N. O., Anufriev, M. N., Trushechkin, A. S., Yunusov, N. N., Kurochkin, Y. V., Lvovsky, A. I., Fedorov, A. K., "Quantum – Secured Blockchain", June 2018, Arxiv, https://arxiv.org/abs/1705.09258 (last accessed 29/10/2022).
11. Gerhardt, I., Liu, Q., Lamas-Linares, A., Skaar, J., Kurtsiefer, C., Makarov, V., "Full-Field Implementation of a Perfect Eavesdropper on a Quantum Cryptography System", *Nature*, June 2011, https://www.nature.com/articles/ncomms1348 (last accessed 29/10/2022).
12. Bennett, C. H., Brassard, G., "Quantum Cryptography: Public Key Distribution and Coin Tossing", *Theoretical Computer Science*, 560, 7–11, 2014, https://core.ac.uk/download/pdf/82447194.pdf (last accessed 29/10/2022).
13. Jogenfors, J., "Quantum Bitcoin: An Anonymous and Distributed Currency Secured by the No-Cloning Theorem of Quantum Mechanics", Researchgate.net, April 2016, https://www.researchgate.net/publication/299749136_Quantum_Bitcoin_An_Anonymous_and_Distributed_Currency_Secured_by_the_No-Cloning_Theorem_of_Quantum_Mechanics (last accessed 29/10/2022).
14. Explodingtopics.com, DeFi Statistics, https://explodingtopics.com/blog/defi-stats (last accessed 3/10/2022).
15. A central limit order book (CLOB) is the main way traditional (and crypto) exchanges operate. Resting sell orders face resting buy orders and are paired up as a match when a buy order has a higher price than a resting sell order.
16. Grassi, L., Lanfranchi, D., Faes, A., Renga, F. M., "Do We Still Need Financial Intermediation? The Case of Decentralized Finance – DeFi", *Qualitative Research in Accounting and Management*, 19(3), 2022, https://www.emerald.com/insight/content/doi/10.1108/QRAM-03-2021-0051/full/html (last accessed 29/10/2022).
17. Dünser, Dr. T., "The Liechtenstein Blockchain-Act", Government Principality of Liechtenstein, 2019.

18. Why 'Dutch panic' surrounding PSD2 & GDPR interplay may be an overreaction (finextra.com).
19. Publicly Available Specification, Code of Practice for Digital Identification and Strong Customer Authentication (PAS499:2019).

Conclusion

This book has been motivated by a deep concern over the way humankind has been evolving in the last few years. Our increasingly digital world risks getting the best of us and doing the worst to us if we do not rein in and bring things back into some kind of equilibrium across the three spheres of the public sector, the private sector and people. But what should that equilibrium be and how can we get there? At the core, it is about maintaining personal agency, re-forging and enabling trust, assuring individual and collective responsibility and providing access and ability to all of us to participate in decision-making on things that affect us all, starting with building a new digital financial ecosystem that underpins so much of everything around us and that can act as a model for other areas.

In this book, we have covered quite a bit of ground. In many ways it has been considering the changing nature of power relations that are leading to economic, political and social changes and fueled by technological innovation. In essence, marking a shift in the way we can arrange our affairs. We have focused on several areas that are important to this turning point that we believe we are at. Redecentralisation is at our doorstep, it is coming and coming quickly as a counterbalance to the current centralisation and its abuse. But thus far it is a reaction to the ills that many are fed up with, and in many ways, can lead all the way right back to centralisation, turning into some kind of never ending cycle from decentralisation to centralisation, to decentralisation and back to centralisation ad infinitum. At the same time, decentralisation has its own issues, too. Not least the fact that most of what is called decentralised is actually centralised, or may likely yield centralised outcomes or is only decentralised in certain dimensions that may not matter when we consider our seven dimensions from Chapter 2. Those seven decentralisation dimensions provide a new way to consider the decentralisation of all kinds of systems we interact with on a day-to-day basis as the system designers, creators and builders that we all inherently are.

Our major concern has been two-fold. First, that trust has been eroded by uber-centralisation that has festered into a trust crisis and second, that decentralisation on its own may well lead to further centralisation either by accident,

R. Wandhöfer and H. D. Nakib, *Redecentralisation*,
https://doi.org/10.1007/978-3-031-21591-9

intent or its very nature. Redecentralisation provides us with the means to build back resilience into the system and put people back into the centre to enable users, consumers, and anyone, anywhere to be able to do whatever it is they need to, to get things done for themselves and without fear of being censored, surveilled, excluded, or discriminated against, and equip them with the technological tools to do so.

We believe and have explored that technology can inspire new ways of doing things to rewrite some of the rules of society through digitalisation in this new wave to address the ongoing trust crisis and allow everyday people to drive towards self-sufficiency with new models of governance and decision-making to do so. But also to be able to work together more collaboratively—locally, regionally and globally. It is against this backdrop that we ended by providing eight desiderata for a new digital social contract that can begin to form the basis for a fully integrated, automated, and efficient digital financial ecosystem in which we can align the values of 'what matters most' to each of the three spheres of people, the private sector and the public sector by recentring the people sphere as being what it is all about and in service of. In doing so, we have a starting point to reach a minimally acceptable reorganisation between the three spheres as a new social construct for the digital world, building new technical solutions around those desiderata that are embedded in the digital fabric that connects our systems.

A good use case is the area of self-sovereign identity and data privacy. Open Banking and Smart Data give us the opportunities of personalised, consent-based, user-centric control, which can transcend into more open everything! The jury is indeed out, but the potential is clearly worth pursuing.

We also see possibilities in the evolution of Web3 and the Metaverse, where embedding identity into everything digital in an accessible way can be the key ingredient to making this new digital interaction work better and more aligned across our three spheres. Digital identity design has to be secure, interoperable and enable ownership with data privacy and protection at its heart.

When it comes to the future of money and payments, we are likely going to see a significant shift in how we buy, pay, invest and save with entire new operating systems being formed that create fully integrated digital financial ecosystems across every area and aspect of finance, accessible at everyone's fingertips. In fact, it will rather be smart digital wallets and their surrounding intelligent agent solutions that will play a role in taking decisions on our behalf, possibly for the stuff that we do not want to be bothered with, such as paying our milkman but maybe also where we can consume research to more quickly get us that highest interest paying savings account. As predicted for many years, we may finally get to a situation where it will be computers talking to computers as autonomous economic agents in order to get some outcome that results in our digital wallets exchanging value or digital objects through central bank digital currency systems to optimise some benefit across multiple parties.

While this may well be the place we are headed, one possible future could be hyper-centralised, where a company or government would be able turn off your electricity, running water, Wi-Fi, electric vehicles, the Metaverse instance you may be hosting, your digital wallets or use of your digital identity because it has been monitoring what you have been doing in every part of your digital life and has deemed some part of it to be against its rules. By taking our eight desiderata and building them into new technological systems and tools, such an outcome can be avoided.

This would indeed hail the next evolution in payments as well, but we do not think that private cryptocurrencies will be the dominant means for exchanging value between machines. Indeed, with security and fraud concerns running rife in the crypto space, it is quite possible that the attractiveness of crypto will continue to suffer. The meltdown of centralised players in the crypto world, such as large cryptocurrency and digital asset exchanges, has ushered in another crypto winter. Clearly more decentralisation and 'earned' trust are the key ingredients to make these types of technological ecosystems work to the benefit of the many, rather than the few, again, more of the same old story.

These incidents are clearly examples of abuse of the system, but given our hyperconnectivity, the degree to which this connectivity within the system can be threatened is also an area of concern. Environmental and human-made systemic risks must also be considered as a threat that can cause shocks against the fragile balance between the three spheres. For example, whilst the world's payment systems concentrate on the menace emanating from organised crime to steal money from the operation of the system, there are other threat vectors with a different motivation to taking down the payments systems, e.g. as a form of geopolitical projection or between the centralisation-decentralisation divide. These would be attacks that are not designed to make the orchestrator any money, but to prevent money from flowing between all other parties, disrupting digital value chains than enable the flow of money, information, data, economic and social activity.

Outside of payments the connectivity itself is sometimes at risk, whether from natural causes, such as solar flares or volcanic eruptions damaging satellite communications or human-made causes, such as anti-satellite missile tests from regimes wishing to cause harm. The threats and risks are rampant, but so are the opportunities to build solutions to support the alignment of interests and values towards self-sufficiency of users of the digital financial ecosystem and all other ecosystems across messaging and information, education, healthcare and more. The eight desiderata for a new digital social contract enable us to build resilience into those systems through a degree of decentralisation by design.

Provided we can keep these risks in mind and ensure our technical cyber security is kept up to scratch, then, hopefully, we have painted a picture of a better way to manage our affairs that is inspired by redecentralisation in order to allow you to be in control of your data, identity and finances, giving you the power of your consent to lead your physical and virtual lives, in all your myriad personae. Of course we also need to make sure that human agency itself is not lost on the way as more and more prolific AI solutions are coming to the fore. Instead, whatever the technology, and whatever the area, there is an array of intertwined and intermingled systems that we touch each and every day across the three spheres of the public sector, private sector and people, where we are all system builders, designers and creators. We all have the ability to reshape them each and every day around our eight desiderata.

This is exactly why delivery of our vision for the basis of a new digital social contract is as essential as it is life-preserving. We need to avoid a new era of trustlessness and instead enter an era of trustedness, with us people at the centre!

Index

R. Wandhöfer and H. D. Nakib, *Redecentralisation*,
https://doi.org/10.1007/978-3-031-21591-9

GPSR Compliance
The European Union's (EU) General Product Safety Regulation (GPSR) is a set of rules that requires consumer products to be safe and our obligations to ensure this.

If you have any concerns about our products, you can contact us on

ProductSafety@springernature.com

In case Publisher is established outside the EU, the EU authorized representative is:

Springer Nature Customer Service Center GmbH
Europaplatz 3
69115 Heidelberg, Germany

www.ingramcontent.com/pod-product-compliance
Ingram Content Group UK Ltd.
Pitfield, Milton Keynes, MK11 3LW, UK
UKHW021422091026
15624UKWH00010B/380
9783031215902